## Also by Benjamin R. Barber

*A Place for Us* (1998)

*A Passion for Democracy: American Essays* (1998)

*Jihad vs. McWorld* (1995)

*An Aristocracy of Everyone* (1992)

*The Conquest of Politics* (1988)

*Strong Democracy* (1984)

*Marriage Voices* (A Novel) (1981)

*Liberating Feminism* (1975)

*The Death of Communal Liberty* (1974)

*Superman and Common Men* (1971)

## In Collaboration

*The Struggle for Democracy*
with Patrick Watson (1989)

*The Artist and Political Vision*
edited with M. McGrath (1982)

*Totalitarianism in Perspective*
with C. J. Friedrich and M. Curtis (1969)

# The
# TRUTH
# OF POWER

## Intellectual Affairs in the Clinton White House

## BENJAMIN R. BARBER

**W. W. NORTON & COMPANY**

*New York · London*

Copyright © 2001 Benjamin R. Barber

Printed in the United States of America
First Edition

For information about permission to reproduce selections from this book,
write to Permissions, W. W. Norton & Company, Inc.,
500 Fifth Avenue, New York, NY 10110

The text of this book is composed in Photina MT
with the display set in Roman Shaded
Desktop composition by Molly Heron
Manufacturing by Quebecor Fairfield
Book design by Charlotte Staub

Library of Congress Cataloging-in-Publication Data

Barber, Benjamin R., 1939–
The truth of power : intellectual affairs in the Clinton White House /
by Benjamin R. Barber.
p. cm.
Includes bibliographical references and index.
**ISBN 0-393-02014-2**
1. Clinton, Bill, 1946– —Knowledge and learning. 2. Clinton, Bill, 1946– —
Friends and associates. 3. Presidents—United States—Biography.
4. Presidents—United States—Intellectual life. 5. United States—Intellectual
life—20th century. 6. Intellectuals—United States—History—20th century.
7. Executive power—United States—Case studies.

E886.2 .B37 2001
973.929'092—dc21      2001030338

W. W. Norton & Company, Inc.
500 Fifth Avenue, New York, N.Y. 10110
www.wwnorton.com

W. W. Norton & Company Ltd.
Castle House, 75/76 Wells Street, London W1T 3QT

1  2  3  4  5  6  7  8  9  0

*To the politicians, one and all . . .*

our fellow citizens, no better or worse than us,
who brave the ambivalent will of the electorate,
the frenzied attention of the media,
and the complacent suspicion of the cynics
in order to serve a democracy
to which too many of us remain
spectators and critics.

# Contents

# Acknowledgments

**ALTHOUGH THE WRITING** of this book was a relatively personal affair in which the primary research was culled from experience and memory, there are a number of people who played a role in its creation. Most importantly, a group of White House staffers who cared deeply about the presidency, the Democratic Party, and the nation and about the role of ideas in shaping them facilitated my modest engagement in the matters described here.

Bill Galston was the intellectual center of much of what transpired under the name of ideas in the Clinton White House; without his spirit of open inquiry and his tolerance for genuine diversity there would have been little to talk about or write about in the domain of ideas. Don Baer was a gracious host to ideas and those who claimed to have them, even where they discomfited conventional wisdom; by insisting that policy and ideology be rooted in serious ideas he gave intellectuals a chance to be heard. Sid Blumenthal, though an adept master of White House spin, never surrendered his openness to contrary ideas and welcomed thoughtful critics to his office and the seminars he arranged throughout his term of service. I take some jibes at him below, which is poor reward for his ongoing hospitality to me and others from the outside.

I also benefited from the openness to my opinions and views of Melanne Verveer, Michael Waldman, Bruce Reed, and especially Ellen Lovell, a White House public servant who exemplified public-spirited dedication to America's democratic ideals. Vice-President Gore and first lady Hillary Clinton not only participated with extraordinary intelli-

9

gence and verve in many of the conversations portrayed below but also showed a remarkable tolerance for the long-windedness and self-certainty with which I promoted my own viewpoint in discussions with them.

Darrell Doan acted as a research assistant to the project in its early days and saved me considerable time and effort through his careful research and fact-checking—though I alone take responsibility for the text that resulted.

In a world of commercial publishing dominated by global corporate conglomerates, I feel very fortunate to have W.W. Norton as my publisher and Alane Mason as my editor. For in a global market society driven by profit and celebrity it is clear that authors need publishers more than publishers need authors—an emerging reality that has corrupted the traditional and healthy codependency of the two. Norton remains a house in which writers and writing are trump, and Alane Mason is an editor who lives that credo by insisting on bringing out the best a writer can offer. If the best isn't good enough, if there are still flaccid passages or sections that read as if they belong in another manuscript, it is not because Alane failed to exercise firm editorial oversight but only because I foolishly resisted her prudent editorial counsel.

Finally there is the president himself. Bill Clinton, as this book makes clear, was and is one of the more problematic if fascinating public figures in American history. But it will hardly escape anyone's attention that I have something and somebody to write about only because the president invited me to participate in the intellectual affairs that are my subject here. In the absence of his appetite for ideas, for challenges, for spirited debate and expansive deliberation, without the ongoing hospitality he extended to me and other intellectuals, there would and could be no memoir, no book about power and truth. Much more importantly, there would and could have been no serious intellectual deliberation in his White House. And whatever the ultimate impact of our ideas, it is clear to me that America was much better off for having a president willing to think about and debate ideas and ideals. In this, the debt I owe Bill Clinton is a debt owed him by all Americans who care about the great civic conversation that defines what is best in our democracy.

# PREFACE

## My Affair with Clinton

**THIS IS A MEMOIR**, an informal political history, an exercise in personal political theory, fragments of an inadvertent autobiography. An account of my affair with Clinton.

This is *not* an insider account of the Clinton years. At best I have written the memoir of an outsider, someone who met with Clinton, mostly in the company of others, perhaps a dozen times in the course of his two-term presidency; and who otherwise was in the White House another several dozen times meeting with friends, staffers, and true insiders, people employed full-time by the president. I cannot claim to be privy to inside information or to harbor secrets I will reveal on the pages that follow. Nevertheless, like almost every other human being who has crossed the glowing path of William Jefferson Clinton, I have the feeling I've had a kind of affair with him. But we are not "friends" in any significant personal sense, and such kindnesses as he has bestowed on me—a birthday card here, a social invitation there—were primarily by-products of my formal relationship as a sometime outside adviser, and can presumably be discounted as normal politics among adept politicians and their donors, supporters, or former counselors. I was in the White House a number of times without ever contributing a nickel—other than to pay for my own fare to Washington for the meetings I attended. I was, however, offered the Lincoln Bedroom—sort of, during a blizzard—but this did not seem to me to be because the White House was for sale. Indeed, during the years of my extremely intermittent affair with the president, I rather worried that I might appear to be for sale: my views, adjusted to accommodate the biases of those in power, auctioned off cheaply in return for a quite trivial access to that power.

I had a rare privilege for an American citizen: I was invited to participate in some significant discussions about large issues with the president of the United States and, as a consequence, to reflect on the relationship of ideas to power. I participated in a continuing conversation about the nature of American governance and the role of the Democratic Party in its evolving "New Democratic" form. On occasion, this conversation even felt mildly historic (although that is a judgment only history can make). It is these conversations, and my reflections on them—some very personal, some those of a political philosopher—and these alone that I can share. On the basis of fairly careful notes, I have offered specific versions of conversations, some in quotation marks. These are not, however, verbatim quotations, but only reconstructions for which I alone am responsible.

Finally, even though the new history as practiced both by gifted historians and by Hollywood muckrakers has licensed me to offer as fact rhapsodic tales I simply make up, Clinton is certainly no Dutch—opaque to all but mind readers and in need of contrived narrators to penetrate the inscrutable core; his reality (and mine) suffices to tell the tale I want to tell.

I waited to publish until the president left office because I believe that there is a necessary balance between what one owes the public and what one owes a president who has allowed one into his confidence. I did not ask the president for permission to write or ask of him sanction for my viewpoint, and since he had no knowledge that I was writing, there is nothing official or authoritative about this memoir. On the other hand, it is not written out of animus or anger (as so many other books seem to be), since I continue to feel toward President Clinton what I felt throughout the years of our episodic encounters: tremendous admiration for his intelligence, his political savvy, and his remarkable personal charm, which I believe to be the quintessence of democratic politics; ambivalence about his leadership, greater, I think, than he is given credit for but finally insufficient in ways not only Clinton himself but surely the country, too, will come to regret; and disappointment that he was not able to live up to his potential for greatness, both because neither his enemies nor the times in which he lived called for or permitted greatness, and because he suffered from debilities of which the sexual scandals were indicators and which might even under more felicitous circumstances have kept him from glory's sparse ranks.

Following his own New Hampshire primary victory last year, Senator John McCain, with whom I had dinner at the White House at a table hosted by President Clinton, observed that President Clinton's presidency was one of "great talent and great waste." Like many of McCain's insights, this is near the mark but not quite on it. For while the president certainly can be indicted for sometimes throwing away with his left hand what he achieved with his right, it is also the case that both the enemies of the president and the country he served helped to "waste" some of what he had to offer the nation. Clinton's story and America's story in the nineties are nearly inseparable. Moreover, while he sometimes disappointed his intellectual counselors with his apparent penchant for Dick Morris–style polling, he was the one who had been elected and the one with the accountability. As David Stockman, Reagan's first budget director, prudently concluded after watching his neoliberal laissez-faire revolution get soundly trumped by politics, "in a democracy the politicians must have the last word once it is clear that their course is consistent with the preferences of the electorate." The revolution Stockman had served was, he finally realized, "radical, imprudent, and arrogant. . . . It mistakenly presumed that a handful of ideologues were right and all the politicians were wrong about what the American people wanted from government."[1] We were sometimes equally imprudent and arrogant in the passion of our convictions, and it may be a virtue of sorts—though we thought of it exclusively as a vice—that although Clinton enjoyed our company and reveled in our ideas, he took his political cues from politics and the polls.

On the way to offering an account of my (to me) memorable affair with President Clinton, the political theorist dwelling inside the activist in me had three larger issues in mind. The first concerns the relationship between ideas and politics, between—in the classical formulation—truth and power. This theme in fact sets the context for the book. Today as twenty-five hundred years ago, when Plato traveled to Syra-

[1] Stockman, *The Triumph of Politics: Why the Reagan Revolution Failed* (New York: Harper and Row, 1981), p. 395.

cuse to enlighten its struggling tyrants, only to be sorely disappointed, it remains the principal obligation of intellectuals and philosophers to speak truth to power. Having no power, we depend on speech. Once speaking, we hope for a simulacrum of truth. The trouble with speaking truth to power is, as what follows will show, that intellectuals rarely have the truth while the president rarely has much power—certainly much less than that with which the office is usually credited.[2] In our postmodern era, where no one can claim to speak truth and where there is no one with absolute power to speak it to, the old cliché turns out to have limited traction. Philosophy with its currently fashionable postmodernist predilections is nowadays devoted to discrediting the very idea of truth, while politics contents itself for the most part with disclosing the bankruptcy of power. Speaking truth to power is simply not what it once was. Perhaps the only truth to which a president can have access is the truth of power.

The second issue that stalked my inner thoughts as I recalled and wrote about my Washington visits speaks to the fundamental change in the nature, ideology, and constituency of the Democratic Party over the last several decades. The party's several earlier iterations moved it from its antifederalist Dixiecrat beginnings as a party that fought and lost the Civil War and then won the battle against Reconstruction; only later, as it negotiated its urban turn and gradually made itself over into a coalition of Catholics, city dwellers, blue-collar union men, immigrants, intellectuals, and minorities, did it become a progressive coalition that produced the great twentieth-century social victories of the New Deal and the Great Society. Yet following the magnificent triumphs of FDR, the party failed to reelect a full-term incumbent for more than forty years. Whereas Eisenhower, Nixon, and Reagan each won reelection, the Democrats watched Johnson, Humphrey, McCarthy, and McGovern take them into a wilderness (Carter tended a dried-up water hole there) from which they were rescued only by Bill Clinton and his New Democrat ideology. Clinton managed to parlay this ideology, which he helped forge at the Democratic Leadership Council (and its think tank, the Progressive Policy Institute), into a formula for electoral credibility. Whether that credibility cost the party the only principles

---

[2] This was one of Richard E. Neustadt's most revelatory insights in his study *Presidential Power*, first published in 1960.

that mattered to its core constituency is one of the questions addressed in what follows.

Finally, there is the matter of the president's remarkable personality. Here was someone gifted with a mien that somehow married a good ol' boy's worst (if most charming) vices with the virtues of a New Age statesman who, alone among modern politicians and presidents, seemed to understand that we were and are living in a new and strange world and moving into one stranger still. Whether or not Clinton will eventually be deemed a historic president (given his impeachment and the scandals that attended his departure from office, the odds are against it, though history has a way of embarrassing prophets), his surely will be seen as a historic presidency occupying a crucial transition in modern history.[3] The times in which he tried to govern were truly historic, ironically enough, precisely because history had ceased to be a useful guide to their daunting challenges.

The "legacy" question will not be settled anytime soon. What seems clear is that the president I came to know was a remarkable facsimile of the people who elected him to power and then through thick and thin, through Clinton hysteria and Clinton fatigue, kept him there for eight years. More than most presidents, he manifested the spirit of those he represented. As a consequence, whatever opinions we have of him we will be constrained to apply to ourselves as well. Me, I don't mind. Because I retain a populist's confidence in the character of the American people, I can continue to allow myself to think warmly of the president to whom the American people remained so loyal. That seems about right for someone with whom I have had so rewarding an affair.

[3] Although polls taken at the end of his second term gave him ratings higher than those of any modern president at a similar moment, his ratings fell after he left office in a cloud of dubious pardons and petty scandal, and a poll of historians placed him roughly in the middle of the pack with respect to performance in office, and at the bottom in terms of his moral reputation. See *New York Times*, February 24, 2000. But even though Clinton lived by the polls, luckily for him, his place in history will not be determined by them.

# The
# TRUTH
# OF POWER

# CHAPTER ONE

# The Road to Camp David

**A WINTRY SATURDAY** in 1995. The weak sun bleached the land-scape along the winding roads of rural Maryland leading to Camp David and beyond—on into memory's interior regions, doubling back into distant personal history. As an academic political philosopher more interested in the culture of power than those who cultivated power had ever been interested in me, I was stepping through the looking glass. I had often peered through that glass with a social scientist's curious eye to catch a glimpse of power. I was now about to become, however briefly and superficially, power's counselor. The president's interlocutor.

Three oversized SUVs secluded us behind darkened windows, transporting us the ninety miles from the White House to the Maryland hillside military installation President Franklin Roosevelt had turned into a weekend presidential getaway during World War Two. FDR had dubbed it Shangri-La, but Dwight Eisenhower renamed it for his grandson David. Although the president could make the trip by chopper in less than half an hour, we followed what seemed a meandering route that created an impression of rusticity and remoteness. The distance allowed us to imagine (as more than one president must have) that we were leaving behind the petty politics and cynical manipulation that defined Washington. And to fancy we were on our way to some Arcadia where ideas, even idealism, might flower alongside the mountain rhododendron.

The impression of rusticity was reinforced by the fact that the participants in our small symposium, though we had first assembled inside the Beltway at the White House, would join the debate with the president well outside the Beltway, out of earshot of its gossiping journalists and career cynics for whom power was the only useful commodity. This was important to us because, while we journeyed to the land of power, we came from the land of truth and fancied that our task was simply to speak truth to power. Our task would be all the easier because we would converse under the firm philosophical hand of Bill Galston—nominally a domestic policy adviser on President Clinton's staff but to us an academic political theorist with a very considerable reputation who, despite service to the presidential campaigns of Walter Mondale and Michael Dukakis and his position in the Clinton administration, had retained a semblance of genuine intellectual autonomy that promised a White House in which ideas might play some role and truth might still gain a hearing.

Our seminar that winter day had originated in a process already in place for more than a year. Prior to the State of the Union Message, overtures had been made to several dozen intellectuals, inviting them to contribute ideas to the speechwriting office. The preceding year, in late 1993, and again in late December 1994, Don Baer (director of speechwriting and after David Gergen's departure, director of communications) along with Bill Galston and others solicited advice and ideas for the upcoming State of the Union from outside intellectuals and academics. We were invited to address our remarks directly to the president, and we were told—and it later became evident—that he received and read them himself. The time was just a few weeks after the 1994 congressional election, in which the Gingrich revolution had wrested the House away from the Democrats with eighty new Republican seats. After less than two years, the promise of 1992 was in doubt, endangered by the successive disasters of "don't ask, don't tell" (an approach to gays in the military that infuriated both gays and the military), an energy tax bill undone by oil state senators in the president's own party, and a universal health care debate undermined as much by poor conception and leadership as by demagogic health industry opposition.

The small group participating in the Camp David meeting this day had been chosen at least in part from a larger group of several dozen on the basis of "audition" comments composed in response to this radically changed political climate. I had met the president when I hosted his visit to our Rutgers service learning program in March 1993 (see chapter 6), and I knew a few of his staffers, including Eli Siegal, Henry Cisneros, and Galston, but it seemed the stuff of fantasy when Galston called to ask whether I might be free to join "a discussion with the president at Camp David."

On the appointed Saturday in January 1995, then, we were heading to Camp David, riding four or five to a vehicle. I traveled with Bill Galston, Alan Brinkley, an earnest, almost dour, young historian from Columbia University, and my collegial friend Robert Putnam, the lively Harvard (Kennedy School) sociologist who was charting the decline of social trust in America as evidenced by the decline of team bowling and other common social and civic activities. Flattering ourselves that we were soon to become the president's tutors, we were already sparring to secure ideological beachheads for the upcoming intellectual campaign to win his ear if not his very soul. Having persuaded myself I might in some small way actually change the world, I was chasing memories from graduate school and recalling the courses in which I had first read the canonical texts on philosophy and power that on this winter day suddenly seemed so relevant.

How many thinkers, far more gifted than our little coterie, had imagined that their cloistered ideals, impressed on the untutored minds of the powerful, might redirect history? I thought of Plato's journey to Syracuse to give unsolicited counsel to its embattled rulers, Machiavelli's courting of the Medicis in sixteenth-century Florence, John Locke flirting with revolutionary politics before England's 1688 "Glorious Revolution," Voltaire whispering into the ear of Frederick the Great, Rousseau issuing unheeded advice to Poland, Corsica, and his own native Geneva (which rewarded him by burning his books): all the foolish and vainglorious and finally aborted attempts by philosophers to cross the great divide separating reflection and action—to descend from the Olympian heights into Plato's darkened cave and force the women and men toiling there in the shadows to contemplate Truth, in whose glow their petty political struggles over passions and interests would simply evaporate. Like these nobly vainglorious predecessors, we would speak truth to power—though in truth their example stood, to anybody willing to notice, as warnings against the hubris of the very enterprise in which we were zealously about to engage.

Thirty years earlier, I had studied with another would-be apprentice to power, a man of worldly ambition cloaked in wordy scholasticism. Pursuing a Ph.D. in government at Harvard at the beginning of the sixties, I watched the first long passion of Henry Kissinger as he awaited his call. How he waited. And waited and waited and waited. Kissinger had written in a popular vein about nuclear policy (initially rationalizing and then condemning limited nuclear war) and had authored the national security report issued by the Rockefeller Commission (Governor Nelson Rockefeller of New York) in 1957. By the early sixties Kissinger was at Harvard, an impatient and importuning intellectual hungry for real-world influence. The gossip was he thought the new Kennedy administration, with its Cambridge fixation—the Boston Irish Kennedys seemed, in their pursuit of "the best and the brightest," nearly obsessed with the Yankee institution across the Charles River that historically had been Boston's critic and nemesis—would whisk him from the ivory tower on the Charles to the white house on the Potomac. There, where the word was daily made flesh, Kissinger's strategic ideas might center a young president who had inherited a war in Indochina, a bitter feud with Fidel Castro, and a nuclear arms race, and who did not seem initially to have an internal compass to guide him in these fateful matters—other than his family's appetite for power and its penchant for unreflective truculence.

But it was not to happen that way. The war in Indochina would end up plaguing three administrations and tearing the nation to pieces, the feud with Castro would help kill the young president (Cuba was a subtext in many of Kennedy's troubles, including his tragic encounter with Lee Harvey Oswald), and the arms race would dominate and (some would argue) distort the nation's political and economic agenda for the next quarter of a century, until it bankrupted the Soviet Union and removed the Iron Curtain from history's stage forever. The call for Kissinger did not come, however, not from Kennedy and not from Lyndon Johnson after him. The brilliant young nuclear hawk who had cut his teeth analyzing Europe's nineteenth-century realpolitik must have wondered whether, had he been brought into Kennedy's circle, he might have identified and treated the causes of all three traumas and so spared the nation several of its modern tragedies.

Kissinger's exclusion from power did not end until he joined the Nixon administration, where the realism that filled him with cold war ardor and enamored him of nuclear posturing was turned to the purposes of making peace in Vietnam as well as achieving détente with China and, in time, Russia too. Kissinger would finally triumph in the world of action, burnishing Nixon's reputation for brilliance in international affairs. Though I despised Kissinger's views and, in my own youthful idealism, distrusted his realpolitik approach to nuclear strategy, I was, in my devotion to ideas with political bite, not so very different from him. Perhaps we detest most the enemies who resemble us. With the same certainty that Kissinger imagined the nation needed his tough nuclear diplomacy, I imagined it needed my radical critique. Professor and pupil, my nemesis and I agreed: ideas mattered.

On the substance of ideas, we disagreed (though I alone noticed). I opposed the emerging war in Vietnam, I chastised the Kennedy administration for its fixation on Castro and its blindness to his impotence (other than as America's enmity empowered him), and I rued the insistence on making communism and the communists into bogeymen whose existence justified the atmospheric testing of nuclear weapons, endless arms expenditures, self-righteous and moralizing foreign interventions, and a curtailing of civil and political rights within this country that did more to legitimate than counter communism's fear of freedom. Of course, he was already Henry Kissinger, while I was just a brash twenty-two-year-old graduate student filled with anonymous conviction.

I do not intend here to try to defend my youthful views, though for the most part I still stand by them, at least inasmuch as they spoke to those times. What counts now is that then, as on the day I journeyed to Camp David, I believed that ideas and even ideals—if well grounded in history and reason—should and could count. Against the "tough-minded" counsel of hardboiled politicos like Harold Ickes, James Carville, and Dick Morris, I thought that a presidency without a moving vision rooted in high ideals could not (and would not) succeed—not even in its own narrow political terms, certainly not in the long term.

That is perhaps why some of us from the Harvard government department who were enrolled in courses with Kissinger felt an ambivalent kinship for a man whose views we could not abide and whose cold pride and seeming self-importance offended our democratic instincts. For Kissinger was engaged in the great debate, in what Machiavelli regarded as an encounter with the dead and what the Burkean British philosopher Michael Oakeshott (my tutor in the fifties at the London School of Economics) had called the "conversation with eternity." We knew that if government was only about men, or simply about laws (the usual formulas), and not also about ideas, we would all be the worse for it. Whether this is actually so is a leitmotif of this essay.

At the Camp David seminar to which we were being escorted that January, the arms race and the cold war (both long since over) would hardly be issues for a president focused on the domestic agenda— although, ironically, nuclear testing would come to haunt Clinton's last year and a half in office, as it had haunted Kennedy's first. The refusal of the Senate to sign the Comprehensive Test Ban Treaty evoked momentarily the battles of the early sixties. But our battles in January 1995, in the wake of the disastrous November elections and the failure of the energy and health care bills, were to be of a different sort: on nearly every issue, from welfare economics to tax reform, old Democrats confronted new. Roosevelt coalition radicals still defended the welfare state against Democratic Leadership Council (DLC) partisans who had helped forge the Clinton agenda around government downsizing and reorganization. The New Democrats were taking credit for winning back the White House by adopting positions in the center after twenty-four years in which the party had languished on the left and there had been but a single Democratic president (the unlucky Jimmy Carter squeezed between Nixon and Ford, and Reagan and Bush). In fact, we were about to debate not merely the character of the Clinton presidency but the nature of the Democratic Party and the relevance of its traditional New Deal and Great Society ideals in a world hostile to government and utterly seduced by markets. Bill Clinton's Democratic Party was to define a new landscape already described in broad strokes by Bill Galston and the DLC. What we said might help determine the form that definition took.

Bill Galston was utterly without pretense, unassuming to a fault. It crippled him to a degree in positioning himself inside the White House, but to his credit he refused to play turf war games. His name does not appear in the index of George Stephanopoulos's *All Too Human*—nor, for that matter, does the name of any intellectual brought from the outside to counsel the president. For George (though George was at Camp David that Saturday), ideas and those who carried them seemed to be secondary. For the president, however, substance counted, and so Galston had the only credential he required.

A University of Maryland political theorist with close ties to the communitarian movement, and the author of a number of books, including
his widely read *Liberal Purposes*, Galston had been issues director for the
Mondale campaign in 1984 and had forged close links to the DLC's Progressive Policy Institute. (Clinton himself had been chairman of the
DLC, resigning only when he declared for the presidency.) Galston had
come to Clinton's attention in 1989, after publishing a striking political essay called "The Politics of Evasion."[1] In that essay, written with
Elaine Kamarck (later a key adviser in the Gore presidential campaign),
Galston offered a potent and controversial critique of the Democratic
Party, suggesting that by clinging to traditional New Deal core constituencies the party had lost the center (and the South); and that until
it once again conveyed "a clear understanding of, and identification
with, the social values and moral sentiments of average Americans," it
would neither regain the White House nor even maintain its hold over
the Congress.

Galston became the political theorist of the 1992 campaign, but
though he served prominently on Clinton's transition team, he felt certain (as he told me during an early visit) that he would not stay on into
the new term, since he had scarcely a single serious ally within the
White House staff he was helping to constitute. Except for one, he later
allowed—Bill Clinton.

Galston was naturally drawn to "big picture" issues of rhetoric, strategy, and vision, even though he worked on more pedestrian domestic
issues with a fellow DLC alumnus, Bruce Reed. He had introduced the
"new covenant" language that had been so useful in defining the president's early interest in public/private partnerships and in cultivating
an approach to responsibility that made citizens and their elected representatives colleagues in action rather than adversarial clients and
providers. The phrase "new covenant" recalled America's Puritan past
and resonated with overtones of the social contract tradition that was
part of the American founding. It was a phrase with iconic value for the
early Clinton agenda, though like so many seeming icons it had a relatively short shelf life in Clinton's restive White House.

Galston occupied one of the power offices in the White House—

---

[1] Galston and Kamarck, *The Politics of Evasion: Democrats and the Presidency* (Washington,
   D.C.: Progressive Policy Institute, September 1989).

advantaged not because of its size (it was a tiny, demeaning closet compared with the palatial suites available over in the Old Executive Office
Building across the driveway from the West Wing) but by virtue of its
proximity to the Oval Office just across the hall. He had been soliciting
outside intellectual counsel for the president from the beginning, especially around the State of the Union speeches. The interactions took the
form of policy briefings, "ideas" breakfasts, and now intellectual seminars. For example, a key theme for the first inaugural had been the
question whether through work and nurture we can "force spring";
according to George Stephanopoulos, the idea had been borrowed from
Father Tim Daley's computer from notes he had made as a spiritual
adviser and friend to Clinton prior to Father Tim's death.

The president's openness to outside counsel began early and endured
throughout both terms, thanks in part to Galston, who understood that
the poor reputation of government provided uncertain ground for
action in the first Democratic administration in a dozen years. Through
outside counsel, Galston hoped to reinforce his own campaign to relegitimize both civil society and government, and thus overturn Ronald
Reagan's widely accepted claim that government was part of the problem facing the nation rather than part of the solution.

In my Harvard years back in the early sixties, government had not yet
suffered the assault on its authority that was to be launched a few years
later and that Reagan was to exploit so effectively. By the late sixties, of
course, things were already changing. Both the Left and the Right were
conspiring in efforts to de-authorize public authority—the Left with its
claim that the government's "imperialist" role in Vietnam, no less than
its "police state" tactics against urban unrest, reflected "illegitimate
authority," and the Right with its nineteenth-century libertarian dogmas equating strong government with economic servitude and individual dependency (dogmas that eventually got Ronald Reagan elected
to the presidency and give Rush Limbaugh his talk radio persona
today). This twin assault contributed in our own era to a delegitimation
of government that encouraged a Democratic president in 1997 to
boast that the "end of the era of big government" had arrived, and
helped put George W. Bush in the White House in 2001.

Forty years ago, when presidents like Eisenhower and Kennedy com-
manded widespread respect, no one questioned the integrity of government or thought to disbelieve "authoritative" intelligence estimates

(later shown to be vastly overstated) making the Soviet Union America's equal in armaments. The Right used these estimates to scare the public into ratcheting up the arms race; the Left used them to warn of Armageddon and urge immediate disarmament—even unilateral disarmament. As genetic engineering and global warming haunt our nights in this era, nuclear winter and the balance of terror haunted our days back then; for those issues dominated not only our national policy debates but ordinary consciousness. That is why, as a young man with a background in physics and philosophy, I could be drawn to graduate study in politics and write a master's thesis on strategic policy. That is why in the fall of 1961, even as I was vehemently protesting the consequences of America's cold war national policies, I enrolled in Henry Kissinger's national security course, the so-called Defense Seminar. That is why so many of my fellow Harvard students with humanities backgrounds plunged into social science graduate training the way, today, students rush into M.B.A. and law school programs.

Now the national security seminar was a course that seemed designed not at all for Harvard graduate students but for the Washington fellows from the State Department and the Defense Department as well as members of the national intelligence community who as "special students" and part-time degree seekers were looking to add intellectual firepower to midlevel careers in the national security establishment. Unlike these fellows, for whom the seminar was an obligatory rite of passage, I was taking the seminar as a critic of cold war strategic ideas and military policies I opposed and reviled.

The material we studied under Kissinger's stern tutelage for our own radical purposes was truly bizarre, but notable because the then fashionable "rational calculus" style of strategic thinking where analysts did cold-blooded assessments of competing nuclear strategies persists today—both in the new debates about a missile shield that preoccupied the last year of the Clinton administration and are on the Bush/Powell agenda, and in the "rational choice" approach to economics and policymaking that is today so disturbingly dominant in our nation's graduate schools. The looney logic of this hyper-rational approach posed such questions as: Should the United States defend itself against the Soviet Union's supposed might with "counter-city" nuclear strategies that envision deterring any form of attack by threatening total nuclear war against civilian populations? ("Hit one of our missile silos, and we'll blow Moscow, Leningrad, and Smolensk off the map!") Or should it deploy a "counter-force" strategy aimed at taking out the other side's nuclear arsenal in a preemptive strike? ("If the Russkies are gonna hit us sometime, let's take out their strategic forces right now, preemptively, before they can put their fingers on the nuclear trigger!") A concomitant of such reasoning was calculating "acceptable casualty" figures in the icy manner of analysts like Herman Kahn at the Rand Corporation. Kahn's strategic ruminations led him to the conclusion that 40 to 50 million civilians would be an unfortunate, even troubling, but not necessarily unreasonable price to pay to "prevail" in a nuclear exchange with the Soviets.

It is hard nowadays to take seriously the doomsday atmospherics such authoritative public thinking generated. Even today, four or five years after our January meeting at Camp David, when nuclear testing is once again on the nation's agenda (with the defeat of the Comprehensive Test Ban Treaty in October 1999) and concerns about nuclear proliferation and nuclear terror by rogue states have reignited a certain nuclear anxiety, the atom bomb remains remote from everyday American consciousness. There were no demonstrations, no nationwide debates, no moral outcries when Senate Majority Leader Trent Lott deep-sixed the treaty. Contrast this with the daunting if comical anxieties that, back in my New York City junior high school in the early fifties, had us regularly enduring civil defense drills in which we practiced eluding the consequences of nuclear holocaust by diving under our desks (the desks were sturdier then) and were taught to look for and obey those murky yellow Civil Defense "Shelter" logos that decorated public buildings.

The fear, some would call it paranoia (but then, the nuclear bombs were real and the threats to use them credible), that enveloped America at the height of the cold war was everywhere in evidence. Pursuing readiness, the government arranged in secret for Arthur Godfrey (Oprah Winfrey's Pleistocine Age forebear) to record a public service message soothingly announcing, "Ladies and gentlemen, America is under attack!" Obviously, the recording never aired, but popular culture refracted the lurking fear over and over again in movies like On the Beach, Seven Days in May, and Stanley Kubrick's 1964 Doctor Strangelove.

Doctor Strangelove's hysterical hyper-rational logic was not only quite mad, but accurately captured the actual doctrine of MAD (mutually assured destruction) being purveyed by Herman Kahn and Thomas Schelling, a game theorist from MIT who visited the Kissinger seminar to discuss the "costs and benefits [sic]" of competing nuclear war scenarios. Yes, there *were* benefits of nuclear annihilation, though it is hard today to recall precisely what they were.

In times when films like these were dominating popular conversation, it did not seem so strange that suburban families were digging and furnishing bomb shelters in their backyards, complete with automatic weapons to fend off desperate neighbors who might lack their foresight; or that some radical academics emigrated to Australia to avoid the nuclear winter they really thought was coming, at least in northern latitudes where the "civilized" world would be busy destroying itself; or that Harvard seminars were being conducted in which alternative roads to global annihilation were carefully depicted and evaluated— including the nightmarish "doomsday machine" scenario, where an imagined planet-destroying superbomb would be rigged to go off without human intervention if it detected any nuclear explosion anywhere on earth.

In this incendiary atmosphere, far more roiling and emotionally destabilizing than anything during the Clinton years, even at the height of the impeachment hearings or the air strikes against Serbia, I was exploiting whatever I could learn in Kissinger's course to serve a saner (or at least a less insane) world. I was in fact an executive committee member of the very active Boston Committee for a Sane Nuclear Policy,[2] and was working with the American Friends Service Committee and other peace organizations on a national campaign to ban the atmospheric testing of nuclear "devices" and to oppose local Massachusetts' nuclear stockpiling ("devices" is what they were charmingly called by people hoping to imprint on the public mind the sense that these devastating weapons of total annihilation were so many new kitchen gadgets that might help make life in America safer and easier).

[2] The National Committee for a Sane Nuclear Policy had been started in 1957 by an ad hoc committee chaired by Norman Cousins and Clarence E. Pickett. There were 130 local chapters with 25,000 members nationwide within a few years, and H. Stuart Hughes, whose campaign for the Senate is recalled here, became its cochair with Benjamin Spock in 1964.

It couldn't have been easy for Kissinger to put up with the peace movement carpetbaggers in his seminar, young hotheads who were using the knowledge gained from his seminar to undermine his reassuring thinking in practice. On more than one occasion I was able to brief peace movement leaders preparing to debate Kissinger and others with material drawn directly from his seminar. Kissinger was, of course, obliged to teach all of us. The Washington fellows required security clearances, but we were bona fide Harvard graduate students and were there to learn firsthand all there was to learn about what we regarded (following the radical sociologist C. Wright Mills) as the power elite or (as that other radical, President Dwight Eisenhower, had described it in his 1960 farewell address) as the military-industrial complex. We were true radicals: critics of government, adversaries of centralized power, skeptics about the "just wars" America was supposed to wage in the name of other peoples' rights, and cynics about universities in the clutches of highly ideologized professors. Today, I suppose, we would be called Republicans.

Our vans pulled up to Camp David around midday Saturday. The complex was elaborately secured, and despite security processing at the White House, we were again ID'd at the gate, our names radioed in from the perimeter guardhouse for confirmation. Even White House staffers had to undergo the process. Camp David was deceptively modest. Scores of frame cabins that everyone who ever went to camp in the 1940s or 1950s will recognize were scattered across a wooded, hillside campground, held together and dominated by a large camp community building ("Laurel Lodge"), which was where the Middle East and Yugoslav peace talks were held in later years and which was to be our meeting venue. Unlike most summer camps, Camp David also offered impenetrable perimeter security and a chopper pad.

While waiting for the president and his party to arrive by helicopter (he never appeared anywhere I ever was at until every guest was present, every notable seated, every detail in place, which means he was always a little late), we were given a brief tour of the premises by an exceedingly polite lieutenant colonel, who after pointing out the tiny cabins in which Sadat and Begin had stayed when President Carter had brokered the first Middle East peace treaty at Camp David in the late seventies, and passing by the chopper pad where *Marine One* would shortly set down, deposited us at the concession stand and café (another of the endless cabins), where we were invited to purchase souvenirs—cups, pens, Frisbees, hats, all inscribed with the presidential seal or the Camp David logo. It felt a little like one of those Friendship Stores in China, terminus of every official site visit and city tour. (George Stephanopoulos reports that even senior staffers go scavenging for matchbooks and coffee mugs on their first visit to Camp David.)

Commerce is the common language everywhere, at Nanjing and at Camp David. Not that we were critical. Reticent philosophers, stolid intellectual aesthetes, professorial ascetics vied with one another like shoppers at a Macy's white sale to stock up on bargains. Not even the appearance of Chelsea Clinton and two of her Friends School classmates, also looking for souvenirs, diverted us from our frenzied binge—though I did notice how entirely relaxed and "normal" Chelsea seemed in this utterly abnormal setting. I hesitated for a very brief moment and then managed in less than two minutes to secure four coffee mugs, two Frisbees, a pen, and what I think were the last cuff links with the presidential seal affixed (a cheap knockoff of the gold links the president sometimes bestows). It was a first and foolish taste of what proximity to power and even the pettiest of its appurtenances can do to mature scholars otherwise devoted to the life of the mind.

Power is an elixir whether aspired to, possessed, or envied; it can intoxicate even when being passionately confronted. However, in opposing power, truth stays honest (the virtue of impotence). In counseling power, it risks contamination (one must often act without knowing). Those who shared my peace actions at Harvard in the early sixties may have been as ambitious as those they assailed, but they retained a certain purity. They included students like Peter Goldmark (later chairman of Port Authority, president of the Rockefeller Foundation, and today CEO of the *International Herald Tribune*) and the NYU sociologist Todd Gitlin. Those two together founded a Harvard peace organization called Tocsin, and both managed in later years to conserve a healthy portion of their youthful idealism, if not their radicalism (and so, ironically, can be called "conservatives" in the best sense). But my fellow peaceniks back then also included men ambitious enough to move as necessity dictated to the center and on to the right, where power felt comfortably proximate and the melancholy of being on the outside in the company of their orphaned ideals no longer had to be suffered—men like Martin Peretz (who in his incarnation as publisher of the *New*

*Republic* seems a complete stranger to the peacenik and radical campaign funder he once was) and Stephan Thernstrom, a graduate student in history who seemed then truly dedicated to ideas that, in his
current role as a dyspeptic critic of affirmative action, have vanished
without a trace.

This is not to pass judgment. Enduring devotion to youthful ideals
may represent integrity and moral consistency. Or it may represent
merely foolish nostalgia or an incapacity to grow or a fear of taking
responsibility for power and its consequences. The journey across the
political spectrum made by so many of my friends and associates from
the generation that gave birth to the sixties has in many cases suggested maturation and a sage acknowledgment of limits. In others it evinces
an attempt to deny Red diaper origins, evade responsibility, or run away
from unpleasant truths. A few have plunged mindlessly (or ever so
mindfully!) from extremism into apostasy without ever having had to
say they were sorry—either for their extremism or for their apostasy.
When I read the Red diaper baby David Horowitz's unrelenting rants
against the sixties generation—most recently in his *Hating Whitey and
Other Progressive Causes*[3]—I shudder, because his charge that the Left
despised not only American policies but also America itself, that it
allowed irrational hatred for government in general to take the place of
prudent opposition to a particular administration's ideas, speaks above
all to his own worst excesses. During a midsixties visit with him in London, to which he had fled (he boasted) out of loathing for the United
States, he was pleased to savage my moderate views. Though I was a
critic of Lyndon Johnson's policy on Vietnam, I had made the multiple
errors of admiring Johnson's domestic record, exonerating draftees
fighting the war from responsibility for the decision to wage it, and
insisting finally on the fundamental legitimacy of the American system
despite the war. After all, the war would in time be ended precisely
because the citizenry refused to support it.

When today Horowitz puts on his apostate's cloak to assail a sixties
movement far more moderate than he was, he is engaged mainly in self-
evasion or (same thing) self-loathing. He may have found patriotism to be
incompatible with his youthful vitriol, but most of us in the peace movement saw opposition to what looked like a reckless strategic logic and a

[3] See also *Radical Son: A Journey through Our Times* (New York: Free Press, 1997).

perilous Asian adventure as precisely the good work of prudent patriots. To be sure, there were zealots among our supporters to offset the zealots of nuclear confrontation, but it is precisely the zealots of that era who today complain most bitterly about the idiocies for which they themselves were responsible. The trouble with zealots, as John Strachey once remarked, is that when they cease being zealots they become knaves.

I was no zealot, though in my attachment to my own personal version of power realism, I was at times knavish. You have to know power's worth to take it on; but as you take it on, it takes you on, takes your measure. It embarrasses me and perhaps should shame me even more than it does (my own realism survives) to remember how hard I was on several genuine pacifists in our midst. They were not anti-American zealots. They were merely moralists (I believe they were American Friends Service Committee members) who had staked out deeply felt ethical positions against war and who were understandably more keen to bear witness to those pure convictions than to make the political compromises that might lessen war's risks.

It was 1961 and SANE had been campaigning to get the Massachusetts State Assembly to take a position against atmospheric nuclear testing (the "Limited Test Ban Treaty" we supported was eventually ratified in 1965) and the construction of a massive nuclear shelter—another boondoggle in that era of boondoggles—at Framingham. We had staged a number of street demonstrations in careful consultation with the handful of Democratic state assemblymen backing our cause. As we neared the day of the critical vote, our political allies in the assembly told us to lay off the demonstrations—that any further street disturbances would be likely to alienate friends previously drawn to our cause. We suspended the demonstrations and then learned that our Quaker Friends intended to march without us. They would hold their own street vigil as witnesses to peace, and damn the consequences in the assembly. Not their problem.

The intentions of these good men and women were pure, and it is possible that their motives carried a sanctity that made them exemplars of what Immanuel Kant and Saint Augustine celebrate as the key to moral being in the world: a good will. After all, there could be no certainty about the consequences of an action; only its intentions could be identified and thus assessed. Good intentions alone are moral because good consequences are always contingent and hard to take responsibility for.

Perhaps the patent display of good will by the Quakers outweighed any short-term political goals our withdrawal from demonstrating could promise. Yet, though we were then all dissidents who stood in opposition to power, even as dissidents we were divided into realists and idealists. The realists among us were sure these saintly figures were selling out real consequences in the name of an indulgent concern for their own moral rectitude, and so we did what political types in touch with power have forever done with men and women of conscience whose principled purity becomes an impediment to the enactment of principled action: we locked them in a meeting room for the several hours it took for the Massachusetts assembly to vote (they were pacifists and offered no resistance). And we congratulated ourselves on our moral realism. The vote was positive. Massachusetts went on record against atmospheric testing. And, who knows, perhaps the assembly's act, which our tough realism had enabled, had some modest influence on the national climate of opinion and so (the logic thins as it stretches out over time) in turn eventually allowed the Senate to pass and Kennedy to sign a treaty banning the atmospheric testing of nuclear weapons. Or perhaps not.

Either way, in taking on the powerful, we had assented to playing power's game on power's terms. Those who wanted to bear witness needed perhaps to grasp more firmly the relationship between their good will and the impact of their behavior on the world. But we surely needed to see more clearly than we did that consequences were always short-term and unpredictable and that, in playing by "consequentialist" rules, we were abandoning the moral currency that was our greatest strength. This battle of personal moral will versus real-world public consequences became a crucible of our political education, and was more than a little relevant to the role I would play in counseling the White House. Uncertainty surrounds every premeditated act aimed at effecting outcomes in the real world. A good will need not consult outcomes, and so will always know itself to be good. The saint allows herself to die rather than to do evil. The ethical realist may do "evil" to prevent still greater evils from being done.

To me, though, there is a critical difference between morals and politics. And between the morality of individual behavior, where intentions matter most, and the morality of group behavior, where consequences count. Only individuals can afford the luxury of the pure-

ly good will. Citizens and politicians caught up in the logic of consequences must reckon the effects of all that they do or do not do on the
world. If you are president, the decision not taken is every bit as conse-
quential as the decision made and executed. For Clinton, not to overturn welfare, to do "nothing," was to embrace and will into the
indefinite future all that the welfare program entailed, even though the
program was not of his making. The decisions I would face in trying to
offer prudent advice to President Clinton were in fact afflicted with
these same perplexing dilemmas, very much like the ones I had faced in
the Boston peace movement in 1961. Clinton would bear responsibility for the paths not taken as well as the journeys he chose to make.

To accept the invitation to counsel the powerful was inevitably to
abandon the goodwilled intransigence of radical opposition. Clinton
himself had made this journey. To say no to power is in a sense easy.
The hands stay clean. To say yes to power's deployment and then try
to guide its trajectory is far more difficult—and costly. The only real
choices are "whose dirt and how much?" That is why Machiavelli
taught the separation of politics and morals. He was not a knowing
teacher of evil (as William Bennett's mentor, the philosopher Leo
Strauss, had insisted he was); he was only a man who knew that what
passed as good among individuals could be calamitous for communities. To decline the invitation to counsel power was inevitably to
acknowledge personal impotence and to sit on the sidelines as the
world with all its possibilities and its perils rolled on by. It was to elude
political choosing and stay with the safety of bearing personal witness
to personal morals where the choice is simply between good and evil.
Politics offers only bad choices—a choice at best, as Hegel insisted,
between greater and lesser evils.

Moralists and philosophers who set the agendas of conscience with
an appropriate antipathy for compromise have no business in politics,
where the only choices are rival compromises and where not good
intentions but merely satisfactory outcomes count. Moralists are the
conscience of a democracy, but their task is to act as irritants from the
outside, bearing witness to truths that oppose complacency but yield no
viable solutions. On the inside, there is room only for those who understand that politics begins where truth ends—where hard, comfortless
choices must be made that inevitably will dirty the hands of the
choosers, whatever they do.

Around 1500 hours (time at Camp David, like the facility's overall administration, remains military), we were shuttled back to Laurel Lodge. There, in a first instance of how seductively power makes its overtures, the president stood, ready to receive and welcome us. Which is to say, to flatter, charm, and overwhelm us. And Vice-President Gore. And Mrs. Clinton and Tipper Gore. And a quite remarkable number of senior staffers, including Chief of Staff Leon Panetta and Clinton shadow George Stephanopoulos as well as Housing Secretary Henry Cisneros (a key participant in the "reinventing government" process and an intimate friend of the president, whom I knew from his days as president of the National Civic League) and Elaine Kamarck, a very well respected policy analyst who had been with Galston at the DLC in the eighties and with Clinton from the beginning. Kamarck insisted, when we met, that she had read everything I had written when she was a student at Virginia. Flattering visiting intellectuals seemed to be a science in this White House, and not a specialty of the president alone. It was an impressive company. How many chips had Galston used up prompting the president to assemble it?

Yet, it wasn't really a question of Galston's chips but of the president's interests and ambitions. In the White House, it is the president and the president alone who holds all the chips. And if someone else is playing theirs, it is only as a surrogate for the president. That is the nature of court power, whether the court is assembled in a European monarch's palace or in the White House. In a democracy it is actually desirable that executive power be concentrated in the hands of a chief executive, who after all is (alone) the elected deputy of the sovereign people. The president's chips consist in the votes he has won, and his power is legitimated by the accountability he owes. The danger of executive autocracy comes when power is shared or delegated or usurped in a fashion that defies accountability or transparency—as when a first lady is feared more than a president (Nancy Reagan?) or when aides leak information without the chief's knowledge and/or permission. Dick Morris's special relationship (just resuming at this point, unbeknownst to either the visitors or the staffers in Laurel Lodge that day) may have fallen outside the normal White House organizational chart, but as long as Morris was advising the president at the president's discretion, exercising power on his behalf and with his knowledge, there was no short-circuiting of democracy. The regular staff might howl and the public might look askance, but as long as the buck stops with the president, it doesn't matter who appears to play his chips. A White House staff at odds (every White House staff?) has been put at odds or allowed to grow at odds because it suits the president, not in spite of his wishes. Power flows from the top down, and when the person at the top is the elected officer, hierarchy is the only acceptable democratic principle.

The president stood with Hillary and the vice-president in a kind of informal reception line so that each of us had a moment to greet and be greeted. Sticking his hand out warmly, he offered us thanks for spending a Saturday with him, making us feel as if it were truly his being favored by our presence rather than the other way around. He might have been spared some of his humility had he appreciated how much— proud intellectuals that we were—we already agreed with him about this. Before I could identify myself to President Clinton, he had spoken my name and seized my right hand with his, dropping his left hand easily on my shoulder in that deeply felt essentialist move the author of *Primary Colors* captured perfectly:

> He is a genius with (his other hand). He might put it on your elbow, or up by your biceps: these are basic, reflexive moves. He is interested in you. He is honored to meet you. . . . He'll share a laugh or a secret then—a light secret, not a real one—flattering you with the illusion of conspiracy. . . . He will lock in and honor you with a two-hander, his left hand overwhelming your wrist and forearm. He'll flash that famous misty look of his. And he will mean it.

I stammered something about Rutgers and his 1993 visit to our service learning program to launch the idea for the Corporation for National Service, but he was way ahead of me (this president is always ahead of you, and it always feels like more than good briefing) and was confiding in me—my "light secret"—with a soft, somber voice, his worries about the future of the service ideal: "You know, national service is in trouble. We have to defend it." Americorps, the outgrowth of a bipartisan idea with roots in President Reagan's and President Bush's Points of Light program, had become a political football. Republicans were now sniping at it precisely because it was President Clinton's signature program, the one he cared about most ardently and personally. Even those across the aisle who admired the service idea had turned on him. It was already apparent that Clinton drove his adversaries batty: they hated him for having his own ideas and detested him for stealing theirs. Voluntarism was, they imagined, one of theirs, so the president's service program was especially aggravating—even though his service ideal was anything but volunteerist and quite at odds with theirs.

In the few seconds available to me while he vigorously pumped my arm, I couldn't rehearse all the things I wanted to say to him about how his service program was about civic responsibility and citizenship while theirs was about noblesse oblige do-goodism, about how service had to nurture public engagement rather than become a private and altruistic surrogate for it. In trying, I probably squandered the precious moment I had. My colleagues were pushing from behind to enter the president's space, and Clinton had let his hand slip from mine, preparing to replay the scene yet again with my successor and then his and his and hers. His gaze had already moved on, and it felt as if a brilliant and warming floodlight had been refocused away from me. Well, there was no need to settle this now. It was to become an ongoing debate not only between Democrats and Republicans but within the White House and the Corporation for National Service, a debate that would culminate years later, at General Colin Powell's service "summit" in Philadelphia.

My ruminations having cost me my time with the president—he was already confiding to my colleague just behind me another "light secret"—I more or less fell into the first lady's extended arms. Standing just beyond the president, she pulled back ever so slightly. She was degrees cooler than her husband, more official, even officious, seeming to be discharging a perfunctory duty rather than enjoying a pleasurable moment. I quickly straightened up and offered a conventional greeting. I can't remember what she said. It would be years before I felt for her what, in a mere nanosecond, I felt for the president. Next to Hillary, the vice-president idled in his now familiar archness. How could a man so comfortable with himself, as he obviously was, seem so uncomfortable with others? He was insisting earnestly and self-consciously that we had met, surely we must have met?—I pretending perhaps we had, so as to flatter his flattery, though we had not. With the president, I was already an intimate—an utter illusion to which, however, he and I had conspired to give the semblance of truth. The vice-president remained a stranger—a much more honest expression of our actual relationship. But, as any experienced politician could have predicted, I preferred the lie to the truth.

Tipper Gore stood next to her husband, more relaxed than Hillary, perhaps because less was expected of her. Her greeting was that of a block association regular welcoming a new neighbor: heartfelt, but fleeting. The formal line trailed off into a bunched coterie of staffers, including Stephanopoulos, Kamarck, and Panetta. Not because he was chief of staff but because he had been a consummate politician, Panetta alone among the staffers seemed wholly self-possessed. Unlike the others, he was no orbiting planet reflecting the president's bright rays; he was a solar body in his own right, generating his own radiant energy. Befitting the summer camp feel of Laurel Lodge, it was the most informal of reception lines, except for that flow of energy emanating directly from the president and pooling in front of him so that, in greeting him, we stepped into a force field.

My thoughts on the ride to Camp David had reflected my sense of the presidency as an office—daunting, imperious, world-consequential. But here in Laurel Lodge it was the man who stood out, a man who dominated the room in a human fashion that made it seem as if he had invested the office with its glamour rather than drawing his radiance from it. As if we might blurt out, even were he but another visitor among us, "*that* man, there's something about him, he should be president!" Perhaps I am merely a sucker for charm or for power (I am), but it was also the unanimous view of everyone else I spoke with—there at Camp David, or in later years.

No revelations here: the president's power to capture, seduce, overcome, and persuade has been universally acknowledged. As the CBS newsman Bob Schieffer would later say, Clinton could charm the bark off a tree. His ideological adversaries were as subject to his power as his allies; those whom he drove mad with his weaknesses could no more resist him than those drawn to and empowered by his strengths.

President Clinton, time would prove, was certainly not a man for all seasons, but when he walked into a room, in the manner of the specially gifted, he carried springtime in his breast pocket, its greening optimism ever at the ready. Reagan's speechwriters had coined the phrase, but Reagan was an old man, whereas with Clinton it always really felt like "morning in America." This man would never be impeached. The most hard-boiled cynics had to be out of his presence to give vent to their umbrage. Indeed, the outrage of those who later declared themselves his greatest enemies, the Ken Starrs and the Christopher Hitchenses, or the irony of critics like Joe Klein (the "anonymous" of *Primary Colors*) and Robert Reich (after he left his Labor Department cabinet post and vented his disappointment), seemed to be stoked by their own vulnerability to his powers. Indifference was not an option. No one hates a seducer like the seducee, once he has extricated himself from the embrace. He reviles the lingering springtime touch because he has given himself to it so ardently. No wonder Newt Gingrich would warn his allies not to allow themselves to spend personal time with the president, and if they had to be with him, not to make any decisions until a decent interval had elapsed.

The Laurel Lodge conference room was not capacious. The oval table could seat perhaps two dozen comfortably. The White House almost always uses place cards for meetings and meals, whether social, official, or business. It is only natural in a place where control is crucial and where (in this particular White House) no externality, no randomness, is ever allowed to creep into arrangements otherwise subject to human intervention and direction. But on this particular afternoon the large conference table in Laurel Lodge offered open seating (I realized only later how rare that was), and after the four principals had seated themselves smack in the middle on either side of the extended oval, the president and the first lady on one side facing Vice-President Gore and Tipper on the other side, we were left to find our own places. Staffers slipped in among the visitors (perhaps the "randomness" was planned?), and Bill Galston took the head at one end, where he could conduct the inexperienced little chamber orchestra that was forming up.

The open seating occasioned a certain frenzy, a kind of civil musical chairs, in which we visitors tried to position ourselves strategically without really having a strategy. I grabbed a seat next to Mrs. Gore as close to the middle of the oval table as I could get, where I could gaze across at the president and Hillary (and be seen by them). Those less fleet of foot ended up down at the ends of the table, feeling just a little peripheral. George Stephanopoulos huddled at one end, far from Galston at the other end. George was scribbling furiously in a notebook before there were notes to be taken, rarely looking up, saying nothing. With the extraordinary influence he wielded in private, he presumably could afford to be silent here. His memoir gives no account of these "seminars," though he attended almost all of them. I suppose for him they didn't matter and so remained invisible.

Before the principals, their names embossed neatly on the covers, lay overstuffed briefing books as large as telephone white pages. They included the fat memos we had submitted earlier (my God we were prolix!), biographical materials, and other items deemed pertinent by Galston. Like quiz show participants, we visitors worked without safety nets, limited in our speaking to what we carried in our heads or had jotted onto index cards. I relied on damp Post-its that inevitably got stuck to the inside of my jacket pockets and could, at the critical moments of need, never be retrieved.

The regimen Galston followed that afternoon turned out to be standard operating procedure for the meetings that followed at which I was present. Not, I believe, because Bill's pedagogical inventiveness was limited, but because this format clearly suited the president and Bill was prudent enough to stick by what worked for the only person in the room who really mattered. We would offer brief presentations around key themes in groups of three or four—about five minutes per person, twenty minutes per group, for a little more than an hour and a quarter of formal presentations. The president would intervene at his own discretion during the presentations, with the conversation accelerating in zones thinly populated by ideas but slowing to a snail's pace in the thickly settled conceptual neighborhoods where the president could get engaged and sometimes, as he waxed loquacious, bring traffic to a complete halt.

Bill had chosen as our organizing themes four topics broad enough in compass and generic enough in description to permit a very general discussion suitable to (in Washington's smart-ass jargon) big-think intellectuals rather than policy wonks. The themes—which turned out to define our conversation over the next several years—were these:

- National Power and National Purpose (defining the administration's vision in terms of the appropriate size of the federal government and the appropriate purposes a nation might pursue when government was downsized);
- Reinventing Government (the Gore-led effort to modernize, slim down, and de-bureaucratize a government apparatus grown heavy and unresponsive under slow-moving welfare state and Great Society programs);
- Civil Society and Public Sentiment (the role of mediating institutions, public trust, and civic engagement in determining a national agenda); and finally,

· Renewing Citizenship (the role of participation, civic education, national service, and social responsibility in re-creating a stronger, more citi-
zen-grounded form of democratic governance).

In fact, our agenda allowed us to ask the most fundamental questions
about what America was, how it should or could be democratically governed, what the distinctive roles of government, civil society, individual
citizens, and the private (economic) sector ought to be, and how the
new Democratic Party and this administration were to implement their
evolving philosophy as it spoke to these questions.

As a political theorist I was elated: I had spent my life wrestling with
exactly these questions, and now I was invited to do it in a place where it
might make a difference. As a citizen I was moved. I had spent a lifetime
insisting that democracy had to govern bottom up not top down, and
here I was, not only positioned to make that argument to the president of
the United States, but by my very presence demonstrating that ordinary
citizens (even if they were intellectuals who sometimes disdained ordinary citizens) had a voice in the highest counsels in the land. Thanks to
this president. But the dilemmas persisted. We were in the lion's den:
Were we polecats and foxes, nipping at the sovereign's heels in the hope
of slowing him down? Or would-be keepers trying to tame his raw power?
Or merely foolish lambs, being led to the slaughter—but paraded first in
all our academic pridefulness to provide a little intellectual cover for
depredations that would continue with or without our counsel? Now that
I had gained the inner sanctum, did I really want to be there?

In the peace movement, the pragmatist in me had tried to walk the
line. Stay on the outside in my criticism and willingness to flout convention, work the inside when reporters or politicians saw things my
way and gave me a chance to achieve something practical. Our small
band of peace pragmatists had worked both sides of the line with the
Massachusetts State Assembly, acting as alienated idealists in conceiving our strategy, but resuming the identity of tough-minded insiders
when we locked up the pacifists who didn't want to play the inside
game. When the Green Party in Germany came of age with its red-
green coalition after the Social Democratic victory of 1998, it faced the
same dilemma: whether to take on the responsibilities and moral risks
of actually exercising power or to hold on to the comfort and moral sim-
plicity of the outsider and remain in comfortable opposition.

Here at Camp David, I had already stepped well over the line. I had grasped the insider's cup and sip by sip was draining it. Except, I told myself, I was still an outsider, an autonomous intellectual here voluntarily, and owing nothing to the powerful man to whom I offered counsel. A few years later, Naomi Wolf would get $15,000 a month to let Vice-President Gore know what women were thinking about (and what they were thinking about him); never mind the alpha male stuff, what she was doing was working the inside. Not us. We were paid not a cent. Said what we thought. We could all stay or go. He could take it or leave it. We had bought our own air tickets into D.C. and were taking no man's dollar for our counsel. We were the president's equals in autonomy (or better—*we* had tenure!). We had spent a day in his lair, but were bound to return to our innocent homes on the outside by nightfall.

Meanwhile, we had participated in an opportunity for democratic officials whose normal thought horizons were defined—in the crisis and response mode of modern government—by tomorrow afternoon or, if they insisted on the long term, late next week, to actually think both big and long-term. Democracies do not do well with five-year plans borrowed from great philosophers, but that doesn't mean they should rely exclusively on five-day whims instigated by trivial headlines and the passing crises such headlines often generated.

We were after the middle ground: a horizon, say, of thirty-six months, something pragmatic enough to meet the president's political needs and the demands of a State of the Union speech, but sufficiently grounded in ideas to allow him to lead as well as to follow. We could not know that at this very moment, panicked by the Republican electoral success in November, the president was reestablishing a backdoor link to Dick Morris and the narrow, poll-driven political horizons Morris represented. But had we known, it probably would have made little difference, since we would have surely persuaded ourselves that we were the weighted ballast for Morris's lighter-than-air prescriptions. Any other interpretation would have compelled us to see ourselves as intellectual window dressing or, worse, as simply irrelevant—though this might have been closer to the actual truth.

In introducing the agenda, Galston allowed himself to "hope" that we might feel empowered in this informal setting not just to edit and elaborate on a philosophy already in place but to help redefine the terms on which that philosophy had been constructed. The president was in effect asking us to help him redefine America and the role of democratic government in it. He was taking governance deeply seriously, and opening to reflection and critique the most fundamental questions about how a democracy ought to function if it is to preserve both law and liberty, to guarantee justice without compromising individuality, to pursue equality and still honor rights. He was asking how the demands of markets and of public goods might be balanced. How a Democratic administration committed to social justice and racial equality might nevertheless get beyond the institutions of the New Deal and the Great Society that had both helped to meet these demands and, in time, come (in the view, at least, of the New Democrats in the White House and a great many voters) to obstruct the way to further success. He was, in our terms, asking us to speak truth to power. All we needed was the truth. All he needed was power. As history was to show, neither of us quite possessed what we needed.

# CHAPTER TWO

# Don't Stop Thinking about Tomorrow

**MADISON SQUARE GARDEN** in a tumult. Balloons everywhere, a gathering roar of voices intoxicated by power and expectation, the band blaring "Don't Stop Thinking about Tomorrow!" through massive loudspeakers—Fleetwood Mac at a political convention!—and two couples dancing madly onstage, the women vivacious and pretty, the two men, mischievous brothers, looking eons younger than politicians who have just been nominated for the presidency and vice-presidency of the United States are supposed to look. It had to be a watershed in the history of American politics. The baby boomers grown up and assuming their rightful station on earth. An antiwar protester (if a rather prudent one), a guy who had smoked a little weed (if rather prudently), the nominee of the Democratic Party. One of ours, up there! A president younger than me!

I don't go to conventions. Or didn't. My participation at the Atlanta Convention in 1988 was virtual—a large print quote plastered over a full page at the back of the Democratic National Convention program booklet. It must have puzzled the delegates who bothered to read the program (a very elite minority, I suspect) to see this rather academic citation, attributed to "Benjamin R. Barber, Author, Commentator and Professor of Political Science" (who?):

> A strong commitment to democracy is the condition for the survival of all that is most dear to us in the Western liberal tradition. To be free we must be self-governing; to have rights we must be citizens. In the end, only citizens can be free.

The road to freedom lies then through democracy, and democracy means above all the capacity for common speech—that distinctive faculty of reasoning the Greeks called logos that sets humankind apart from the animal kingdom and bestows on it the twin gifts of self-consciousness and other-consciousness. To strong democrats, the right of every individual to speak to others, to assert the right of being through the act of communication, is identified with the precious wellspring of human autonomy and dignity.

Thus it was that in ancient Greece, isogoria—the universal right to speak in the assembly—came to be a synonym not merely for democratic participation but for democracy itself. Thus it is that democracy, as it struggles to flourish in a shrinking world of ever greater complexity and interdependence, has to nourish the power of the people to speak, to decide and to act.

For in the end human freedom will be found not in caverns of private solitude but in the noisy assemblies where women and men meet daily as citizens and discover in each other's talk the consolation and strength of their common humanity.

Don't ask how this prolix inscription got in the program. Or about its impact on the convention. At best, it was the kind of vanity moment that let me feel a certain connection with a Democratic Party from which I was otherwise alienated. That was precisely why I was content to watch the conventions on TV, where, from the outside, and with the help of the skybox commentators, you can catch all the nuances and turnings of politics you miss if you're on the inside. But in '92, I went. It was in New York (my town), and I had friends who could get me in—like Mike Levy, once an astute student of political theory at Rutgers and in 1992 an even more astute chief of staff to Senator Lloyd Bentsen (Bentsen would become treasury secretary and Mike would become deputy secretary for political affairs) and after I became a Clinton counselor my own tutor on Washington politics. Lots of good reasons to go. Besides, this one had a historic feel to it. A sea-change year. A Democrat who actually planned to win.

The Democrats had spent two dozen long years in the wilderness with only the administration of Jimmy Carter to show for it. Carter was a good man on whom the gods had visited endless bad luck. His single, misbegotten term had only deepened the sense of the party's historical marginality. But now the Democrats had actually nominated someone with the charisma and vigor and vision and youth—and, most significantly, the knack for accommodation otherwise known as the politics of compromise—to take victory away from the complacent Republicans, who were featuring a seemingly tired one-term president and a vice-presidential candidate with a reputation (probably undeserved) for preternatural dumbness. Clinton alone, this small-state hick governor known nationally only for an endlessly *boring* convention oration in 1988 had alone among the notables (and he wasn't one) thought it worth running. With the odds against him, Clinton, the candidate who in January had gone on TV to apologize for an affair and in May was featured on the cover of the *New Republic* under the title "Why Clinton Can't Win!" (with a contribution by Sid Blumenthal, who would later serve in Clinton's second administration), had made the race. He had run hard where Mario Cuomo and Bill Bradley and all the other smart could-be/would-be front-runners had packed it in to wait for more propitious times, and he had pushed an impossible campaign to victory. He hadn't just backed into the race because everyone else was running the other way. He had entered resolutely as a self-persuaded must-be who knew he could win and would win. A New Democrat with a new program calculated to win because it was so unlike what Democratic programs were supposed to be like and took accurate aim at all those centrist Democrats who had become Reagan supporters in the 1980s but whom Clinton knew he could recapture. When he was through winning, he had made it look so easy that everyone immediately forgot how impossible it was supposed to have been.

In fact it had been pretty daunting. A week before the New Hampshire primary, Clinton had been 20 points down, scandal already plaguing him. Yet he came in a strong second, dubbed for the first time "the comeback kid," a title he earned again and again over the next eight years. The general election was very close, and one could say that as Ralph Nader cost Gore the 2000 election, Ross Perot cost Bush Sr. the 1992 election. The forty-second president of the United States was in fact elected with only 43 percent of the vote in 1992. Even the doomed Dukakis had done better. In June, weeks before the convention, Clinton had been running third behind Bush and Perot. The convention marked another turning point.

Clinton was there, big time. And so was I. Thinking about tomorrow.

And all the lost-opportunity yesterdays. I was supposed to have been at
the other "big one" of the century—the '68 Democratic convention at
which the party imploded and took itself out of competition for a couple of dozen years. I was to have been there—as a delegate. Not for
Humphrey, but for peace and Eugene McCarthy. I ran as a "peace" delegate from Philadelphia's Second District and campaigned in a
McCarthy-friendly but independent manner. Back in these years, before
the Democrats reformed their party rules, we were practicing exactly
the kind of maverick politics to which the 1972 rules changes would
put an end. Like the Mississippi Freedom Party in 1964 (whose civil
rights inclined members were barred from participation in that LBJ
convention), our peacenik races in 1968 were challenging the centrist
party—pulling it away from the center to which Clinton would aspire
to return it nearly a quarter of a century later. We wanted to nominate
Eugene McCarthy, a genuine "peace" candidate who, unlike either
Humphrey or Nixon, had pledged to end the Vietnam conflict and otherwise was encouraging the idea of international disarmament.

When the McCarthy nomination strategy failed, some in the peace
party (like some supporters of Ralph Nader in the 2000 election) hoped
to take enough votes from Hubert Humphrey to hand the election to
Richard Nixon and prove to the Democratic Party that it had better
start representing the radical wing of the party if it wanted the radical
vote. Unfortunately, that strategy worked rather well (both times). We
defeated Humphrey. But we also helped plunge our party into twenty
years of self-recrimination and defeatism. In the end, I could not be true
to these cockeyed radical politics. My realism and dislike of Nixon
trumped my radicalism, and—to vote against Nixon—I voted for
Humphrey. Still, the die was cast: like so many other Democrats, I had
been propelled into an era of voting for highly principled losers. And
feeling proud of it. As Tom Lehrer had written about the Left's role in
the Spanish civil war, "they won all the battles, but we had all the good
songs." And our principles wholly intact.

These were years of political ardor, however, and it probably isn't fair
to ask for prudence. I entered the race for delegate to the Democratic
convention on a peace ticket friendly to but not pledged absolutely to
vote for McCarthy. In Pennsylvania the primary took the form of a non-
binding preference poll (in tribute to the Constitution's embrace of federalism, every state had and has its own electoral rules—and, as we

recently have learned, sometimes with disastrous consequences). Those delegates actually elected could do as they chose at the convention, even if it meant turning their backs on the candidate to whom they were pledged on the primary ballot.

Most Americans pay no heed to primary politics, which vary from state to state and seem hopelessly arcane. But it is in the primaries that the contours that define national political choice are determined: imagine if Bradley and McCain had been the nominees of the two official parties in 2000—or Nader and Pat Buchanan! What happened to put the Democratic Party beyond electability until Bill Clinton took up its cause, decades later, happened in the 1968 primaries. You could write in, say, Bobby Kennedy. Kennedy was not on the ballot in Pennsylvania, but had inaugurated a campaign that brought together what today would be the Buchanan and the Nader constituencies. He managed to ignite the passions of both right-wing populists who formerly supported Alabama's racist governor, George Wallace, and left-wing populists too radical to have supported JFK, let alone Bobby in his earlier tough-guy attorney general incarnation. In Michigan, the spinners had it, he was garnering the support of ethnic racists and union populists.[1] But it didn't really matter what you thought about him, even if you were "his" delegate, because that committed you to nothing. Whether you ran in the name of Kennedy or Humphrey or McCarthy, you could vote at the convention for whomever you pleased. Real democracy. Real chaos. The way party politics used to be before nominees locked everything up in a couple of superprimaries, and conventions became scripted prime-time extravaganzas devised by spinners and publicists hoping to put voters to sleep.

Most of us in the peace movement preferred McCarthy to Bobby

---

[1] This view was challenged even then by many progressives, who refused to admit that Bobby was one of them. Bobby Kennedy was not only still associated with his tough-talking attorney general days; he had been a "carpetbagger" in New York. Those challenging Kennedy's liberal credentials were reinforced again recently in Ronald Steel's biography, *In Love with Night: The American Romance with Robert Kennedy* (New York: Simon & Schuster, 2000), which challenges the liberal theory that Bobby was getting a combination of George Wallace votes and minority black votes in Indiana that made him a putative "healer" across the political and racial divide. On the other hand, I actually heard Bobby campaign in 1968, and he *was* talking about black/white coalitions and uniting right and left populism in a campaign against the elites that normally kept them divided.

Kennedy. Kennedy might have had a chance to win it all, though many in the civil rights and peace movements found it hard to accept at face value his conversion to populism during the Lyndon Johnson years. The Kennedys were certainly the darlings of the liberal or "vital center" represented by Arthur Schlesinger Jr. and Harvard's "best and bright-est" memorialized in David Halberstam's book of that title. But for those on the left, Bobby was the attorney general who wiretapped Martin Luther King Jr. and whose brother had deepened the involvement in the Vietnam War and risked nuclear conflagration over Cuba (we blamed Kennedy not Khrushchev, although it was Khrushchev, of course, who had made the near-fatal miscalculation of installing medium-range nuclear missiles in America's backyard). Bobby was also that carpet-bagger who, like Mrs. Clinton more recently, challenged for the Senate in a state not his own. (He's the historical legitimizer for her run, but his own campaign was assailed in much the same way.) The authenticity of his new views was never subjected to a vote, however, because just a month after the Pennsylvania primary he was gunned down by Sirhan Sirhan, joining his brother in martyrdom.

Me, I stuck with McCarthy that spring. It's not just that I ran; I was elected. In a primary that gave McCarthy over 400,000 votes, two of eight delegates running as peace supporters in Philadelphia were elect-ed. We had bucked the party machine and run in open hostility to the party's mainline candidate. Hubert Humphrey was Lyndon Johnson's vice-president and though a true liberal on most issues—he was brought up in Minnesota's populist Farmer-Labor Party—on Vietnam he'd become a hawk. Whether he was acting out of true conviction (we thought he was) or stewing in the bitter juices of loyalty to a president with whom he didn't really agree (the problem Nixon had had before him and George Bush and Al Gore would have in later years), Humphrey was pledged to the war in Vietnam. And so, we reasoned, it wasn't Humphrey but the war that we were out to beat.

In the books kept in Party Heaven, I was elected a delegate to the 1968 Democratic convention. But like certain ballplayers, with aster-isks after their names because they hit a record-breaking number of broken-bat doubles in nineteen-something-or-other except that nine-teen-something-or-other had a shortened season because of a war or a strike or a change in the rules, I was a delegate-cum-asterisk. Meaning that, living in my first house with my first wife and first child, holding my first real job as an assistant professor at the University of Pennsylvania, I was duly elected by my fellow citizens of Philadelphia's Second District. But (asterisk) there was a problem. Well before the actual election in April, my nomination petition had been declared invalid by a hack state judge out in Harrisburg, and so my "election" didn't count. I got the votes but was "illegally" on the ballot, and no majority, though it might propel me to victory, could propel me to Chicago. I never got to the Windy City that summer. Which means I never won my sixties spurs, never got hectored by Mayor Daley, never joined the Chicago Eight or the Friendship Park 800, never rioted and smoked dope (and got a chance not to inhale) outside the convention hall, never got arrested by Daley's rogue cops. The tear gas others inhaled deeply, I never even got to breathe.

The judge out in Harrisburg who sat in judgment on what must have been an injunction filed by the regular party seeking to assure we couldn't win, even if we won, as much as admitted that his ruling was arbitrary. He was a hard-ass Democratic pol, and he knew exactly what he was doing. He didn't like amateurs, which is what I suspect he thought most citizens were. (Citizens *are* amateurs; that's the whole point of democracy!) He let me and Gina Hartell (who would win with me on the peace

*Benjamin Barber, Gina Hartell, and presidential candidate Eugene McCarthy in Philadelphia in 1968. (Photo by Martin Smith.)*

line and be declared illegitimate as well) know that whether or not we won in April, our candidacies were dead in the water. That we had every right to fight the injunction and that we'd likely win if we did. For—and he smiled broadly when he said this—there was considerable doubt about the standing of the regular party's objections as well as to the credibility of its challenge to various signatures on our nominating petitions. Given the crowded dockets of the Pennsylvania court system, however, the spring primary would come and go, and we might be duly elected, but that election, based on his current ruling, would be invalid, and by the time we got our case heard on appeal—why that would be, say, five or six months hence, which, count the months on your fingers, would be well after the summer convention was over. And, he concluded with a broad, malicious grin, that would serve us goddamn peaceniks right for affecting to "challenge illegitimate authority" (as the peace slogan of the time had it). "Ya want illegitimate authority?" his every quiver seemed to say, "I'll give ya illegitimate authority. How's it feel? Pretty illegitimate, huh? Good!"

I was incensed, but we didn't bother appealing. As a social scientist I have a certain appreciation for the role of minor corruption in keeping bureaucracy from paralyzing a political system. One of my teachers at Harvard, Carl J. Friedrich, who had helped write the constitution of postwar Germany, liked to say corruption was like arsenic: every living body needs a small dose to thrive, but—caveat emptor!—more than a little was always fatal. My hard-won place on the ballot as a potential delegate to the convention may have been arbitrarily annulled. But (I consoled myself) political parties were still essential instruments of democracy in this era before television destroyed party solidarity, and party regulars could hardly be blamed for using every bent tool of governance available to bend the system in their favor. Without political parties, disfavored by America's original founders who regarded them as fractious seedbeds of discontent and faction (they were right there), the American system would have become inflexible and oligarchic. Parties were big, bright, brassy buckles, which, however, allowed ordinary citizens to feel bound to government. With respect to our case in '68, it was sort of too bad for the separation and balance of powers that the state judiciary had become a crooked tool of the state party system, but it made for a degree of stability and continuity in an otherwise too anarchic decentralized electoral system. The same kind of thing Bush Jr. loyalists probably were telling themselves in the fall of 2000 when they were successfully working the courts to prevent a Florida recount that might have kept Bush from claiming the presidency.

Besides, how was a twenty-nine-year-old assistant professor making $7,800 a year going to pay for an appeal anyway? The state Democratic Party obviously had deeper pockets than a kid academic representing a peace movement driven by ardor rather than dollars and with no pockets at all of its own. So I didn't go to the convention, and missed the massive demonstrations and Daley's reactive shenanigans. I had already had a taste of Democratic machine politics in Harrisburg and didn't need to travel to Chicago to be exposed to Daley's regional hyper-variations on the same theme.

I was over fifty when I finally got to my first political convention, in New York in the summer of '92. And if our political conventions no longer entail those seven-ballot backroom bargaining marathons by which the Democrats once resolved the angry regional and ideological differences forged by divisive and inconclusive primaries, this one still resonated with a theatrical magic that television viewers were unlikely to fully feel. Conventions are, of course, loyalist congresses where faithful campaign workers and local party officials and diligent union stewards who have pledged their lives to the welfare of the Democratic Party are rewarded, along with sundry elected officials, hangers-on and fellow travelers. The mood is one of willed chaos: a participatory spectacle in which no real decisions are any longer taken, but everything feels good. Over the course of the second half of the twentieth century, they were transformed. They had long been active arenas of debate and decision-making, where nominees had to run the gauntlet of vote after vote before winning a majority, where vice-presidential nominees were negotiated only after a presidential nominee was finally chosen— where, in short, delegates actually had several jobs to do and where their work would last into the final day of the convention.

I was grappling with puberty in 1952 when Adlai Stevenson, the intellectuals' favorite egghead, was "drafted" by the Democratic convention at Truman's behest. Having lost that election to Eisenhower, he four years later duked it out with Estes Kefauver, Al Gore's forebear as a senator from Tennessee, who after endless ballots became Stevenson's running mate in 1956. Between paying rapt attention to the radio soap operas my mother was writing (*Ma Perkins, Just Plain Bill* [a prophecy of presidents to come?], and *Helen Trent* ["Can a girl from Kansas City find happiness in the big city?"]), I listened in those years to my first campaigns, in which it seemed that literally dozens of candidates were still politically alive going into the actual conventions. In the early spring of 1952, Stevenson rode a train into Pittsfield, Massachusetts, and I got a glimpse of him, standing on the rear car platform and waving a little self-consciously to the small crowd. Even at thirteen, I thought of myself as a kid intellectual and was drawn to the man with ideas. Even if he couldn't make up his mind, even if just ten years later he would fall down dead in Mayfair outside the American embassy in London, having sold out his principles on the way to trying to get those principles heard (as U.S. representative to the United Nations, he had to rationalize Kennedy's Bay of Pigs invasion he had opposed with all his heart). Hopeless dreamer that he was, he was my man; the last Democrat I deeply admired . . . until Clinton—by which time I'd grown tired of being a utopian dreamer whose favorite candidates lost every election they contested.

If the conventions of the fifties were still free-for-alls, in which delegates often voted as they pleased, by the sixties and seventies the more "democratic" idea of citizens choosing delegates in primary elections who were actually committed to vote for specific candidates was spreading and nominations gradually were being decided in the primaries. In 1960 Stevenson's name was still alive, so Kennedy's nomination was not altogether certain going in. The new maverick Eugene McCarthy (the wild card in 1968) would nominate the old maverick Adlai Stevenson one last time, with Eleanor Roosevelt stumping for his candidacy. But that was the last time there was any real contest, any mystery about the outcome. In 1968 Hubert Humphrey's opponents were all outside the convention hall. Conventions were losing their drama, becoming rubber-stamp celebrations of candidates already chosen, so that balloting became an empty exercise and backroom debates a thing of the past.

By the 1980s conventions had been wholly drained of theater and were becoming those public relations spectacles we are familiar with today, directed as much at television audiences as at delegates on the floor. Ronald Reagan's famous 1984 "Morning in America" convention video provided the benchmark for success in these new "virtual" conventions, while the 1992 Republican convention, torn to shreds by right-wing pontificating and images of cultural war, became a permanent warning to party elites about what could happen when conventions escaped the care of prudent spin doctors (Clinton could happen, the "Man from Hope" who borrowed his tactics from Reagan). The results were all too dully visible in Philadelphia in the summer of 2000 when the Republicans pulled off the safest and most successful nothing-can-possibly-happen convention in their long history, and went on to win (sort of) the presidency.

In the year 2000 the conventions not only made no decisions; they no longer were organized for the benefit of delegates or the purpose of making decisions at all. They were wholly scripted television mini-series that occupied three or four prime-time evenings aimed at national viewers who may not even have been regular voters, let alone political junkies or convention delegates. The 1992 Democratic convention in New York may have been the last national gathering punctuated by a degree of spontaneity. When President Clinton bade farewell to the Democrats in LA in 2000, the best he could do was to remind them of his 1992 theme-song convention-stopper "Don't Stop Thinking about Tomorrow"—invoking the spontaneous future by appealing to the stale past. For Al Gore it perhaps seemed more like "Yesterday, all my troubles seemed so far away."

Back in 1992, however, "Don't Stop" felt fresh. The floor of Madison Square Garden had been cleared for the tide of delegates who would wash into New York from every part of the country and were distributed in the manner television viewers have become familiar with in colorful sections, their state banners and homemade as well as professionally designed placards and posters bespeaking a federalist and proud parochialism of a kind one could never find in unitary nation-states like England or France. E pluribus unum indeed! The broad stage where key events unfolded that television cameras brought into your living room just across the coffee table were a distant apparition when viewed by delegates, whose immediate world comprised the gossip-driven nattering of fellow delegates, the sudden eruptions of neighboring delegations cheering for reasons that were never apparent, by milling reporters and boisterous floor managers who would shout unintelligibly into the mobs of delegates, trying to arrange interviews or orchestrate floor demonstrations. So that when you were on the floor, you might bend an ear only occasionally to the overhead speakers to try to hear what was happening on the far-away podium whenever a new face seemed to appear at the microphone. The speeches that are front and center on television droned on here as comforting background noise.

Much more exciting was the potted grandiloquence of the deliciously histrionic roll call of states—"the great, green, good state of Podunkia, where weeds grow like flowers and politicians like weeds, is proud to cast one vote for native son Herman Hucksterson, the beloved and all too recently deceased mayor of Podunkia Junction, and all of its remaining three votes for the next president of the United States, Bill Clinton!" These were the only floor speeches that could really be heard. The acoustics of Madison Square Garden are better suited to fan hullabaloo than to classical rhetoric, and it was much easier to listen to a ward organizer from Brooklyn wonder whether Chuck Schumer (then a tough congressman from Brooklyn and my son Jeremy's boss after the '88 Dukakis debacle) would get a subcabinet post than to hear a report on a platform struggle over campaign finance. Why listen to Paul Tsongas give up the ghost in the name of party unity when you could giggle at the South Carolina mayor who was shouting that if Mario Cuomo was offered a Supreme Court seat, that would be the end of the Democratic Party in the South? As if it wasn't already the end of the Democratic Party in the South. LBJ had wept when he signed the Civil Rights Act in 1964, predicting that his courage would cost the Democrats the South for generations to come. And it had.

Most of the speakers—Clinton's erstwhile rivals whom his hard-assed campaigning had sent to defeat, along with Ted Kennedy, who came to recite the liberal catechism—were relegated to CNN and C-SPAN, out of prime-time network coverage. A few got special attention from their cliques on some part of the Garden floor—like radical California's professional weirdo Jerry Brown, the Ralph Nader of that time, who spent his time in the limelight denouncing what he called "the smug custodians of global finance" (he got that right!) and pointedly ignoring the nominee (he got that wrong!). The crowd also would pause to look at (if not listen to) celebrities like President Carter, who offered his blessing for a guy he didn't much like and later criticized, and Nelson Mandela, who made a beatific impression merely by being there. But it took a true orator to claim the attention of the floor. Someone like the Seneca of the modern Democratic Party, Mario Cuomo, when he took the podium to place Bill Clinton's name in nomination. One of democracy's more ironic, if wholesome, practices insists that losers eat public crow by saying nice things about, campaigning for, or even nominating those who vanquish them in the primaries. But Cuomo's appearance was different.

With the governor of New York at the mike, the vast throng fell silent. The networks, who managed to ignore most podium speakers, were head over heels in love with Cuomo (that man could *talk*!) and finally panned away from their own jabbering commentators to show the public something that was actually happening inside the Garden. There was drama in Cuomo's rivalry with the man whose name he would place in nomination. In a taped phone call Clinton had made to Gennifer Flowers, there had been a reference to "Mafioso" and how Cuomo seemed to "act like one." Cuomo fumed. The governor from backwater Arkansas had also suggested initially that holding the convention in bigtime New York might be a mistake. Cuomo went ballistic. So how would he play it now? Would he use his eloquence to elude a real embrace of Clinton and talk past him to the larger issues of principle that always exercised him and aroused his audiences?

Fear not. Cuomo was Cuomo, too noble for petty revenge. His speech was reason enough for a Hyde Park ward leader from Chicago to spend three days on the home court of the New York Knicks, enough for a disciplined shop steward from Des Moines to dwell for nearly a week in the belly of anarchy that was Manhattan. As circuses go, Ringling Brothers had nothing on this one. Howard Kurtz of the *Washington Post* called the nomination speech a "rhetorical tub-thumper," while E. J. Dionne (perhaps Clinton's most sensitive journalistic interpreter) dubbed it Whitmanesque. In bringing down the house, it raised up Bill Clinton, whose poll numbers surged, even before his acceptance speech, from well behind his Republican rival to a 45 percent to 28 percent lead over Vice-President Bush.

It was not Cuomo's magnificent riff on poverty and race that captivated the audience, though his line about kids' being more likely to hear gunfire before they ever get to hear a symphony orchestra was surely captivating. It was the unexpectedly warm embrace of Bill Clinton. Other speakers walked around the nominee gingerly, because he had trounced them in the primaries; or as if they were still not sure he could win for them in the fall, what with the scandals and uncertainties along the campaign trail. Cuomo, his arch-rival, with every reason to still be smarting from the "Mafioso" garbage talk, showed no such reserve. He knew a winner when he saw one.

In his very first words, uttered in the unfamiliar hush, he said to the delegates, "This is not a matter of *wanting* Bill Clinton; it is much much more than that. We need Bill Clinton because he is our only hope for change from this nation's current disastrous course."

Cheers, placards waving, hats aloft dancing in the lights. Don't stop thinking about tomorrow! Yeah! Then a long, poignant account of America's woes, conspired in by harsh and complacent Republicans. Some pointedly New Democrat words about the hope kindled by the man from Hope when he places his faith in work, in jobs, in an opportunity for every American. A new path of public works tied to personal responsibility. And then the final ascent up the rhetorical mountain— Cuomo knows how to finish!

"I'd like to march with you behind President Bill Clinton through cities and rural villages where all the people have safe streets, and affordable housing and health care when they need it."

Delegates are thrusting their fists in the air, clapping wildly. Cuomo seems to be reading their every move, anticipating the frenzied action.

"I want to clap my hands and throw my fists in the air, cheering neighborhoods where children can be children . . ."

Cheers, truly thunderous, chants too, a warm feeling of gratitude to this orator who reciprocates the pride people feel in him.

"I want to sing, proud songs, happy songs. . . . I want to march behind Bill Clinton in a parade that sends up fireworks. . . . I want to march with you. . . . I want to look around and feel the warmth, the pride, the profound gratitude of knowing we are making America surer, stronger, and sweeter."

Yes, now it is our time! Time for *our* America! The Reagan era is *over*! Cuomo continues to read our collective mind.

"So step aside, Mr. Bush. You've had your parade! It's time for a change. It's time for someone smart enough to know; strong enough to do; sure enough to lead: The comeback kid. A new voice for a new America!"

It's bedlam now, the crowd's voice tracking Cuomo's final words in a crescendo of cheering:

"Because I love New York, because I love America, I nominate for the office of the President of the United States, the man from Hope, Arkansas, Governor Bill Clinton!"

Maybe this is Clinton's epiphanic moment. And ours. The highlight, the climax, as good as it will get—this moment of ecstatic expectation before the candidate has even offered his acceptance speech, before the rock 'n' roll party featuring Fleetwood Mac and Clinton and Gore dancing with their wives with an abandon that tells us they know they will win, before the heady days of transition when everything seems possible, before the first term's unfulfillable ambitions are boisterously raised up and ignominiously shot down, before the showdowns with Newt and his obstreperous Congress, before the scandals of Whitewater and Monica and the ultimate bittersweet victory of surviving Ken Starr and impeachment—before any of this even is begun, we arrive at epiphany. History is ours again. The gods smile. There will be no better moment in the two terms of governance that lie ahead. Not until eight years later, when Clinton again mounts the podium of the Democratic convention on the other coast—now playing Cuomo to Al Gore's Clinton, using nostalgia for all his achievements in all his own yesterdays to propel Gore into tomorrow—will Democrats hear rhetoric this passionate.

Cuomo's rhetoric is, of course, nearly unique in an era where rhetoric is out of fashion. Clinton's a brilliant conversationalist, even when talking to the whole nation, but he is no classical orator. He inhabits his speeches and brings them to life, but if you examine the words the next morning they feel like a dead carcass. He simply knows how to "communicate" in the way that moderns think of as modern: low-key, personable, example-rich, point to point (like the Internet). But no arching narrative structures to achieve a series of linked agons. No Gettysburg, no Four Freedoms. Not even a Kennedyesque turn of the kind favored by traditional presidential speechwriters like Goodwin or Safire or Peggy Noonan. Cuomo is of this old school—older even than Safire and Noonan—because he does it himself. How can even the most hardened cynics not listen? How can the political veterans of the Democratic Party, losers now for two dozen years, not take heed and heart?

Cuomo is the master: sublimely corny, uplifting by reaching down, calculatingly earnest, unabashedly familiar in his self-conscious self-distancing. He engages in despondent diagnostics in order to leaven despair with irrepressible hope. There is in his just-below-the-surface religiosity an odor of salvation—a not quite wholly secularized redemption. He uses America's predicament as a platform to re-launch its promise. He uses its promise to pummel its problems into submission.

The last time I'd heard the likes of Cuomo's speech live was nearly thirty years earlier. Martin Luther King Jr. on the Lincoln Memorial. Not going to Chicago in '68 had in fact broken my modest string of attendance at sixties-defining national demonstrations, including most notably that March on Washington in 1964, at which King gave what was arguably the most sublime oration in America's modern political history—certainly the most ringing political sermon on behalf of America's as yet unfulfilled promise since Lincoln's Gettysburg Address. I listened from a perch I had secured early in the day on the lower steps of the Lincoln Memorial, from which powerfully appropriate podium King captivated the nation. As deeply affecting as King's simple words was the sea of bodies stretching away from the Memorial and running up either side of the reflecting pools to what seemed like the horizon marked by the Washington Monument.

This quiet but potent ocean—a black, brown, and white sea of expectant faces—lay calm, ready, for once, not to be disappointed, ready for the first time to believe that the American promise might include all Americans, that little white children and little black children might truly walk and work and live hand in hand. Martin Luther King's prophecy that noontime would one day, long after he had given his life to its claims, animate the politics of President Clinton as well. On this day in March of 1963, America turned a corner. The days of an all-white, all-Anglo-Saxon, all-male America were numbered. King was a prophet of too often deferred dreams, but in Washington that day he was also an observer of a changing country, and his prophecy of little black children and little white children walking hand in hand had an aspect of anticipation about it: not that this must happen if America is to be whole, but that it is going to happen because that's where history and destiny and (least dramatically, most importantly) demographics are taking America. Today King's prophecies ring true, not as moral shibboleths but as demographic realities. The nation's largest state no longer has a white majority. America's urban schoolchildren are now majority nonwhite. Multiculturalism is no longer an aspiration but the first fact of American life. King's prophecies of hope have become the new stubborn political facts of our national politics.

So it was that thirty years later Cuomo's nomination of Bill Clinton seemed to take up, perhaps for the first time, the hope engendered by

Martin Luther King that spring day in Washington, the hope buried with him three years later with his assassination. Cuomo's speech, the nomination of Bill Clinton, was a match rekindling the fire of America's promise, but fueled now by hard demographic data. We were back. Reaching out to the new constituencies, the Democrats were moving again. Bill Clinton would take up King's torch and use it to light America down the shadowed path—and would be loved for it by the heirs to King (the African-American community has been his most faithful constituency) and despised for it by those being left behind, the ones for whom the thirty-year hiatus provided by Nixon and Reagan promised an illusory respite from change, a seeming haven for reaction; the ones for whom the very thought of a multicultural, multigendered, multisexual, multicolored nation was too much to bear and to whom, therefore, Bill Clinton could only appear as a traitor and an enemy.

That was the radical moment defined by Cuomo's convention speech. For many of us listening, for liberals and progressives whose time never seemed to come, between the two moments defined by King's dream and Cuomo's aspiration lay a lifetime of unrewarded struggle. Far more typical of these frustrating years between King and Clinton was that other March on Washington—the so-called March on the Pentagon—that had occupied so many of the warriors of '92 back in our youthful days of radicalism in the sixties.

Rhetoric had been in short supply since King was gunned down. The war in Vietnam, the breakdown in America's inner cities, the turmoil of Watergate seeded far grimmer responses. Talk meant little in a tumultuous era when action meant everything. The 1967 March on the Pentagon was a far less consensus-forging event, at which an impressive, if motley, coalition of peace movement organizations came to Washington not to talk but to demonstrate. No gifted speakers, only angry actors, no burning words, only burning draft cards, no assault with rhetoric and metaphor but an actual assault on the Pentagon, clambering over police barricades, scaling side walls, braving tear gas and fixed bayonets! This was the beginning of the end for the old Democratic Party, the inflicting of wounds that would not heal until Clinton secured the nomination in 1992.

I was no prophet, however. For me, the March on the Pentagon in 1967 was the culmination of the commitment I had made at Harvard at the very beginning of the sixties. In the course of a long day, we had

moved from agitated demonstrations in front of the Lincoln Memorial
to a rapid march across the Potomac to lay siege to the portals of the
five-sided fortress on the Potomac. Where many Americans identified
the Pentagon as our nation's rock of national security, we saw in it a
symbol of the cold war, the war in Vietnam, and the runaway defense
budget that—on the way to bankrupting the Soviet Union—was also
undermining America's economic stability. It drew us across the bridge
to Virginia like a magnet.

We were less of a threat than we wanted to be. Eventually things got
out of hand, and we were all gassed, and then rushed by the police and
the National Guard and sent fleeing helter-skelter back across the
Potomac or (for the ones intent on the gesture) got ceremoniously
busted. In the meantime, we worried away the hours confronting the
rows of soldiers defending the Pentagon. Most were even younger than
we were. We were predominantly middle-class university types from
Westchester County and Connecticut hectoring poor kids in uniform
from rural West Virginia and inner-city Baltimore. Not that any of us
on either side of the picket lines were anxious to serve: we were all Bill
Clintons; on the protest side, many of us had lucky draft numbers or
were conscientious resisters. Many of them were in the guard so as to
avoid conscription, these boys with daisies sticking out of the M-1's
held rigidly in their hands, their bodies frozen into the riot-ready positions they had been taught but never actually employed. We planted
the wilting yellow- and white-topped greens that gave us our flower-
child name wherever we could, dropping them into the upright, vase-
like gun barrels to seduce or taunt the kids. God, they really didn't
seem much over eighteen. They were discomfited, not knowing
whether to ignore these peace offerings or to remove them—ending up
too embarrassed to do either. These were the years when cops were
pigs, and in our righteous arrogance some of us thought it clever to
foment what we ourselves would have to call a divisive class war (our
adversaries would just call it stupid politics). We turned radical priori-
ties upside down by transforming working-class men in whose name
the Left was supposed to operate into underlaborers of hegemonic
elites, and treating rural teenagers in uniform as "the enemy," while
we, the children of a more privileged segment of society, affected to be
their sanctimonious liberators.

We stood that afternoon at the Pentagon on the fissure that the war in Vietnam had opened up, separating American from American, and it seems a wonder today that the breach was ever healed. Perhaps the true lesson of the Clinton years is that it wasn't and hasn't. Not if you listen to Rush Limbaugh or Curtis Sliwa on talk radio or to John Ashcroft or Vice-President Cheney or Trent Lott in Washington. Twenty-five years after the assault on the Pentagon, the heirs to these unforgettable protests—blacks, countercultural intellectuals, hippies, consciousness-raisers, feminists, gays, and an army of immigrants who had spent their sixties years in foreign lands but who would benefit from a defining sixties achievement, the end of discriminatory and racist immigration laws—had come to define an emerging American majority that was neither silent nor invisible. This new majority first nominated and elected and then stood stubbornly by William Jefferson Clinton. It was targeted by both Gore and Bush in 2000—there would be no victory for either without this new center.

In the eighties the Right had been screaming bloody murder because sixties radicals were supposed to have taken over the media and the universities, turning Harvard and Madison Avenue, Yale and Silicon Valley, Rutgers and ABC, Berkeley and Hollywood, into exclusive fiefdoms of liberal extremism. The political philosopher Allan Bloom cursed "the closing of the American mind" being perpetrated by what he fancied were radical academic know-nothings and politically correct feminists and brain-dead television addicts and a variety of sexual perverts who could "feel" everything and "think" nothing and consequently confounded principles that should have stood in opposition with matters of taste to which everyone had an equal right.[2]

The charges were as overblown as the puerile antics they took too seriously, but Bloom and his hysterical allies on the cultural right did understand that America was turning a corner—not ideologically, or even just culturally, but demographically. In 1965 the rigid rules that for forty years had kept our shores "safe" from the successive waves of immigrants that would surely have followed the earlier ones that had given America its twentieth-century energy before 1925 were lifted. This small victory of the Great Society played a far more significant role in America's future than the March on Washington or the March on the Pentagon could ever have done, and it was as significant as any of

[2] See Bloom, *The Closing of the American Mind* (New York: Simon & Schuster, 1987).

the Great Society's many progressive reforms. America has always been more multicultural and heterogeneous than its Protestant curators wished, but with the opening of the floodgates in 1965, the country was set to become the first truly global society. And when the kids who marched on Washington and then on the Pentagon, who campaigned for McCarthy and Bobby Kennedy, and then for McGovern, grew up, they inherited and increasingly took their cues from a multicultural country. They didn't really want to close the American mind; they wanted to force American society wide open—open in the way that Sir Karl Popper had described those free nations that had vanquished fascism; open in the way George Soros recently defined free-market societies that are both democratic and pluralistic.[3] One of the kids Bloom was implicitly complaining about was Bill Clinton, who would drive those fearful of openness stark raving wild. Those with agendas of opposition such as Dan Burton and Newt Gingrich and Pat Buchanan.

Pat Buchanan, running again in 2000, had been ranting about a decisive "cultural and religious war" inside America since the late eighties and would go on ranting into the new millennium as a recovering Republican and the Reform Party's not altogether welcome successor to Ross Perot. From the perspective of the '92 Republican convention, the nineties were to be the last battleground, a "Custer's Last Stand" on behalf of that other older America under assault. Buchanan, ironically, was himself an emblem of the great-grandchildren of Catholic immigrants who themselves had once been barred from America's shores by Protestant Know-Nothings insisting that America could not absorb these Catholic refugees from Italy and Ireland. Now here they were, joining the old Wasps who had tried to keep them out of America, insisting that America could not withstand the new tide of Latinos and Asians, could not stay whole in the face of the new "onslaught." In the late nineties Samuel Huntington's rabid book decrying the "clash of civilizations" actually made American multiculturalism a culprit in a supposed weakness that would make our "civilization" vulnerable to Chinese and Muslim hordes that would gang up on us in a violent civilizational showdown! Buchanan was Clinton's polar political antipode, bearing the standard of a raving politics of fear as

[3] Popper's classic discussion of liberal democracy *The Open Society and Its Enemies*, 2 vols. (London: Routledge, 1945); and Soros, *Open Society: The Crisis of Global Capitalism Reconsidered* (New York: Public Affairs, 2000).

Clinton waved the bright banner of inclusion; Huntington was his intellectual polar opposite, using Kiplingesque "civilizational" rhetoric against the idea of global interdependence.

In fact, Bill Clinton was elected president of the new America precisely by those most feared by Buchanan and Huntington, working women and new immigrants and gays and lesbians and unmarried mothers and people of color who had jobs but not the respect that was supposed to come with jobs. They aspired to the open society—a society seeking to heal the very rifts Buchanan intended to use to rend the nation in two. Cultural healing, not cultural war, was their ideal. Clinton would become this new nation's first antiwar president, its first openly reefer president (he didn't inhale? yeah, right), in the remarkable words of Toni Morrison, its "first black president."[4] Anyone who attended the 1992 convention knew that in five minutes. You needed only remember where you were—in America's immigrant capital, its urban epitome, its one true cosmopolis, the heart of America no heartland American wanted to acknowledge, New York, New York. And yes, of course, "Jew York" to bigots, anonymous electoral sanctuary to stateless progressives like Robert Kennedy and Hillary Clinton seeking a new political home, a maverick iceberg of an island many Americans wanted to set adrift so they could watch it float out into the Gulf Stream and melt, founder, vanish. You had only to look at the faces in Madison Square Garden and compare them with the faces on-screen a few weeks earlier when the Republicans gathered in a for them equally appropri-

---

4 Morrison's bold comment captures Clinton's capacity to represent existentially groups for which he did not necessarily deliver the goods—a vital point for identity politics. Civil rights leaders complained at the end of his presidency that Clinton did little for them but talk (despite the commission on race chaired by John Hope Franklin), but Toni Morrison wrote ever so tellingly, "White skin notwithstanding, this is our first black President. Blacker than any actual black person who could ever be elected in our children's lifetime. After all, Clinton displays almost every trope of blackness: single-parent household, born poor, working class, saxophone-playing, McDonald's-and-junk-food-loving boy from Arkansas. And when [Clinton's] body, his privacy, his unpoliced sexuality become the focus of the persecution . . . who could gainsay these black men who knew whereof they spoke? The message was clear: 'No matter how smart you are, hard you work . . . we will put you in your place or put you out of the place you have somehow, albeit with our permission, achieved.'" "Talk of the Town," *New Yorker*, October 5, 1998, pp. 31–32.

ate Texas convention hall to nominate George Bush (the elder) to what this other America was certain would be an inevitable second term.

It was all there plain as the faces visible in Madison Square Garden in August 1992. You could look at them, and they looked more like that multihued sea in front of the Lincoln Memorial than like the colorless sameness that stared from the floor of the other convention. The demographic was younger, browner, and newer to America than a convention had ever before been. This did not necessarily mean more liberal or progressive or union-based (the ideology of an earlier wave of now fully integrated Irish and Italian [i.e., Catholic] and southern European and Jewish Americans).

Not at all. Part of Clinton's New Democrat leanings came precisely from his understanding of the need for an ideology that did more than mimic the politics of an earlier generation of Democrats—the storied "Roosevelt coalition" of rural blacks and urban Catholics and southern Whites and liberal Jews who had declared war on fear, and who heroically took America from the Great Depression to the New Deal and on through World War Two to the Great Society, Robert Putnam's generation of joiners and good citizens whose virtues today we so sorely miss. The New Democrats wanted not a class society tilted their way (fear was no longer their adversary) but an open society where everyone had the same chances ("opportunity" would be the key term). These children of change, wedded to no traditional ideology, "working families," but no longer necessarily union families or nuclear families, were to be his constituents, and they would hang with him through thick and thin, scandal and impeachment. They were there in New York at the convention to mark the beginning. They were there in the unprecedented poll ratings to mark the end. Given the chance, they probably would be there still now, electing him to and sustaining him through a third term.

I went home happy. I hadn't met the president, and figured I never would, but I'd witnessed his role in midwifing the rebirth of a party that I had watched die when I was run off the Pennsylvania delegation to the Chicago convention in '68. And now I'd been given the chance to watch the new America midwife his nomination. We were back. The Democrats were back. But with a difference. We had a president who knew how to win, who had figured (and figured right) that until a Democrat won there would be no Democratic agenda—progressive, centrist, or conservative—worth debating.

# CHAPTER THREE

# Arguments at Laurel Lodge

**BY THE JANUARY AFTERNOON** in 1995 when I was engaging with the president at Camp David, he was already being chided for his seminars—the endless college-style talkathons in which Clinton himself was always the best listener, the most loquacious talker, the quickest wit, the deepest thinker. Bill Clinton was simply always going to be (it seemed more a matter of boyish pride than presidential prerogative) the best student in the room. Staffers who admired the process suggested his affection for seminar debate revealed the president's penchant for serious scrutiny of important issues, as well as his willingness to listen to a wide variety of viewpoints before taking decisions on them.

Staff enthusiasts were probably in a minority, however. I had the sense that even the admirers secretly felt they were being dragged back into schoolrooms they hoped they had left forever, and that the whole exercise was a waste of precious time for them and the president. In fact, critics inside and outside the White House insisted the seminars brought out the worst in the president. It was avoidance masquerading as pseudo-intellectualism—evidence of sophomoric self-indulgence and an unwillingness to take decisions at all. George Stephanopoulos would later complain that Clinton suffered from "chronic bouts of indecision."[1] Elizabeth Drew suggested the president makes decisions only "when he absolutely has to" and argued that talking was a form of pres-

---

[1] Stephanopoulos, *All Too Human: A Political Education* (Boston: Little, Brown, 1999).

idential evasion.[2] He was, even sympathetic critics concluded, a ponderer: one of those masters of the nondecision who, like that great intellectual avatar (and perennial loser) of the 1950s Adlai Stevenson, was just too intelligent to be a politician.

Yet this view of the president seems patently absurd. Can anyone really accuse Bill Clinton of being insufficiently political? If Clinton sometimes tiptoed around decisions, it was surely because he was too political rather than too intellectual or too cerebrally remote from politics. He never played the egghead and, though altogether comfortable with ideas, wasn't a fan of the abstruse and impractical. There was nothing of Adlai Stevenson about him. He did not prefer ideas to decisions; he preferred keeping the two apart.

In the seminars in which I took part, the questions we raised were not of a kind that birthed legislative proposals. We were engaged in political philosophy. Big questions for which there were no particular theoretical answers, let alone policy consequences. Did "putting people first" (Clinton's campaign slogan) mean *more* government (his social investment package) or *less* (the deficit reduction strategy for which after 1994 he had abandoned social investments)? Could one support a notion of strong national government, as Professor Sam Beer of Harvard advocated in one of our meetings, and still be a critic of overbearing, dependency-breeding "big government"? Teddy Roosevelt actually had done so historically (as the ex-neocon Michael Lind was quick to add). How about communitarianism? Was it an invitation to bureaucratic interventionism on behalf of tyrannical collectivities or merely a way of thinking about the neighborhood and about civil society? What was the appropriate relationship between government and business, between the political and the economic sectors? If the Democratic Party abandoned its polarizing "class war" stance, could it remain progressive? Was civil society—that new darling notion of Third Way politics— a progressive notion? Was it a cross between the government and private sectors or some genuinely third domain quite distinct in character, one that might possibly mediate between the two? What exactly was the Third Way? Debating such questions might help define parameters and show what was at stake in forging a long-term direction for the administration, and it might even inflect policies with a certain

[2] Drew, *On the Edge: The Clinton Presidency* (New York: Simon & Schuster, 1994), p. 67.

accent. But it obviously would not determine whether the defense budget should be raised or lowered, or whether a key welfare concept like aid to families with dependent children created dependency in the children's parents or not.

Even as our session was just getting started, it was apparent that the president treated it more as intellectual calisthenics to keep his mind nimble than as a part of the policy process. God knows he was a superb thinker; but he seemed to actually take critical decisions in a manner pretty well insulated from thinking of a philosophical kind. Polls and pondering are worlds apart. His intelligence and curiosity as well as his capacity for sustained argument were all on display in this and subsequent seminars and those powers were for the most part regarded with awe by those who were privileged to witness them. But whether the debates themselves ultimately enhanced or undermined his capacity to take decisions—indeed, whether they had anything whatsoever to do with his decision-making—seems at best moot. For, as is well known, the president took key decisions mainly in the conspiratorial company of one or more of his tough insider politicos, men like Dick Morris or Harold Ickes or Leon Panetta, pollsters like Stan Greenberg and later Penn and Schoen, or cabinet officers with clout (Bob Rubin) rather than those with ideas (Bob Reich).

Those who worked communications and speechwriting, such as Don Baer, Michael Waldman, David Gergen, and, in the second term, Ann Lewis and Sid Blumenthal, certainly didn't boast that they were consulted at the crucial moments when specific policy decisions were taken. The more substantive work of Bill Galston, Bruce Reed, and the domestic policy staff obviously was crucial to legislative innovation, but that work found Galston and Reed in the policy mode where philosophy kept its own company, for the most part inside their heads. No discussion I was in ever put under philosophical scrutiny the "small incremental change" approach of Dick Morris that took issues like school uniforms and television V-chips and food safety and forty-eight-hour hospital stays for moms as markers of public concerns appropriate for micro-legislative action. Or subjected "triangulation" (the method Morris used to locate these very small and very safe concerns at the very center of the political spectrum) to critical examination. Or even raised specifically the pros and cons of deficit reduction or the earned income tax credit. What, then, *were* we doing at Camp David?

Technically, we were there to help weigh language and ideas for the State of the Union Message. In practice, we were hoping to use what was primarily a presidential diversion (mental golf) to leverage a little influence. A very little influence. Perhaps a shaping of the rhetoric in which, once taken, decisions were to be justified and defended; a general strategic direction, such as "more public-private partnerships," if not a specific policy outcome, such as turning national service into a state by state program. The president himself wrote in one of the many flattering thank-you letters he sent (this one dated January 22, 1998, in reference to what he called the "Leaders and Thinkers Dinner"), "These types of sessions are helpful not only for my State of the Union preparations, but also for thinking through how to carry out our plans over the long term." To this degree, he perhaps shared our illusions about the power of truth as an antidote to the truth of power.

Since we were for the most part pedagogues and academics in love with talk and wedded to debate, whether or not they issued in action, the talk was for most of us more than enough, even if we were to look mostly in vain at the actual State of the Union speech for traces of our ardent debates. And who would look too hard after receiving a printed copy of the actual speech with a handwritten inscription from the president thanking us for our contributions? I suspect, by the measure of the volume of such inscriptions in circulation, each one of Clinton's State of the Union speeches has a hundred authors. And, come to think of it, they all read that way. This was not only the "meetingest" president ever (as Lloyd Bentsen said), but the "thankingest" president of all time. Gene Sperling has a framed copy of the 1994 State of the Union reading, "To Gene, whose dreams and ideas are here."[3] One of mine reads less dramatically, "To Ben with thanks." Another carries the inscription "For Benjamin, with appreciation." The pollster Mark Penn reportedly has a *Washington Post* front page headlining Clinton's Senate acquittal with Clinton's "Thanks" scrawled on it. A brilliant touch: a hundred men and women, each thinking he or she authored a State of the Union! And how many more persuaded they have actually saved the Union? Or, at least, saved the president?

From other seminars I later attended or heard described, it is safe to

---

[3] Matthew Miller, "Trapped: The Education of Gene Sperling," *New Republic*, December 6, 1999, p. 22.

conclude that the Saturday afternoon and evening gathering at Laurel Lodge in January of 1995 pretty much defined the genus. What would most Americans make of it? A long yawn. Too serious, even academic, for the broadside style of talk familiar to the public from talk radio or scream TV on the model of *Crossfire* or *The McLaughlin Group*. Bill Maher would shudder at our earnestness, while Charlie Rose would wonder what the relevance was to the real world of money and power. C-SPAN political junkies and social science policy wonks would question whether what we were doing was even politics. Many Americans would presumably envy the tour of Camp David, and the reception line with a brief private moment with the president of the United States. But for the rest, they'd probably take a pass.

Yet, though most of our prudent fellow citizens (save the C-SPAN junkies among them) would probably surf right by us if we were on cable, they might still be at least a little pleased to learn that government could hold a thoughtful and serious debate about the philosophy of governance. Those many Americans persuaded that politics is little more than a corrupt pursuit of special interests, ambition, and power for their own sake, interrupted by the occasional pursuit of sexual favors, might even have found their cynicism mildly challenged had they witnessed the public-spirited and earnest, even patriotic, tenor of our conversations.

Imagine yourself at a large oval table of the kind that a very large family might use at Thanksgiving—seating up to twenty-five or thirty but with an intimacy that makes it feel as if you and all the aunts and cousins were sitting at one rather small table engaged in a single conversation. We are talking about a group of approximately the same size as your third-grade class or the senior honors seminar you took in college. The President presides, but in the manner of a principal sitting in on the third-grade class, or a visiting celebrity scholar in the honors seminar. The class teacher is Bill Galston, who runs the show, trying to capture the relaxed intensity of an advanced graduate seminar without forgetting that his boss is in the room and will judge not only the proceedings but *him* as well. So while the pretence is that we are all there for a no-holds-barred open debate about the issues, with the president looking on curiously—first among equals perhaps, but no more than that—the reality is that the whole thing is designed for and directed toward the president, who is a great deal more equal than everyone else.

Americans boast about the "Everyman" quality of their presidents and indulge in the illusion, especially with populist presidents like Carter, Reagan, and Clinton, that they are more like us than different from us. But power democratized is perhaps more rather than less awesome. Sitting with the easygoing Clinton was a little like joining a banquet table at which a very large lion is seated, and being told by a trembling host (Galston in this case), "Don't worry, the lion isn't hungry; he just likes to *watch* people eating."

What makes our Saturday conversation in Laurel Lodge engaging, and worth rehearsing for readers who probably don't much care for the details of the debate, is that it was America itself that was under the glass that afternoon. How to define the country and the appropriate boundaries of its government; how to define the roles of progressives and of the Democratic Party. Most of us at Camp David, certainly the president—his wife still more so—felt a twinge of nostalgia for the solace of the era of benevolent progressivism. We had our baggage. We were of a time when every American who had felt robbed of a job, every immigrant deprived of a voice, every black man stripped of rights, every worker victimized by a predatory monopoly, had seen in government a friend and protector. Whether through Social Security or antitrust, Roosevelt's Civilian Conservation Corps or Kennedy's Peace Corps, Head Start or Pell grants, Aid to Families with Dependent Children or the Civil Rights Act, government legislation and government regulation and, yes, the government "bureaucracies" that made and enforced those regulations were seen by a majority of Americans as keys to greater freedom, achieved justice, and manifest dignity. These convictions elected activist Democrats to the presidency and the Congress regularly from 1932 to 1968, a period when Democrats still controlled the preponderance of Congresses and yielded the presidency only once, for a two-term stint by a popular general without partisan leanings.

Throughout this era, whatever the problem, government was likely to be seen as the first and obvious road to a solution. This remained true whether or not it actually solved the problems directly. Many would argue World War Two and not the New Deal was what revived America's industrial might, just as some would regard the Vietnam War rather than Great Society programs as the engine for the prosperity of the sixties. Either way, the government made the wars as well as the peace, and nothing was possible without it.

From the New Deal to the Great Society and through the Carter administration into the era of the Democratic Congress that had resisted President Reagan's new version of Republican libertarianism, the Democrats had been the party of government—whether in areas of little controversy like transportation, housing, and Social Security or in realms of greater controversy like education, welfare, income redistribution, and the environment. In the nineteenth century, when it was the party of Jeffersonian antifederalists, states' rightists, and Dixiecrats, and the Republicans were the keen moralists of national union, things had been otherwise. But ever since Teddy Roosevelt abandoned the Republicans, it has been the Democrats who are the statists.

The baggage Democrats carried got noticeably heavier in the sixties, around the time I was working in the peace movement to ban atmospheric testing, the time when John Kennedy got shot and American boys started going to Vietnam to fight a war nobody could fully understand or defend. Political assassinations, urban breakdown, the struggle for civil rights, the escalating war in Asia and the resulting "counterculture" radically altered the political climate and called into question the coalition politics of the New Deal Democratic Party. Those on the left who had once most trusted government (my father worked for the WPA and was the first director of the Federal Theater in New York and did not think it improper to continue his government career during the war by helping administer a Japanese relocation center in Cody, Wyoming) had kids like me who became government's detractors.

On the right, the same thing was happening. Richard Nixon's election in 1968 signaled a shift in political philosophy among Republicans, who through Eisenhower and Nelson Rockefeller (governor of New York in the late fifties and a wannabe president who never quite made it) retained some of Lincoln's and Teddy Roosevelt's Republican faith in national government. Though by the standards of Reagan, Nixon was an activist and interventionist who actually increased government spending on welfare and other government programs, he initiated a move away from trust in the federal government with new "block grants" to the states that shifted responsibility to them. This move was accelerated by the constitutional crisis his illegal behavior in the Watergate scandals precipitated. The Nixon years accompanied and reinforced a dwindling trust in government, business, and collective action that Robert Putnam has charted as the erosion of "social capital" in his seminal study "Bowling Alone." These tendencies left Democrats who still believed in government increasingly abandoned on both flanks.

The once "invisible majority" became visible enough as a new Republican constituency took root in the South and among Catholic workers and other ethnics across an unraveling urban America. Whites traditionally tied to the Democrats bolted their party, while the South embraced a Republican Party that had defeated it in the Civil War. By the time Reagan had secured the White House for a second term, the Democrats were without a viable political philosophy and in danger of becoming a minority party. President Reagan evoked an America without government, an America of individuals all pulling their own load. He held up the sixties as proof that government didn't work. Conservatives paving the way for his election claimed that federal programs had done little to change America's poverty profile, and instead had aided the growth of dependency and abetted the breakdown of traditional families and eroded the influence families could exercise over their children through its aggressive paternalistic practices. Surely, the new libertarians of the Reagan revolution concluded, no one any longer believed that law could change the nature of women and men or that government could change the face of America. Law imposed by a busybody government was the death of liberty. Government—big, bureaucratic, and inefficient—was part of the problem, not part of the solution. Its vaunted programs were spendthrift and ineffective. Temporary public assistance bought only permanent private lassitude and dependency, sapping the will to compete not just of businesses but of individuals, especially those conditioned to the dole.

Whatever meanness President Reagan's ideology concealed, on the surface its account of a storied nation glowing in the warming rays of an omnipresent rhetorical sun triumphed at the polling booths and in the hearts and minds of a majority of Americans. It was always morning in America. And even when dusk threatened, the landscape was still illuminated by a thousand points of light—one for each man with enough gumption to light a candle and make his own way by its shimmering flame.

The new Republicanism, incubated in conservative think tanks in the sixties and seventies, was about a mood and a mind-set. Never mind that government and its staggering national debt actually grew precipitously under Reagan; attitude was everything. The Hollywood actor could grasp as eastern political "realists" could not that America had been from its very inception a movie: an inspirational dream and a collection of hopeful myths that infused abstract ideals like "the city on the hill," "the second Eden," and the "new American man" with a magical sense of concrete possibility—as long as America was led by dreamers and mythmakers who knew how to kindle dreams and inspire hope. Whatever the facts, however disconcerting the realities.

America has always been the land where hope trumped realism and soft ideals beat hard facts—which accounts for both its remarkable success and its persistent hypocrisy, its capacity to kindle expectation in those it excludes, permitting it to turn an indifferent, even complacent, eye to their exclusion. America is the only country in the world where people vote not their circumstances but their dreams—the class to which they aspire rather than the class to which they belong (hence 90 percent of Americans describe themselves as "middle-class"). Reagan's understanding of this truth, whatever his deficiencies of understanding and compassion otherwise, accounts for much of his success. It also generated the challenge to the Democrats that Bill Clinton was to take up with equally stunning success. For it was just this Reaganite feel for the power of positive myth that Bill Clinton used to turn around his party and get himself elected to the presidency. And it was this insight that he used to remain standing, against all odds, when as president he sustained a combination of enemy-inflicted cuts and self-inflicted wounds that should have felled him. As liberal Democrats hated Reagan for enveloping their constituents in a dreamy fog in which they strayed unwittingly from their principles, Republicans would come to hate Clinton for "stealing" their ideas and seducing their constituents into heresies of their own. Both betrayed sets of partisans recited a similar litany: "Don't they understand? He's not really *their* President!"

This was the backdrop for our conversation at Camp David. The Democrats of the early eighties had remained mired in the past, playing at an unrealistic realism by complaining that dreams were only dreams and myths were but myths and that the poor were getting poorer and that national debt was getting bigger and that the Reagan "revolution" was a charade and a bust. Reagan's deep cheeriness made this penchant for the reality check look like whining. As would happen to the Republicans a decade later as they kept sputtering to an unmoved majority about how "that man Clinton" was a liar and a crook and a lecherous incompetent to boot, who should be voted out of office or impeached or hit with whatever it took, so the Democrats in the eighties sputtered to another equally unmoved majority about how "that man Reagan" was talking one game and playing another, that his morning was a dark midnight for minorities, that this champion of family values had children who wouldn't talk to him, and how could any decent, thinking American vote for such an imposter?

In this way, during the Reagan years the Democratic Party became associated with a constituency of "losers" and the "culture of complaint"—for what better way to dismiss the claims of justice than to associate them with a party of whiners? The Democrats became a losing party—at the polls and in the hearts of too much of middle America. Old radicals (like me) could scream that it was precisely the linkage of the party to minorities that cost it its constituency in what we saw as a permanently racist nation, could complain that once ethnic whites made it into the mainstream, they moved over to the other side of the political spectrum, leaving behind those still poor (mostly people of color) without a voice in national politics. We were probably right. But right or not, it made us sound like lethargic whiners and envious losers and helped pushed the white ethnic "winners" over to the other side, costing the Democratic Party its majority-party status. To middle America, the Democrats increasingly seemed to blame crime on society and hence more on its victims than on its perpetrators; they seemed to blame poverty on economics and hence exonerated the individual from any responsibility. They blamed social vices on dysfunctional families and thereby contributed to the disempowerment of the family. By focusing every program on minorities, Democrats gave the impression that minorities were special-interest groups rather than carriers of universal-rights claims. They even made the concern with equality look like the politics of envy and turned the quest for justice into a celebration of "How are you gonna fix my problems?" lassitude. They made democracy look like paternalism and allowed paternalism to father dependency.

At the darkest moment in the Democratic Party's exile, in the middle of the triumphant Reagan years, when it looked as if the Democrats might never return another liberal to the White House, a group of congressional Democrats founded the Democratic Leadership Council (DLC), dedicated to the proposition that Democrats didn't have to be permanent losers to pursue their permanent principles. Because they didn't have to be "liberal." Not in the old sense. This didn't mean simply tacking to the center (which was what every American political party did in general elections), though many thought the New Democracy was nothing more than a new centrism. What they had to do was to acknowledge the need for fresh thinking about progressivism, thinking free of cant. What they needed was a willingness to probe their own traditional beliefs and recast liberalism.

Enter Clinton. The Clinton we would argue with all afternoon and evening at Camp David. Bill Clinton was one of the first governors to sign on to the DLC project and subsequently (in 1990) to become its chair. (Tellingly, Senator Joe Lieberman, Gore's vice-presidential nominee in 2000, was a recent DLC chair.) Bill Galston was one of the first intellectuals to sign on to the DLC. Clinton and Galston effectively met by indirection. Bill Clinton read an essay by Galston and Elaine Kamarck, then researchers at the DLC's think tank (the Progressive Policy Institute). Their piece, written in the immediate aftermath of the Dukakis campaign fiasco, challenged the party to figure out why so "many Americans have come to see the party as inattentive to their economic interests, indifferent if not hostile to their moral sentiments, and ineffective in defense of their national security." After a brutal analysis of party complacency, Galston and Kamarck concluded, "Above all, the next Democratic nominee must convey a clear understanding of, and identification with, the social values and moral sentiments of average Americans. The firm embrace of programs, such as national service, that link rights to responsibilities and effort to reward, would be a good start. The consistent use of middle-class values—individual responsibility, hard work, equal opportunity—rather than the language of compensation, would also help."[4]

This is not in retrospect merely a prescient guess at what the next president might look like: it was a stunning definition of the profile Bill Clinton would assume and the program he would embrace and which would carry him to the White House. And it is a statement of the new principles that we would seek to elaborate at Camp David to relegitimize the very idea of government. Me, I was a fan of government and

[4] Galston and Kamarck, *The Politics of Evasion: Democrats and the Presidency* (Washington, D.C.: Progressive Policy Institute, September 1989), pp. 1, 28.

a child of the New Deal and the Great Society. But my years in Switzerland when I first studied and then taught at a small international
seminar called the Albert Schweitzer College (run by Unitarians and
Swiss liberal Protestants and actually founded with the active participation of Albert Schweitzer) had taught me something about confed-
eralism and the devolution of power, about the importance of
citizenship in the neighborhoods as a foundation for government in
the capital. Although I had (and still have) doubts about the DLC's
approach, which at times looked more like opportunism than fresh
thinking and which risks justifying policies that pander to the privileged in the name of challenging those that hurt the marginalized, it
was also clear to me that the Democratic Party could not regain the
presidency without new thinking and could not keep it without showing its new colors.

Bill Galston had helped some of us who were there at Camp David and
were attuned to communitarian and new civil society modes of thinking to convene a White House conference entitled "The New Citizenship" in the first year of the Clinton administration. We had met
without the Clintons, but with several key deputies who continued later
to be engaged in White House dialogues, including Deputy Secretary of
Education Madeleine Kunin (the former governor of Vermont and later
Clinton's ambassador to Switzerland, where she had family) and Housing Secretary Cisneros, and a host of others, in the Roosevelt Room in
the White House. The populist organizer and scholar Harry Boyte and
I had prepared "The New Citizenship" document, and with Galston and
Kamarck actively participating, we began a discussion among ourselves of the themes demarcated in their 1988 article. Boyte and I were
a good deal more populist than the DLC, and we talked about government as a function of the public work of citizenship. Boyte honored the
"commonwealth" tradition, and I urged "strong" or participatory
democracy. But like the DLC, we questioned welfare statist politics as
usual as insufficient to the challenge of governance in the face of globalization, technological innovation, and the changing relationship of
work to status and power. The progressive politics of the twentieth century had been born in the industrial economy of the nineteenth, with
its embattled classes and its labor-intensive mode of mass production,
and the Democrats from Roosevelt to Johnson were wedded to its
rhetoric. Yet the new, technologically based global information econo-

my had eroded traditional class boundaries, internationalized production and distribution, and transformed the landscape of politics.

The strong interpretation of what we were doing at Camp David that January afternoon was to join and extend the debate, begun in the Roosevelt Room a year earlier, about how progressives could move beyond nineteenth-century rhetoric in pursuit of just solutions to twenty-first-century challenges. That, at least, is what I was thinking about as we sat down at the conference table in Laurel Lodge and Galston introduced the agenda, the four encompassing discussion points of National Power and National Purpose, Reinventing Government, Civil Society and Public Sentiment, and Renewing Citizenship.

We opened with sets of arguments, four at a time, grouped around our themes. But the real architecture of the meeting was provided by the combat between the old liberals and the New Democrats for the hearts and minds of those of us unwilling to acquiesce in that particular dualism. Those unwilling to let go of what they thought the New Deal and the Great Society had done for America went first. Galston's initial group included Alan Brinkley, Theda Skocpol, Paul Starr, and Eddie Williams.

Alan Brinkley was a Columbia University historian who wrote on the New Deal era and, as a fine teacher, gave the president a sparkling three-minute mini-lecture. (In grim tribute to the irrelevance of good teaching in the modern research university, Brinkley had won Harvard's Levenson Memorial Teaching Prize a few years earlier, which carried the unexpected reward of his being denied tenure and invited to leave the university.) He pointed the president to examples from Roosevelt and Truman, making the case for how government could be forceful on behalf of rather than at the expense of liberty. It was a pretty opening performance, but lacked the New Democrat tone (its virtues and its vices). Theda Skocpol, a Harvard sociologist with gumption who had written on health and social policy and was militantly principled and hence unpolitical in a fashion that made her views seem admirable and futile at the same time, defended government as an idea against its "disablement." Although in later years she moved beyond them, here she still argued for the legitimacy of class issues, suggesting that the attack on them and on government was proof of their continued relevance—a proof that New Democrats were too anxious to dismiss. Paul

Starr, an extremely thoughtful and soft-spoken sociologist from Princeton who had won a Pulitzer Prize for his 1984 book *The Social Transformation of Medicine* and who was a cofounder of the progressive biweekly
*American Prospect* (which he continues to coedit today with Robert Kuttner and Clinton's former labor secretary, Robert Reich), also argued for
a more confrontational posture. After all, he had worked on Clinton's
disastrous health plan strategy and could hardly be other than defensive. He nearly defeated the tough substance of what he said with the
gentle meandering way in which he said it, however. Too nice by half.

It wasn't easy to make an impression in this gathering. It was apparent how brief our time would be, and how easily we could fail. Succinct-
ness can sometimes render necessarily complex issues simplistic and
reductive, but clearly it was indispensable here where, as with television,
one had perhaps a sentence or two to capture attention, and a paragraph or two to pay off on it. Like democracy in the wider world, democracy here meant in theory a chance to have a say: but only those able to
command speech would get people to listen. And democracy in practice
is not simply about the opportunity to speak but about the ability to get
others to listen. Eddie Williams, a modest and soft-spoken African-
American who had taken a few minutes between Skocpol and Kuttner,
had rambled amiably through what should have been a fiery call to justice. He spoke just that once, falling silent for the balance of the afternoon, our seminar's "invisible man." Voicelessness is sometimes a state
of mind—a reflection not of inarticulateness but of too acute an aware-
ness of the incapacity or unwillingness of others to listen.

The old, if refreshed, liberalism of the first group help draw battle
lines—big government had a legitimate role to play in our lives, these
four speakers were saying, and those who assailed it often did so to protect not liberty but their own special interests. So if we were being urged
to disable or even to reinvent government, we should ask why and for
whom. They had an air of defiance. These scholars knew that the new
administration was looking for a way beyond such arguments. Well,
don't look to them: they were there to recall what the old liberalism
stood for.

The president listened intently, and occasionally nodded, though
much less intently. His manner said, "I know these arguments and why
you make them. And I respect you and your high ideals. I'm a Democrat too, and my wife's an outspoken liberal. But this is no longer

enough. This is how we went into the wilderness for two dozen years. Tell me something new." But in fact he said nothing. And when Galston invited his comment after the first group concluded, he replied, "This is real good. I think we ought to just keep going." Which is what we did.

Galston had contrived the dialectic perfectly: following the old liberals, he gave the New Democrats from the DLC their opportunity to counter the moving logic of old-style liberalism. Al From, a Carter administration and Capitol Hill staff veteran, was founder and president of the DLC. I associate him more with its highly effective politics than with the articulation of its innovative ideology, but he did quite well doing exactly what I thought he couldn't: he articulated the ideology. "You can't make politics from class war anymore. You can't win elections when people think you're tax-and-spend maniacs who are going to screw up the economy. You can't keep the middle class in your camp making war on middle-class values. The engine of prosperity is in the private sector, so don't attack business. Talk responsibilities as well as rights. Don't attack the winners, enlarge the winners' circle." It was sound-bite ideology, but no less effective for that, especially in this setting, where loquaciousness was a vice.

Before we heard the other principal at the DLC, Will Marshall, two DLC-style "reinventing government" interventions were made by David Osborne and Henry Cisneros. Cisneros, a brilliant Harvard-trained Chicano lawyer who had been mayor of San Antonio and then the president of the National Civic League, was one of Clinton's favorites (mine too). He enjoyed an access to the White House rare among cabinet members in this second tier of posts, although he would eventually resign under pressure from still another personal scandal distorted into a public political challenge (he went on to become CEO of UNIVISION, the largest Spanish-language telecommunications conglomerate). Though he was a cabinet member, he appeared at the seminar as one of us, an "outside intellectual," and he used the opportunity to offer a rather too long and complex three-part memorandum on the relationship of government to the private sector. Clearly reflecting his experience at the endlessly bureaucratized Department of Housing, Cisneros was oddly off message and at the same time oddly pertinent. Reinventing government had to mean reinventing government relations to the economy. Reinventing the relationship of government and economy turned on vital details that a housing secretary faced every day . . . and that is where Cisneros left the general conversation. The devil in his details took him on a road to minutia hell, leaving us behind. Everyone seemed to like him, but nobody quite got what he was saying.

Having written *the* book (*Reinventing Government*, 1992) and administered Vice-President Gore's program on behalf of making government "more flexible, creative and entrepreneurial," David Osborne hardly needed do more than say the words to make the point. His mind on the State of the Union speech, he devoted his five minutes at Laurel Lodge more specifically to the reinvention of communications in the digital age. Presidential speechmaking, he insisted, could and would no longer dominate the media. Everyone of importance was on the Internet; no one of importance was watching televised press conferences, and so it was a waste of time to focus on the old modes of rhetoric. Directed at a president so gifted in political persuasion and informal rhetoric, this seemed to me to be disastrous advice, though it perhaps was prescient in foreshadowing the release of the Starr Report on the Web. But Clinton's finest and most affecting moments in the presidency were probably his traditional televised speeches like the ones on race (the Memphis speech) and on the tragedy of Oklahoma City, while his Internet interventions (where he responded in scrolling text to conventional queries) seemed only to reduce him to the digital triviality of one more computer nerd. In computer-speak, all men are truly equal—and it isn't pretty.

Going last in the group, Will Marshall, the director of the DLC's think tank—the Progressive Policy Institute—acted as a bookend to Al From. Marshall was a likable person, someone I came to admire for his openness to those like me to the left of him who worried that his wish to charm capitalism into the Democratic fold might end up folding democracy into the capitalist pen. No, he would say, we can appreciate what competitive markets can do for productivity and efficiency without becoming naïve about their perils. But we have to stop thinking about "losers" in the new economy and think rather about how to equip people to win through education, retraining, and vocational learning. His speech this afternoon was, however, less about the economy than about the middle ground between government and the economic sector. He was pointing us to the intermediate civic associations and the forms of local citizenship that defined the alternative to "big government" as a strategy.

At this moment Galston again invited comment from the president. Still no dice. "I think we're in a listening mode. Let's just move on." That was it. Garrulous as we were, we were only too pleased to comply, though the dynamics of the debate would have benefited from a break. Instead, the afternoon wore on with extended comments from Yale's Stephen Carter on the role of black churches in building a healthy community not dependent on government for its sustenance—a continuation of the civil society themes introduced by From and Marshall. Carter had clerked for Supreme Court Justice Thurgood Marshall and was the author of such best-sellers as *Reflections of an Affirmative Action Baby* and *The Culture of Disbelief,* as well as a President Bush appointee to the National Commission on Judicial Discipline and Removal. A student of law and religion in the Tocquevillean manner, Carter worried with us about the political impact of affirmative action. He cited the sociologist Bill Wilson's argument that class and jobs rather than race were the real issues for inner-city Americans and urged fresh thinking. Carter was giving the conversation a twist I could exploit—there were issues of civil society and the economy that now trumped old issues of race and class. My turn was coming. But we were losing steam as we lumbered into the late afternoon shadows of an awful lot of condensed talk.

Sometime after four, the collective biorhythms of the group seemed to bottom out. Tipper Gore leaned into a brief nap, her head nearly resting, ever so lightly, on my shoulder. The president didn't bother to stifle several deeply felt yawns, and his nonintervention strategy began to look like a "Let's get it over with!" ploy rather than a commitment to genuine listening. Staffers, who had been scribbling notes, dropped their Bics, as their eyes wandered to blank walls, theirs minds trailing along just behind. Only George Stephanopoulos wrote on, at a furious pace unrelated to the failed energy in the room. Perhaps he was working on something else: a presidential speech or a press release or a memo staving off Dick Morris (Did George *know* Dick was back? Did anyone?). Or maybe he just scribbled on in order not to have to listen. I was tiring, too, depressed at the notion that the seminar was out of gas a full half-hour before I would begin to speak. Would I even be heard, over the snoring?

We were rescued by Bob Putnam. Think of Marcus Camby (the Knicks' high-energy scarecrow rebounder) coming off the bench when the starters are falling down; or, if you are not a basketball fan, think of an unexpected late entrance by Jack Nicholson in a film you thought was about to expire of lethargy. Life! Energy! An ardent academic! Slack jaws snapped closed, eyes blinked open, bodies lurched to attention. We were back. Bob was a playful intellectual from Harvard's Kennedy School of Government—who says Harvard and Yale do not continue to dominate American academia?—who loved what he did. He didn't just explain how civic engagement was dwindling and social capital was in decline; he rehearsed the statistics he had made famous in his wonderfully named essay "Bowling Alone" as if he were reading late-inning World Series scores to a roomful of overseas GIs.[5] Americans don't bowl in leagues anymore, he declared. Where once they forged communities of common interest, they now bowl alone, solitary consumers in an anonymous civic landscape. That's bad for voting, bad for social trust, bad for citizenship. Where our moms and dads played bridge, we are lodged in front of our television and computer screens as disengaged solitaries. Where Aunt Tilda volunteered for active work in the hospital, her niece Emma sends a check to Medecins sans Frontières and gets on with her life. Putnam was on a roll: PTA memberships are down— the percentages exploded from his mouth like popping bubble gum—50 percent or more! And voluntary charity work at hospitals, down 40 percent! Or 60 percent. Other indices, down 40 percent. Down, down, down! The culprit? Workaholic men, women driven from home and civil society into the workplace by ambition, changing mores and needs. And, above all, television: that pixilater of communities was turning the country into a land of solitaries. Never has so depressing a message been delivered with such joy and élan. Each time Putnam spit out another statistic pointing to the decline of social capital and the death of civil society, we felt more awake and alive. Morticians salivating over the numbers on runaway growth in environmental carcinogens. Uncanny.

Perhaps Putnam's experience in the Carter White House, where he had spent some time on the National Security Council back in the late seventies, had taught him that bad news had to sound an opportunity for good news if it was to be useful. A passionate warning about trends if we don't get down to business is one thing. A dour reference to the

[5] Putnam, "Bowling Alone," *Journal of Democracy* (1995). Putnam's book-length version of the argument about declining social capital has been published by Simon & Schuster. Readers can find my extended discussion of it in "The Crack in the Picture Window," *The Nation*, August 7–14, 2000.

ineluctable spread of malaise, as President Carter learned, is another. When leaders turn diagnosis into accusation, the public quickly loses patience and responds with counteraccusations and cynicism. Clinton understood this better than anyone else and had gotten elected by turning diagnosis (It's the economy, stupid!) to the purposes of hope (Don't stop thinking about tomorrow!). Putnam's happy-warrior sociology, grim though its message was, refreshed and energized the room. Both the president and the vice-president were again alert.

Alan Wolfe was next—not an enviable post, because Putnam's was a hard act to follow. On the other hand, people were at least awake. Wolfe was another of those Americans who had drawn the Left out to the radical margins in the sixties and then retreated in horror and, over the next twenty years, migrated toward the center. Unlike Horowitz, however, Wolfe was no apostate blaming calmer peers for his own excesses. Still, it has been strange to watch this once naïvely zealous advocate of radical change turn into a churlish critic of leftist incaution and its misplaced faith in the purity of the people. So many former radicals who expected more from the "people" than the overburdened people could possibly offer had turned on populism and—like those nineteenth-century anarchists who blew up railroad stations to make a point to common folk who wouldn't follow them—allowed excessive distrust to displace excessive trust. For those who still believed in our better angels, Wolfe was there to caution us: his new study (published in 1997 as *Marginalized in the Middle*) would dispel any illusions we retained about the potential of Americans for robust democratic action. There was no reason to think that anything other than a gentle meliorative politics was to be drawn from average Americans. Americans were fine, but they were no heroes; yet there was nothing wrong with meliorative politics. Wolfe, perhaps without knowing it, was giving Clinton a reason to trust Dick Morris and Morris's micropolitical incrementalism.

As Wolfe drew to a close, I drew a deep breath: me next. Galston, looking my way, nodded. He was not going to make his earlier mistake. "I'm a quick study," he announced, glancing at the president. "I believe the point is now to go right on to the next presentation." Wrong again. "Well actually," interjected the president, playing the good-humored contrarian, "before we go on, I *do* want to say something." I exhaled. Not yet. Clinton looked out at us, taking us each in quite personally. "We've been talking here very clearly about a number of issues that will affect my State of the Union speech. But there is a larger question. It's not just a matter of the State of the Union, but what happens afterwards. How can I address the sorts of issues you are talking about on a continuing basis? How ought it to affect my presidency?" Enlarge your perspective, that was the president's subtext. Take the moment to speak of the character of my presidency. I stared at my damp, yellow Post-it notes. Perfect for where we had been, but not expansive enough if I was to respond in the manner the president's pointed remarks seemed to require. I abandoned the safety of prepared notes for what I hoped would be relevance. How often do you have the president and vice-president of the United States listening to you?

"Nobody is better suited to answer the large questions the president has asked than Ben." That was Bill Galston, something in his challenging voice making the compliment seem more like a threat.

"I wish the president had chosen some other moment at which to speak," I offered, rather lamely, trying to break the ice and gather my thoughts. There was some supportive laughter around the room, a tittering that said, yeah, it's tough to follow the president, tougher to answer a broad nonquestion about the shape of some indeterminate fateful future. The president himself remained straight-faced, peering directly across the table at me, his gaze felt almost confrontational (I regretted my pushy grab for a seat in the middle of the table for the first time), as if to say, "Don't equivocate, Barber. Just answer the question."

The little yellow squares went back in my pocket. I would respond to Clinton's big picture question by drawing out the earlier discussion of civil society and civic partnership and locating the president's terrain on the new civic geography it suggested. For a long time we had conceived ourselves, I began, for a long time we Americans had conceived ourselves as caught between two behemoths: government and the market, a singular public sector marked by coercion and bureaucracy and a singular private sector marked by freedom and competition. But in truth, the government was also about freedom, and the market could be about coercion. The old binary of government and market wasn't sufficient. We lived our daily lives in neither, but in a third, civic sector between the two. The places where we played and prayed and went to school and to church and synagogue, where we volunteered our time and worked with our neighbors—these were "places for us," the ordinary venues of civil society that Tocqueville had equated with American liberty, places that defined us more completely than our roles as voters or consumers. I had offered these words to the room generally. I turned now directly to the president, looking at him across the table. The presidency was often seen as an embodiment of popular government—the people's tribune—and as an embodiment of government's role in regulating the economy, the people's watchdog. But in this era where government and the private sector were no longer strictly adversarial and Democrats were seeking new forms of partnership, the president also had to become an embodiment of civil society—to express in his actions and policies the public/private partnerships he talked about, to commit to and help government facilitate the commonality we forged as neighbors, friends, members of groups and associations.

Addressing him as if we were alone, with as dramatic a tone as I could muster, I said: in this role, Mr. President, you can bridge the sometimes conflictual relations of government and market, you can reengender a sense of connectivity without depending on the limited notion of formal citizenship (taxpaying and voting) about which Americans have become skeptical, even cynical. You are fortunate in the times, Mr. President. The Republican victory in Congress has a silver lining: it leaves you free to occupy the bully pulpit and minister to the nation's needs for visionary leadership. Now I turned back to the room, summoning everything I knew about theater to fix attention on my words. Had not the great presidents acted as teachers to America? Had they not explained the nation to itself, reflecting back to the people the visionary sense of themselves lost in the quotidian struggle to live one day to the next and make ends meet? Those milestones of an unfolding American dream, the Gettysburg Address, FDR's Four Freedoms speech, even Reagan's Morning in America, each one spoke not directly to politics and policy but to a fresh, deeply energizing self-portrait of the nation. A self-portrait in which Americans could find themselves limned in a way that offered hope and purpose and integrity. Now a turn back to the president: freed from the responsibilities of legislative leadership by the Republican victory, Mr. President, you don't have to tinker with small-bore legislative policies. You can become a national leader on another plane—one sufficiently above policy quarrels to assure that you can transform the debate and, in doing so, mark your presidency for all time. No one is better suited to this higher task of addressing the nation's deeper aspirations than you.

The flourish of rhetoric in which I concluded, if a little overdone, was intended to manifest the spirit of the rhetorical presidency I was urging. The president stared, expressionless, as if there might be more. I suspect, in retrospect, that he must have been taken aback because I had just used the front parlor to dismiss as tinkering the very incrementalism Dick Morris was busy selling him from his back porch perch. The choice between big vision and small bore was in fact the real question about the fate of his presidency he would have to answer. Which did the country really want? Need? Did the essence of leadership lie in reading the country right or in leading it right? I might not have given the correct answer, but I had addressed the right question.

Even as I contemplated my impact, a little self-indulgently, the conversation moved on. My friend Harry Boyte was on. Harry was the director of Project Public Life (later the Center for Democracy and Citizenship) at the Hubert Humphrey Institute at the University of Minnesota and the partner with whom I had organized our White House conference on the New Citizenship two years earlier. As I had cut my teeth on the peace movement, he had come up through the civil rights movement, having served Martin Luther King Jr. as a Southern Christian Leadership Conference field secretary, and was one of the few realistic idealists (or idealistic realists) left in our generation. Like me, he had maintained his youthful convictions because, like mine, they were sufficiently pragmatic to endure the ideological vicissitudes of the Left over thirty years. If I ever held office, high or low, Harry would be my first appointee as chief-of-something-important, as I hope I would be his. He usually spoke with a kind of eloquence of the ordinary, making the common work of political problem solving seem like a sublime activity. At five in the afternoon, however, he appeared a little weary, perhaps a little anxious, finding himself at the end of the line. Too many swings of mood, too much rhetoric already on the table. So, pragmatist that he was, though no mean orator when he wanted to be, Harry dialed down the rhetoric and talked about his real experience with storytelling as a way to get people to reveal and enhance their civic lives. If I had tried to portray what a great president might do, Harry portrayed what a great citizen could do. He put the burden and the expectations back on ordinary Americans. This, in a democracy, is finally where they belong. Democracy can survive inept leaders, but it cannot survive an inept people.

Only Os Guiness was left to speak. Guiness, like Stephen Carter, had made a career of writing and speaking thoughtfully about religion and faith in America, in books such as *Time for Truth* and *The Call*. In his brief remarks, he allowed as how his presence at this gathering was "something of a mystery" to him, hence turning it into something of a mystery to the rest of us. But in truth, I knew how he felt. Being at Camp David had to feel like something of a mystery to each of us in attendance. For myself, being there trivialized an otherwise grand and remarkable event. Like my distant cousin (really) Groucho Marx, in one quite marginally but very noisily self-loathing corner of my soul, I found it hard to respect a supposedly august company that had deigned to admit me to its inner sanctum. That's probably what Guiness meant. He was an agreeable man, and agreed with all of us. Wolfe was right, he said, the country was divided, more so even than his native country, Ireland (big laugh); Carter was right, it was in need of spiritual sustenance; Putnam was right, indicators of social engagement were disappointing; Barber was right, the president needed to use the bully pulpit more, use his formidable powers of persuasion to heal and harmonize. Boyte was right, we needed strong citizens as well as strong leaders. A perfect summation.

Galston surveyed the room and proposed—not without a hint of trepidation, since the president had by then managed to contradict just about every procedural suggestion Galston had proffered—a ten-minute break. It was already after six, and we had had no debate or discussion. Just our riveting but (same thing) overblown narratives. For a change the president nodded assent. "This is wonderful," he enthused and stood to take the break. The vice-president and Tipper rose, and Gore turned to me and murmured, "That was marvelous, what you said."

I know that flattery is a politician's cheapest and most effective tool, perhaps above all with vain intellectuals, but I allowed myself to believe him. "I know you're a political philosopher," he continued winningly (he is remarkably handsome, something his public awkwardness sometimes disguises). "Do you think Gingrich really understands the social contract tradition when he talks about the 'Contract with America'?" Gore, I knew, had studied political theory when he was an undergraduate at Harvard under the tutelage of Martin Peretz, then an instructor responsible for a freshman seminar on social and political theory

(Marx, Freud, Weber, C. Wright Mills) that Gore took. Although in transition, Peretz was at that moment still closer to the radical I knew from the left progressive Stuart Hughes senatorial campaign in which we had both worked (against Ted Kennedy's first Senate run) a few years before Peretz became a tutor to Gore than to the hawkish conservative he later became as the publisher of the *New Republic* and enemy of the enemies (especially the communist ones) of Israel. Peretz is today far more conservative than his famous tutee, but he remains a fan in the manner of mentors proud enough of their progeny to overlook a heresy here or an apostasy there, and he has promoted Gore's career in the pages of the *New Republic* ever since—more ardently than ever in Gore's recent presidential campaign.

"No, sir, you're right, Gingrich got it wrong," I ventured, studying the vice-president's face to see if he was making conversation or really interested. He seemed profoundly interested. Less facile than Clinton, he is perhaps more serious, treating ideas less as recreational foils than as sources of genuine political utility. Yet there was also something of the struggling scholar about Gore. I had already concluded from the couple of hours I'd spent with them—drawing on my professorial experience in quickly assessing my students' capacities—that President Clinton was the smart, seat-of-the-pants, quick-study underclassman who scored straight A's without seeming ever to crack a book, a "dazzler."[6] The vice-president was the stubbornly studious graduate student who, although he worked harder at it (both because he took it more seriously and because he was less facile), managed a B+ only by dint of pluck and fortitude. Spontaneity versus heavy lifting; a sometimes squandered gift versus a strenuous achievement. Where Clinton would have diverted me at that point with a witticism, the vice-president leaned in, listening carefully, prompting me to continue, calling me "Professor" where the president always said Ben. (Alone in his freshman seminar, he had called Martin Peretz, just a few years his senior, "Mr. Peretz" while everyone else said "Marty.") "See," I

[6] "Dazzler" was a title former classmates gave to the most brilliant members of the freshman seminar in which Gore had sat for Peretz. Gore himself was not included, yet managed to out-achieve all his dazzling rivals from that period. See David Maraniss's and Ellen Nakashima's account of Gore in Peretz's seminar, "The Thrill of Discovery," *Washington Post Weekly Edition*, January 24, 2000.

continued, seduced by his interest into that wayward pedantry that is always ready to invade an academic's response to a perfectly pleasant social question, "what Gingrich gets wrong is the whole idea of the social contract. I mean the social contract tradition in Hobbes and Locke and Rousseau is about citizens contracting *with one another* to yield their liberty *to one another*. It's not about citizens contracting *with* government; it's about citizens *founding* a government through a mutual contract *with one another*." I was edging into a mini-lecture, saying too much, stressing the key words, but the vice-president remained remarkably attentive, as if preparing for a doctoral exam, and I lectured on. "So when Gingrich talks about a contract 'with America,' he turns government into some anonymous 'other' rather than something that belongs to us, something we establish through our mutual contracting. That may suit his hostility to government, but it gets democracy and the social contract quite wrong." I stopped abruptly, aware suddenly that I was talking to the vice-president of the United States rather than Peretz's hardworking Harvard freshman. But Gore smiled and seemed pleased. He returned later in our public discussions to the philosophical distinction between a contract among citizens and one between citizens and a paternalistic government. Gore was less quick on the draw than Clinton (who could boast to be as quick?), but he was a formidable learner, which meant a very apt listener and a politician of unusual depth. Yet he seemed always to be on an earlier or later page of the common book we all were contemplating, a tad tone deaf to the obvious in his acuity about the esoteric.

Galston pulled us back into the conference room and, after rewarming us to our task with a few well-conceived words summing up the afternoon, invited us to debate. He had made it easy to focus on the New Democrat civic themes on which Marshall, Carter, Putnam, Boyte, and I had enlarged. We congratulated ourselves on our fresh thinking. Until Leon Panetta spoke. If the State of the Union speech took as its motif the role of partnerships, active citizens, and a robust civil society—he asked in pleasant tones that only partly masked the hard-boiled impatience of his political realism—how would such themes (such baloney, I imagined him thinking) define the political and legislative tactics of the coming year? Panetta, the former congressman and in my book Clinton's most successful chief of staff, had pulled from Clinton's pre-break general question its political core. "We took a beating in the last election. Now, I like the sound of philosophy we've been talking about, but how's it gonna help us with the voters? Is it going to contribute to the reelection of the president?" Nothing like a reminder, in a roomful of intellectuals at play with fascinating ideas, of what is really at stake. "Don't blow away my president with some fanciful new idea," Panetta seemed to implore, "if you can't show me how it will play to our core constituency."

The cynical interpretation of Panetta's question, of course, was that all the pols care about is power; get my man elected any way you can, and I don't care what they stand for or what they do. But in a democracy the question of how new ideas and fresh principles can win the support of a core constituency whose right it is to exercise its sovereign function at the polls is more than legitimate: it defines the difference between Plato's regime of wise men who know the Truth and democracy's regime of deputies chosen by men and women both wise and foolish who think politics is about conflicting interests and values rather than about truth; and who, whatever the truth, believe they must be governed in a manner consistent with their liberty.

Panetta posed the questions of a blunt politician. But what we had to remember was that politics is a nasty word for democracy, and if we thought more about it we might show more respect for politics and less naïveté about democracy. Morris might take politics to a foolish extreme where there is no leadership, no principle, no ideas at all—just trolling for votes, even when elections are years away. But regimes of great ideas like the dictatorship of the proletariat and the thousand-year reich of Aryan hegemony that lay on the other side of the divide are far more dangerous. The journalist Joe Klein (the author of the "anonymous" *Primary Colors*) represented many frustrated liberal intellectuals (me included) when in his *New Yorker* profile he faulted Clinton for abdicating leadership in the name of a politics of polling and, at least after the defeats of the first two years, for being unwilling to take bold and visionary actions.[7] But when I think carefully about the quotidian meaning of democracy—which is government by consent rather than government by sagacity—I remind myself that polls are another form of democratic accountability. They may appeal to triviality rather than truth, but in the realm of human governance I will always prefer triviality to

[7] Klein, "Eight Years: Bill Clinton and the Politics of Persistence," *New Yorker*, October 16 and 23, 2000, pp. 188–210.

tragedy, ordinary interests to heroic ideals. And so, where some of my friends bristled, I welcomed Panetta's intervention.

His question gave heart to the old Democrats left behind in the New Democrat complacency with which we had opened the second part of the afternoon debate and allowed them to rejoin the fray. Was not the supposedly antiquated language of class and old-fashioned distributive economics still the bread and butter of core Democrats? Skocpol was back in her element, insisting that the only prudent political course was to draw a line in the sand: to take Newt Gingrich at his word and accept his challenge. If Panetta wanted a political course of action, Starr added, that course was to defend the women and children and minorities and the poor who would be victimized by the Gingrich revolution, not to sell them out by mimicking Gingrich with some soft patter about civil society and welfare reform. Defend the traditional interests of the traditional Democratic coalition. Upon whom else could Democrats depend at election time?

Admirably tough. Admirably on point. Except, several proponents of New Democracy shot back, it was on the basis of exactly this strategy, now fervently endorsed by Starr and Skocpol, that the party had lost a succession of electoral contests, including the 1994 congressional election. Theirs was the disappearing Democratic base. How could they look at this sad history and respond, "Let's have more of same!" Clinton's '92 surprise victory rested precisely on his willingness to move beyond more of same. We can't just defend old battle lines; we have to occupy new territory, try out new strategies.

After all, Clinton had already jettisoned his own preferred campaign interest in "children" and "children's issues" because, polling showed, talking about children aroused images of welfare in the public's imagination. You had to wrap kids' issues in the language of, say, "working families" to draw attention to them in legislatively viable ways. The earned income tax credit, one of the president's most successful programs, helped children without making them its centerpiece.

My gut was with the traditionals: one out of five kids remained in poverty throughout the Clinton years, "working family" talk notwithstanding. The powerless are a minority, and unless the majority can be made to care about them, majoritarian politics will ignore them. Yet my social science realism and pragmatic interest in ideas that could make headway against history's tide found the New Democrats seductive.

The vanishing base could be served only if those deserting it returned to the fold. And for that to happen, more was needed than class struggle formulas. You couldn't help kids by marginalizing them rhetorically. Their very identification was rhetorically challenged and had to be pulled into a conceptual category larger than those favored by the old Left. It was a tribute to the power of American myth that so many Americans ignored their real economic status and defined themselves on the basis of their hopes. It was not just convenient for the wealthy to deem the poor "middle class." The poor themselves preferred to think this way. Rather than writing them off as duped by "false consciousness," why not try to find ways of serving them through their middle-class aspirations? However illusory the hopes of its would-be "middle-class" members might be, the poor could not be served by a party of the minorities that became a permanent minority party. And so, I reasoned (and said aloud), if Americans have lost confidence in their government and no longer respond to the old truths about government as a friend of the people because they have lost confidence in their governors, what this really betrays is a loss of confidence in themselves. Look at term limits, look at the proposed constitutional amendment to require a balanced budget. People are saying, "We don't trust ourselves! Don't trust us! We might vote some jerk in over and over—so limit his term! We'll never balance the budget on our own—make us do it through the courts!" If we want to restore faith in government, I concluded, as if it were a matter of a syllogism, then we have to restore the faith of citizens in themselves. And that means addressing the realm where they live their lives and still can feel some sense of power—civil society, the communities and neighborhoods where they live. Get people to feel they can make a difference right there where they live, and maybe they will begin to realize they can make a difference in government as well. That will help them remember that government itself can make a difference, that it is their common tool. It is civil society's executive branch as it were. But start with the neighborhoods and with community responsibility and work back up the ladder. Don't defend government, I finished (wanting to persuade rather than arouse Skocpol and Starr), empower people where they live, and draw them back into a world of politics they will want to defend. They will come back as Democrats, but as Democrats who believe in democracy. Skocpol started to reply, aroused not placated.

"Hold on!" said the president, growing visibly uncomfortable with the dissonance in the room. What was to us merely a tribute to the liveliness of academic minds at play seemed to disconcert him. "We don't have to choose one or the other." He looked around, like a referee. "I think I can do both. Defend government, yes, I have to in order to defend myself. I can't just throw all the responsibility on the American people—it would be like I'm evading responsibility. But at the same time, we need to go further, do more than *just* defend ourselves. We have to have partners in responsibility."

The president didn't like hard choices. That much was clear. I paid less attention at the time to his discomfort with disagreement, although later it came to sum up both an obvious political strength of his presidency and a glaring weakness in his leadership. He wanted to placate our two quarreling groups. Defend the old? Pursue the new? We can do both. Old Democrats? New Democrats? We don't have to choose. This was a president who believed deeply he could always do "some of both." He was, in speechwriter Michael Waldman's tantalizing phrase "a one-man coalition." To the extent he succeeded in doing both, he was remarkably efficient, with a series of political victories won under the most trying political circumstances to his credit. He could make war on the congressional Republicans, and he could work with them. He could dazzle and seduce the media, and he could detest and revile them. He could contemn Newt Gingrich, and he could strike deals with him, sit with him in New Hampshire and promise to break the gridlock he was helping to create in Washington. He could tack to the center and please the Left, and tack to the left and propitiate the Center. He could pursue a grand vision made up entirely of small changes.

Yet politics is also about hard choices and unpopular principles. Clinton sometimes seemed like my distant cousin Groucho: "Yes, I have principles," Groucho boasts to a skeptic, "and if you don't like them, I've got others." Reaching out to the two sides of our argument around the oval table in Laurel Lodge, Clinton was Groucho: yes, we have to defend the great old principles of the old Democratic Party, and if you don't like them, I have others fashioned by the DLC. Meet the claims of both old and New Democrats? "I can do both." Please Skocpol and please From. (Later, around this same table, he'd try to please Israeli Prime Minister Barak and Palestinian chief Arafat with results that were catastrophic.) Was this a necessary politics of compromise, or was it bad politics, what

Bill Galston had called the politics of evasion? Yes, democracy means doing politics, but politics is about making choices. Admirers would say Clinton did in time "do both," for he took on Gingrich directly in the closure of government debate and won hands down, destroying the Republicans' hope of extending their 1994 congressional victory into the White House in '96. And at the same time he pursued an affirmative politics of new citizenship and small reforms and social responsibility, punctuated by a (for old Democrats) hard to swallow welfare reform bill. Against the old Republicans, he played by the old Democratic rules and won. With the general public, he assumed a new posture and won. Maybe he could do both. On the claim that he could, the reputation of his presidency would rest.

Behind his penchant for arbitration and inclusion was more than (in the jargon of the psycho-biographers) a wish to please, to accommodate warring parents and appease an alcoholic stepfather. That was clear from the president's own answer to Panetta's question, which followed our debate and for me was the high point of the day, a moment when the president's astuteness rose to the level of sagacity. After Clinton told us he could split the differences between us, Hillary had jumped in with her own response to Panetta, speaking with warrior forcefulness on behalf of traditional Democratic politics—a habit she had to unlearn later, when she entered politics in her own right. Hillary seemed here to be playing conscience to a president who sometimes was all politics. One could wish she did it privately rather than publicly and that she didn't so often seem to stand in judgment of the people to whom she wanted only to be an example, but her role struck me as vital (and when, in her own campaign for the Senate seat from New York, she later grew more discreet and "political," I saw it as both necessary and regrettable). She referred feelingly to the oligopolies and monopolies, the special interests trying to manipulate the average American into thinking they represented the common good, manipulating him to obstruct the progressive agenda. Her hard, angry rhetoric resonated with the ancient ardor of class war. She was with Starr and Skocpol. She was not persuaded that the soft, if well-meaning, language of civil society could contend with the hard power of well-entrenched socioeconomic groups. If working white men and white women in the South no longer wanted to support the president, if ethnics were continuing to jump the Democrats' ship, then—she looked her husband in the eye—"screw 'em. You don't owe them a thing, Bill. They're doing nothing for you; you don't have to do anything for them." This was liberalism at its fighting best. The point was not to heal in the name of soft consensus but to attack in the name of hard justice.

The president stepped in, calm and judicious, not irritated, as if rehearsing an old but honorable debate he had been having with his wife for decades. He looked at Starr and Skocpol, but seemed to address Hillary.

"I know how you feel. I understand Hillary's sense of outrage. It makes me mad too. Sure, we lost our base in the South; our boys voted for Gingrich. But let me tell you something. I know these boys. I grew up with them. Hardworking, poor, white boys who feel left out. Feel that our reforms always come at their expense. Think about it, every progressive advance our country has made since the Civil War has been on their backs. They're the ones asked to pay the price of progress. Now, we are the party of progress, but let me tell you, until we find a way to include these boys in our programs, until we stop making them pay the whole price of liberty for others, we are never going to unite our party, never really going to have change that sticks."

Nor win any more elections—that was the subtext.

In my six or seven years of occasional interaction with Bill Clinton, I don't think I ever heard a more profound piece of straightforward political wisdom. Or one that better summed up what Clinton hoped to do with his presidency—why he wanted to do "both," why he thought he had to honor reform and honor those who paid its costs, why it had to be blacks and whites, not blacks or whites. This was a road other Americans had taken. Martin Luther King had talked about little white children and little black children walking hand in hand and then put the rhetoric into action by asking why poor white adults and poor black adults had to be pitted against one another in getting education, housing, and jobs. That was what he was doing with his "Operation Push" housing program in Chicago right before he was murdered. It was how Bobby Kennedy was talking around the time he was assassinated.

Ronald Steel doesn't buy it, but I heard Bobby campaign in '68, and he
was talking about bringing together black folks and blue-collar whites
and making a stand against those who used their divisions to maintain
hegemony in America. It was even how Malcolm X had begun to talk
after coming back from Africa convinced that race might not be the key
to overcoming deep injustices in the American system after all, that
economics was the critical factor (Malcolm X foreshadowing Bill
Wilson).[8]

Back in the seventies, without quite becoming a conspiracy theorist, I had even developed the quasi-conspiratorial notion that the
assassins who felled so many American heroes in those years had chosen their targets with an unerring, if unconscious feel for who really
threatened the status quo. The ones who got shot had all begun a shift
away from a purely race-based politics to one in which have-nots,
white and black alike, joined forces. Not Dixiecrat racism, but this
truly radical politics is what exercised the elites and ultimately mobi-
lized the assassins. Now here sat a president of the United States in a
post-assassination epoch, offering an eloquent and gentle version of
exactly this radical argument—an argument whose radicalism was
disguised by its seemingly conservative poll-pandering electoral tactics (don't punish those good ol' non-union, white working boys who
abandon the party, woo them).

The problem with so many liberal approaches to reform—busing or
affirmative action or crime prevention, for example—was that in each
case, oh so conveniently, they set poor black against poor white, aspiring minority against aspiring immigrant, non-union entry worker
against entrenched union member. Crime victims, white and black,
were disproportionately poor, so refusing to be tough on criminals had
greater consequences for poor than for well-off communities. Busing
within cities or between cities and first-ring suburbs forced the residents
of such communities to bear all the costs of dislocation. The wealthy
lived mostly in far suburbs safe from busing or sent their kids to private
schools to avoid it. Insulated from its costs, such liberals found it easy to

---

[8] Steel has offered extensive evidence showing that Bobby Kennedy's claim to represent
both blacks and white ethnics who otherwise supported George Wallace was pretty
thin, and that his 1968 campaign was mostly opportunism. What is striking here,
however, is the perception, for it was the perception that drove the campaign, whatever the "reality."

embrace busing.[9] Affirmative action righted historical wrongs, but by seeming to penalize those just ahead of poor minorities on the social ladder. It was white ethnic public school kids being pushed aside to make space for minorities, kids named Bakke and Silvio from Jersey City, not high SAT–scoring Choate graduates from Greenwich, Connecticut and Evanston, Illinois. The logic of New Democrat policies followed directly on: let's get tough on crime without forgetting that a majority of criminals are school dropouts, and that if you build more prisons than schools, you may serve safety but you can't serve justice. Let's keep affirmative action to honor a pledge to racial justice, but find ways to spread its costs so that aspiring whites from poor backgrounds are not pitted against aspiring blacks from poor backgrounds. Let's not turn community busing into an excuse for community busting, and secondary and tertiary rounds of white flight.

All these thoughts flew through my head as Clinton spoke those few wise words about why he could not and would not make war in '96 on "his boys," the redneck white guys with whom he had grown up.

We finished the afternoon focused again on the State of the Union. In keeping with my argument for the bully pulpit, I reminded the verbose president with what I hoped sounded like wry irony, that the Gettysburg Address had been but 284 words. In a great speech, less could be more; perhaps it was now time to retire the annual kitchen sink of a speech in which every government department got a single parochial paragraph and coherence was a matter of stitching together the paragraphs with an otherwise irrelevant ideological thread. Putnam later told me that Panetta had winked at the president when I cited Gettysburg's 284 succinct words. Was he also a champion of brevity? It didn't really matter, in the course of things, the speech Clinton gave several weeks later was one of the longest in history, replete with a cornucopia of policy recommendations from every cabinet department and agency inside the Beltway. So much for the power of good advice.

As the evening wound down—hunger stalked the room—the vice-president wound up. He had played an appropriately backseat role to Clinton, but clearly did not want the meeting to end without contributing something. It's not that he wanted to weigh in on the main debate,

---

[9] This is the essence of arguments made recently by Jim Sleeper in his *Liberal Racism* (New York: Viking, 1997).

for he would probably have focused on quite different issues, had it been his seminar. But the vice-president was a warrior of sorts, even in peacetime. His awkwardness stemmed in part from his posture as a fighter out of the ring, slightly uncomfortable in the absence of political combat. Adversaries like Bill Bradley and George Bush Jr. would, as a consequence, underestimate him and find themselves startled when his sharp-edged aggressiveness was unleashed from the tight little box in which it was usually contained. If only he were less self-conscious about unleashing it! If only he were not so easily dissuaded from being who he was by those who thought they knew exactly who he ought to be! If only the layers of assumed identity had not become so thick that Al Gore no longer could figure out where they stopped and he started! But President Clinton seemed to understand and appreciate his qualities, and he looked on benignly as Gore went through a rather routine reply—as if Gore had pressed a button and a thoughtful paragraph on civil society and its virtues played out—understanding that this disquisition was necessary even if not quite pertinent. What he said would have been more pertinent two hours earlier. He challenged government to shape up and respond to the emerging dynamics of civil society. People say, he quipped, we are encumbered with "a mainframe mentality in a PC society." Well, that's not the metaphor we need, he continued. It's not personal computers against the old lumbering mainframes; it's the "parallel computing" implicit in the many-sidedness and interconnectivity of civil society against the linear computing of one big government trying to do it all.

We stared at him. Gore may not have invented the internet, but he used tech metaphors adeptly and accurately. To the degree that he puzzled or irritated audiences, it was more than just his penchant for singsong pedagogy; it was our era's impatience with substance driven by the media's quest for endless drama. Television refused to recognize that substance had become indispensable to politics in the new global information society. Clinton knew how to disguise his intelligence as mere facility, to humanize his intellect by advancing it under the banner of empathy. Gore wore his knowledge like a zoot suit, in your face. He was often right, but right at the wrong moments, distracting from his point by drawing listeners to what felt like a smugness of the arcane (even though it wasn't).

Our debate had peaked with Clinton's peroration on behalf of his boys and the need to stand by them, and nobody quite knew how to follow up without seeming either sycophantic or irrelevant. Gore appeared not to have noticed, however, and lectured on, making points relevant half an hour earlier with an enthusiasm suitable to our upcoming cock- tail hour, but all wrong for where we were now. Galston glanced around, taking the measure of our impatience. Then he simply adjourned us. Dismissed the vice-president the way a majority would do in the 2000 election when it opted either for an unlikely Bush Jr. or for an even more unlikely Ralph Nader rather than put into the White House the most eligible and governance-ready candidate ever.

Drinks and dinner, Galston said. It was over.

Not quite over. In a group like this one, "drinks and dinner" was code for more talk. We had broken for dinner so late that we had only a few minutes for cocktails. I found myself with the first lady, who stood opaque and unsmiling. At this first meeting, she struck me as a formi- dable woman, nearly unapproachable. Feeling preemptively defensive, wanting to soften her, I said sincerely, "My wife is a great admirer, as so many women are." She stared. Realizing I might be sounding vaguely sexist, I quickly added, a little foolishly, "I am too, and there are a lot of men who admire you too." Finally, as if she had finished testing me, she grinned broadly, seemingly more out of pity for my discomfort than out of pleasure at my silly remarks. It was one of the few times she had smiled all day. When Harry Boyte stepped in to offer a brief lecture on the importance of citizenship—a seeming rebuff to her old-style liber- alism—she turned abruptly away from us, tossing over her shoulder the words "I think it's time we all go in for dinner."

Dinner was buffet style. Again, it felt like summer camp as we circled the pine serving table surveying the array of Oprah specialties (from his appearance, it was clear that this was one of those periods when the president needed to diet). Five large round tables had been set, and I joined Don Baer, then the chief speechwriter for the president. Our con- versation that evening at table sealed a relationship that endured for the balance of Baer's tenure in the White House (later as director of communications after David Gergen had left that post). Baer was a *U.S. News & World Report* editor who was by far the most modest, soft-spo- ken member of the president's senior staff. He had, however, parlayed these gentle qualities into a kind of enduring influence in the adminis- tration, able, for example, to champion Dick Morris without alienating

Morris's many adversaries. When he finally left for the private sector well into the president's second term, he earned the highest praise from the president and feelings of warmth from his colleagues few others enjoyed.

Sitting with Baer and his assistant Michael Waldman (who later became chief speechwriter), I pursued an intense debate about the strengths and weaknesses of the afternoon debate. A familiar voice quipped something or other, and when I turned to my left, the president was taking a seat accompanied by a generous helping of Oprah's delectables. More casual than in the seminar, but exuding the same easy charm, he chatted through dinner, urging me to join him at the dessert table twice—"They're all Oprah's, you can eat as much as you want!" I did just that, seduced equally by Bill Clinton *and* Oprah Winfrey.

Hillary had joined Chelsea and her school friends at an adjacent table. The steely concentration in the first lady's countenance had been replaced by a warming maternal glow. Chelsea, as attractively unpretentious a teenager as one might ever imagine, was oblivious to the surroundings, deep in an animated exchange with her mother. It occurred to me that in the world she had inhabited since Yale, Hillary's tough exterior might be absolutely necessary armor in the face of vulnerabilities associated with her role as Chelsea's mother—a role she exuberantly embraced. Women who cherish their public lives but refuse to relinquish their roles as wives and mothers do not survive outside or inside their families without shields. Misogynists insist there can be nothing there but the essential mother (how dare she demean baking and Girl Scout cookies!). Piggish rivals notice only the tough shields (whatta bitch!). Hillary has always been assailed from both sides, making both the White House service and the autonomous political career she later was to nourish more risky and difficult than they should have been.

Don told me over dessert that he had particularly liked the image I offered in my written comments a week earlier of how the West was settled. Ronald Reagan (or his brilliant speechwriter Peggy Noonan) had it wrong, I had said. It was not a single lonely pioneer heading into the sunset on a solitary Conestoga wagon, but wagon train after wagon train of moving communities. We settled the West together, not one by one, but town by town and school by school. And that was how we had to take on America's challenges.

It was after nine-thirty when the president rose and said to us with a kind of wink, "I want to thank you all for coming. If the speech is a success, yours will be the credit. If it fails, I will get all the blame." Kennedy's line about success having a thousand fathers and failure being an orphan. As we departed Laurel Lodge, we rehearsed in reverse our reception line formalities. Except we all felt like veterans of a common campaign, old friends. Clinton clasped my shoulders in his large hands. "Benjamin, I'm truly grateful to you for coming and for what you gave us." Babbling again, I muttered something about how, no, it was *me* who was grateful . . . grateful for . . . grateful that he was the president of the United States. Then I was out in the night, cold and damp, looking for the SUVs. A Secret Serviceman playing doorman held out an umbrella. "Your van's up on the left. Be careful. It's dark." A few colleagues joined me. With a half smile—I hope it was a half smile—our security man added, "Don't turn right or you're dead." We turned sharply to the left and walked smartly to the waiting vans. The admonition seemed quirkily inconsistent with the metaphoric message that had come through loud and clear all afternoon at Camp David, a message that read, "Don't turn *left* or you're dead."

# CHAPTER FOUR

# The Art of Speechwriting

**ON JANUARY 24, 1995,** just a few weeks after we had shared a day with him at Camp David, President Clinton delivered his State of the Union Message to a joint session of Congress. The most telling moment of our seminar turned out to be the one when Clinton had interrupted our debate with the remonstration "We don't have to choose. . . . I can do both." He paid homage to the old-time Democratic moralists hoping for a line in the sand, and he assumed the more amiable posture of the New Democrat center, asking for collaboration from and promising cooperation with a recalcitrant Republican Congress. He would do both. In fact, in the nearly hour and a half he ended up taking (so much for my little joke about a 284-word speech and Panetta's complicit wink), he promised not just to do "both" but to do everything and anything that anyone anywhere in the executive branch of government thought was worth doing. Every cabinet and subcabinet department, every general and special interest, every foreign and domestic agenda, got equal time. A lot of equal time. Time equal to the longest State of the Union Message in the history of the Republic. There were high points: a passionate defense of the Brady Bill on handgun control, an attack on the attack on the poor, a denunciation of violence in the movies (the Hollywood that loved him hated that), and a defense of his signature project on national service (though not nearly so stirring as the many speeches he had offered on its behalf on other occasions). And there was the cafeteria menu of policy options, flattening the speech where its passions might have let it sing. Trying to offer something to everyone, he tired out listeners and wore out his welcome inside the Capitol. Our concern with citizenship, civil society, and public private partnerships certainly inflected the speech, allowing us to feel our time at Camp David had been well spent, even historic in some trivial sense. But there was no arc to the narrative, no direction or structure in the daisy chain of programs, no ultimate vision holding together the host of good ideas.

The Washington pundits didn't like the speech any more than we did, pointing to the very weaknesses we had tried to warn him away from at Laurel Lodge. But the American public, and with them David Osborne, carried the day. Osborne had insisted that heroic rhetoric was no longer needed or appreciated in this new and leveling era of television and the Internet. The polls bore him out: nearly 80 percent of viewers liked what they heard, responded to the very minutiae we students of high oratory dismissed as trivial. Clinton made them feel comfortable. His audience actually increased in the course of the long message. The only casualty of his long-windedness had been the Republican response to the State of the Union. Governor Christie Whitman of New Jersey had been pushed out of prime time into a late-night hour. Her abrasive remarks to a group of local Trenton shills (who she seemed to want us to think were Republican congressmen) were lightly reported, and left no impression. Clinton had foiled the experts, us among them again. He played well with the only constituency that mattered, the American people. As with his presidency generally, he had a better feel for what Americans wanted, what they would tolerate, than all of his advisers and media critics put together. That was his genius—and his weakness. He was as good as the American people, but incapable of making them better.

Lolling in front of the TV and listening to the president ignore all the advice we'd given him, I again wondered if we hadn't been engaged in a pointless exercise at Camp David. Whatever we'd achieved, it had nothing to do with speechwriting. Speechwriting in the conventional sense seemed about the last thing in which the president was interested. Benjamin Disraeli had proclaimed "with words we govern men," and Clinton's earnest speechwriters understood that "the words that are chosen can define a Presidency."[1] But Clinton himself was impatient with them as anything other than ciphers of ordinary conversation.

[1] Michael Waldman, *Potus Speaks: Finding the Words That Defined the Clinton Presidency* (New York: Simon & Schuster, 2000), p. 15.

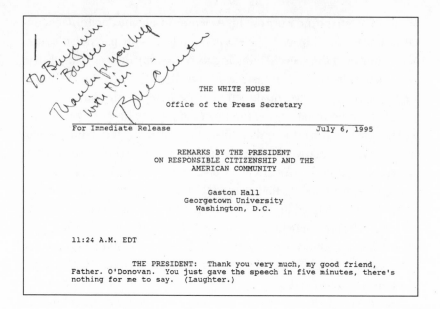

THE WHITE HOUSE

Office of the Press Secretary

For Immediate Release                                    July 6, 1995

REMARKS BY THE PRESIDENT
ON RESPONSIBLE CITIZENSHIP AND THE
AMERICAN COMMUNITY

Gaston Hall
Georgetown University
Washington, D.C.

11:24 A.M. EDT

          THE PRESIDENT:  Thank you very much, my good friend,
Father. O'Donovan.  You just gave the speech in five minutes, there's
nothing for me to say.  (Laughter.)

"Words, words, words," he had screamed at George Stephanopoulos during the 1992 campaign, "all you write is words—they don't mean anything."[2] Michael Waldman, later the president's chief speechwriter, himself acknowledged that the president's "strength was never soaring rhetoric. . . . [Rather it was] the intensity of his connection to the audience before him."[3] I made up my mind to forget about the speechwriting dimension of counseling Bill Clinton.

Until the calls started coming, some months later. They would arrive unheralded, often when I was traveling in Germany for a seminar or giving a speech in LA. "Hey, Ben. It's Michael. The president is going to give an education speech at the Princeton graduation next month. I'm sure you'll have some good ideas." Or "Don Baer here. We're going to respond strongly to the Oklahoma City bombing. You can imagine how touched the president is, he really feels strongly. Anything you can suggest that might help. . . . I know he'll be grateful." And I'd drop everything, put my own about-to-be-delivered speech on automatic pilot. I immediately forgot all the doubts raised by the State of the Union, and

[2] Stephanopoulos, *All Too Human: A Political Education* (Boston: Little, Brown, 1999), p. 90.
[3] Waldman, *Potus Speaks*, p. 17.

started writing. Writing about whatever I was asked to write about. A talk linking higher education in the Ivies to the classical American common-school mission of education for citizenship; or thoughts for the president's elegy to Oklahoma City—was there a way I could stitch together from the names of all the small, devoted government agencies blown to smithereens in the Federal Building a quilt of the diverse, common, everyday reality of public service? Could not such a portrait of ordinary Americans serving their fellow citizens stand as a rebuke to those whose antigovernment venom had helped create a climate for terrorism? The terrorists in Oklahoma had murdered government by murdering public servants caring for working families' kids; when you affected to assault government in the name of some cockeyed anarchist dogma, you took out not some symbol of military might or some arch and arrogant president, but a child care center run by and for your fellow citizens.

I loved writing for the president—or at least contributing materials to his speechwriting staff—simply because I loved to write. Whereas the seminars required only thinking, speechwriting called on the writer's craft. I had started in writing at about the age of ten, after reading Albert Payson Terhune's dog stories, from *Lad of Sunnybank* to *Wolf,* collies and more collies, and then was transfixed by an old classic about a bull terrier gone to heaven called *Beautiful Joe's Paradise.* I'd been writing ever since. At Harvard, I felt a natural affinity for Rousseau and Voltaire because they eluded categories and wrote seamlessly about whatever interested them, whether it was stagecraft, botany, belles lettres, politics, or physics. They were wordsmiths, insisting on the root power of words as illuminators. With words, they gave birth to a self-consciously designated Age of Enlightenment. I imagined I might bring a hint of the Enlightenment to speechwriting (I flattered myself that I was Voltaire at—I flattered Clinton—the court of Frederick the Great: I would interest him in the words he so distrusted). Enlightenment ideas rooted in reason's new authority may seem a provocation to skeptics today, but not even postmodernist cynicism can refute the incandescent power of meaning invoked by words, for it is precisely words with which postmodernists wage their irony-laden campaign against meaning.

My earliest memos for Clinton were *written*: not jotted down, not noted and observed, not typed or word processed, but written—written

down, written out, written up. Despite my own early skepticism, I wanted to convince him that rhetoric counted, could work for him, make an
impression that would persist on paper days and months later. The writing counted as much as the content: how something was phrased and
where it was placed in a narrative structure counted as much as its elementary meaning. So when I realized I had a chance not just to chat
with the president but to be read by him, I wrote my heart out, for the
most part without hesitation or forethought, without concealment or
reserve.

My transition from seminar participant to writer was easy, quite
seamless. The Camp David seminar and its successors had had as their
object the fixing of a text for the State of the Union addresses (even if
nothing we did ever had much to do with the actual texts that were fixed
for the State of the Union). So even then our concern was ostensibly
with words and speeches. Moreover, the lively interest staffers showed
in my words made me suspect almost immediately that the naïve clear-
headedness of the outside could be of some benefit to the cynical clear-
headedness of the inside. The speechwriters would always assure me
about the importance of contributions like mine, though I would search
in vain for traces of what I wrote in the finished products. Still, they kept
coming back for more, so I kept on writing.

Whenever the calls came—"Hi, it's Michael again. We're working on
some stuff for the president on technology. He's speaking at MIT. Is there
a way to relate new telecommunications themes to democracy and citizenship?"—I'd leap right in. It was almost as if Clinton himself were making a late-evening call via an emissary; it was the fact that it was his
errand that made it so seductive. "The president's hoping you can contribute something," the voice would say, and in a second I'd be plumbing
Michael or Don or whoever it was for clues about exactly where the president wanted to take it, how I could be useful. And then I'd stretch for
some esoteric but useful quotation: "You know, Michael, the president
might like that passage where Aristotle argues a democracy is limited in
scale by the territory a man can traverse in a day to get to the assembly,
because then Clinton could remind us of how the global reach of the
Internet let's us be global citizens!" My interlocutor, the president's go-
between, I liked to think, would welcome my esoteric reference but
remain a little vague about what his colleagues were after; they were in
the early stage, fishing for ideas and themes and images. The president

wasn't really weighing in on it yet, they'd allow. Nonetheless, I'd usually get a hint here, a provisional idea there, enough to flip open my laptop, flattered, invigorated, and write not a paragraph or two but my version of the whole speech, imagining the president scanning my words.

It was more than just vanity, however. I wrote whole speeches because a speech is pointless without an architecture, and you can't devise an architecture with just one section of a speech, or one zippy paragraph, or a couple of quotes, so I figured why not write the whole thing? I suspect the speechwriters used my self-consciously architectonic whole speech texts as little more than raw resources to be pilfered for the useful factoid, the historical reference, the little story, occasionally a fat phrase that had the ring of originality because it wasn't theirs, the ones they'd gotten too familiar with. "Oh yeah, Aristotle, that'll be a change," I figured they were thinking. Or "What was that epigram from Thoreau? The one about how we mustn't become tools of our tools? That's real good." The denizens of the White House, whether they were advance men for events or assistant speechwriters for the Saturday morning radio speeches or deputy chiefs of staff calculating the impact of an address to a joint session of Congress—it didn't matter who—they all loved the lucid little epigrams and pithy little stories with a personality at the core and a simple moral issuing from the story's central action. Fables and fairy tales on the models of the Brothers Grimm were for them the stuff of political speeches: an imagined anecdote rooted in a possible reality, one or two central characters carrying the ethical weight of the story, a turn of events often untoward and unexpected, a spiffy moral easily extracted from the story's outcome. Such fables were the written equivalent of the overachieving soldiers and everyday heroes sitting with Hillary in the balcony at each State of the Union, ready with the help of an artful metaphor in the president's speech to morph into human illustrations of overachieving and heroic policy initiatives.

To be sure, the speechwriters knew their business: there's no good speech without a good story. Fables were a vital part of their craft. Yet much as they loved the stories, the White House writers disdained the architecture, perhaps because they sensed the man for whom they wrote had no feel for it. He was an informalist. That was his strength as a seductive conversationalist but his and their greatest weakness as writers. Too bad. Because to think speechwriting is about stringing together a series of small narrative pearls, a mere telling of sequential stories, misses its essence. To think that way is to think like all those failed aspirants to the glories of the theater who insist that playwriting's easy because "all you have to do is write down conversation, you know, how people talk, because that's what actors do—right?—just talk." So lift some gab off a Web site or report a conversation over the barbecue about the neighbor's really ugly new pool or capture that fight with the wife after you bought the Camry without consulting her first and, bingo, theater! Well, there are playwrights like David Mamet (try *American Buffalo*) who are very good at talk; and there are playwrights like Eugene O'Neill who are not very good at talk. But Mamet and O'Neill alike know that talking is so much fleshy pulp on the body of drama and that without a narrative skeleton on which to hang it, it slips down the play's unsupported body and ends up a useless blob on the floor.

You really shouldn't be a presidential speechwriter unless you're a writer. You can't be a writer unless you understand narrative architecture. Clinton was an extemporaneous speaker extraordinaire, and it spoiled him for understanding the demands of speechwriting. And made the life of his full-time speechwriters a kind of hell. He had the seducer's gift for heartfelt gab but lacked the statesman's gift for true narrative; hence, he had no real need for writers, except as research assistants. As Michael Waldman came to realize, "for all the glory of writing for Bill Clinton, everybody knew that he gave his own speeches—rewriting, improvising, making them his own."[4] He could feel out an audience and extemporize the hell out of a topic or a story; he was at his best when the television prompter went dead or displayed the wrong text (as it did at the beginning of one of his State of the Union speeches and he riffed brilliantly for seven or eight minutes until the text was restored and he was brought back down to earth), or when he had spent the day rewriting and revising, and threw the whole thing away just before he got up to talk. But while you can woo and seduce an audience extemporaneously, there's nothing there when the event is over. As a devastating comment from a sympathetic critic had it, he was a fabulous communicator who never said anything memorable. A shoot-from-the-hip facility that lets you feel with and for your audience is to that audience like a really tasty fast-food snack, fun and easy to eat, but without lasting nutritional

[4] Waldman, *Potus Speaks*, p. 264.

value. Why has a president so gifted with words left so slight a written legacy? Why, as the historian Michael Beschloss commented on PBS following Clinton's farewell address to the Democratic National Convention in LA in 2000, did so effective a live talk always vanish a few days later when read on the page of yesterday's newspaper? Because, unlike Jefferson or Lincoln or Roosevelt, Clinton mistook talk for drama, confounded well-chosen sentiments with speechmaking, mistook seduction for leadership. His "ritual complaint" (Stephanopoulos) was about how "nobody on the staff could write a speech" but in fact he asked little of his writers and less of his listeners. No wonder there was no Ted Sorenson (JFK) or Bill Safire (Nixon) or James Fallows (Carter) or Peggy Noonan (Reagan) on the staff.

It struck me as especially odd that Clinton wasn't much of a writer, because he was a committed reader. Yet there's little evidence, for all his interdisciplinary literacy, that he read other than to garner information and fuel his brain cells with the empirical data they required to fire effectively. Reading for reading's sake, for literary pleasure or love of style, was not his thing. His favorite books were *useful*. He was a utilitarian. That is why the arts and humanities never stayed long on his horizon. Neither Clinton nor his speechwriters were really writers; the latter provided outlines for the organized talking at which the president excelled. They wrote long for a guy who couldn't stop talking—Clinton's notorious windbag effort at the 1988 Democratic convention (during which he first used the phrase "the bridge to tomorrow") set a standard from which later, more fluent efforts didn't really depart. And they wrote short for a guy who never had enough time and had to give more than two thousand speeches during his two terms—which meant an average of nearly a speech a day for seven years straight. (Think of the highly effective and even more forgettable Saturday morning radio chats that tried to capture the informality of Roosevelt's firesides, but were generally limited to some Dick Morris micro-issue or an upcoming event like library week.) Long or short, though, the speechwriters wrote in disappearing ink, and a month or a year after the president had mouthed the words, the parchments were all blank. What's your favorite Clinton speech? Yeah, Memphis on race was terrific and the Oklahoma elegy comforted the whole nation, but can you remember a choice phrase? A lasting epigram? An enduring paragraph? I can't, and I supposedly helped to write some of them.

Yes, the speeches at Memphis and Oklahoma City were exceptions. Here the spontaneous event so inspired the extemporaneous president that his words rose to something more than grab-the-audience charm and took on the power of the architectonic. At Memphis his response to the church bombings in the South bespoke a kinship that perhaps only a white southerner could evoke; and after the terrible bombing in Oklahoma he wept on behalf of all of us and in the arc of his speech gave to a city that suffered a brutal tragedy some semblance of dignity. He also gave a couple of big-think speeches at Georgetown that rode a dramatic narrative to heights he otherwise rarely reached. When he ascended to a pulpit to suffer with and for his country, he seemed able to reach beyond himself, and then not even Lincoln's moral empathy was beyond him. His impassioned haters have been quick to mock his "I feel your pain" solicitude, but most Americans know that to have the deep pain evoked by a public tragedy felt and articulated movingly by a public figure is the essence of inspired leadership and no small part of consolation. With the help of his writers, Reagan mourned the martyrs of the *Challenger* disaster with a powerful empathy no one dared ridicule.

Effective speechwriting cannot merely exploit the natural affect of great events, however. It must also invest ordinary events with rhetorical grandeur. For such rhetoric, President Clinton had neither the taste nor the gift. Not that it's easy. Not in these self-consciously ordinary times where postmodern irony makes every inclination toward the heroic look merely foolish. And certainly not for the protagonist. For the bystander like me, modeling a speech in the calm of a university study, one carefully chosen phrase at a time, is to real presidential speechwriting under pressure as plotting a virtual voyage by computer across the Atlantic Ocean is to actually sailing the Atlantic alone in a dingy. For the White House speechwriting department, the reality, I quickly learned, was one of disorder, confusion, chaos, and uncertainty. I approached the job like an airline pilot flying clear vectors between two continents; the pressured speechwriters, from what I could gather on the occasions I actually sat with one or another of them in the Old Executive Office Building, felt more like New York taxi drivers trying to score half a dozen fares before the cab had to be back in the garage, wanting desperately to figure out how to do the airport job in Queens without losing the theater crowd over in Manhattan.

Any writer likes to write—that's certainly why I responded gladly to requests for text. But there was little time for the art of writing or even the base craft of scribbling in the whirlwind of 10,000-word days that were required to keep up with a proactive president addicted to talking. Remembering a founding, memorializing a death, defending a success, explaining a failure, introducing a visitor, taking leave from a conference—all those proclamations, celebrations, explanations, clarifications, policy summaries, and legislative proposals, not to speak of the grand occasions, special events, national tragedies, that had to be turned into words. Two thousand speeches: it was truly staggering. And here I go on about narrative structure and the Aristotlian art of rhetoric.

The asymmetry was inevitable: overwhelmed presidential speechwriters would hassle me (and dozens of others) for assistance, flattering us to engage in a prudent day or week of labor, and then take our well-thought-out and measured paragraphs and plunder them for a single thought or solitary metaphor, only to assure us that we had made a vital contribution to the president's eloquence. What we had in common was an appreciation for words. For words were and are a president's only real currency, which is why Disraeli insisted it was with words that nations are governed. Spoken, written, shouted, or whispered, they made up the president's army. As commander in chief, he had real troops, but he couldn't shoot his way to legislative achievements; as chief executive officer, he had appointments, but once appointed, subordinates went their own way until they felt superior to their benefactor. ("Every time I make an appointment from a dozen candidates," President McKinley had muttered, "I make eleven enemies and one ingrate!") As the people's tribune the president had the power of public opinion, but only if he marshaled it to his purposes with rhetoric. In the end, he had his words. And so he needed his generals of verbosity—the harried speechwriters—who in turn needed foot soldiers (even if the foot soldiers pretended they were the real generals). Why not me?

Words were more than surrogates for action; they were its presidential essence. Those leaders who knew how to use them (or how to empower the writers who knew) were successful—to the degree they succeeded—because of their words; I think of Jefferson, Lincoln, Wilson, Franklin Roosevelt, Kennedy, and Reagan. Those for whom words were adversaries—Eisenhower, Nixon, Carter, Dan Quayle, and the

Bushes (*père et fils*), for example—were damaged to the degree words failed them. George W. Bush has employed a gifted speechwriter, Michael Gerson, and benefited enormously from the unexpected fluency this has given a few of his early speeches, including his inaugural. Eisenhower actually used verbal awkwardness to strategic advantage, but that's another matter. Clinton was somewhere in between: he had the facility but not the gift, the gab but not the art.

The presidency is a bully pulpit by default. In a democracy, which is government by words rather than by force, there's really nothing else. Policies are words enacted, programs are words implemented. I fancied myself speaking truth to power, but the president's power depended on his words and the power of his words depended on their truth. Therein lay his strength and his weakness. His strength, because of his facility with words. His weakness, because the words he spun so effortlessly were not always strongly linked with truth.

Clinton's way with words was the lawyer's (he who loves winning arguments for the sake of winning, he whom Plato denounced as the Sophist), not the philosopher's (he who is in love with truth, Plato himself). When he proposed that the exact truth depended on what the "meaning of 'is' is," or denied an affair with "that woman," the American people knew him to be clever and precise, but also small and duplicitous. He was using words to elude rather than to establish truth. And hence, during the sexual scandals and the impeachment trial that followed, his reputation for verbal facility was turned against him. He turned the sacred word profane and brought speech itself into bad repute. His adversaries could say, "If you can't trust him to tell the truth about his marriage, you can't trust him to tell the truth at all." It was not that the man who lies about his private life necessarily lies about his public life (there's no necessary connection, as Clinton in fact proved). It was that the man so skilled in the arts of verbal misdirection exposed the fragility of words and their ambiguous relationship to the real and the true. That is perhaps why there was no means for the president to talk his way out of the difficulties he had talked himself into (the alleged crime was not the deed but what he had said about it). Having tainted words, he reinforced our suspicions every time he opened his mouth. The old and bitter joke about Nixon—"How do you know when he's lying? When he moves his lips!"—could now be applied to Clinton. The trustworthiness of his words could be reestablished only by action and behavior. The words by which he otherwise might have repledged himself to truth were themselves the culprits in his fall from grace.

It was not I but the president who had to speak truth to power, and he drove a wedge between speaking and truth that made this nearly impossible. He had to talk us into believing again in his words, using only the medium of talk he'd led us to mistrust. He was a lawyer trying to prove he was a philosopher. Imagine, then, the pressure on the journeyman wordsmiths. But that was only later. Still, the hint of what was to come was there from the beginning in this president's slippery and seductive facility with words detached from larger frames.

The president's strengths and weaknesses with words were also related to historical developments in the executive branch's increasing complexity and fragmentation. George Washington's executive staff included a couple of secretaries, a postmaster, and a handful of cabinet officers to head up Treasury, State, and the War Office. Today's executive branch is a fat corporate bureaucracy that grew to its current gargantuan proportions (even after the "end of big government") during the Reagan and Bush years of talk about government downsizing. Like so many other executive functions in this corporate bureaucracy in recent decades, speechwriting has been outsourced. Once it was an inherent presidential responsibility demanding a commensurate presidential talent: imagine Wilson or Roosevelt or Lincoln without their proprietorship over words—no "four freedoms," no "house divided" that cannot stand, no "nothing to fear but fear itself." Now it is merely another delegated task of hirelings (the president himself in Clinton's inadvertently trivializing self-portrait: "hired to do a job"). It was only in Calvin Coolidge's administration that a chief executive first thought it necessary to hire a "literary clerk," as Judson Welliver (the first speechwriter and the namesake of today's elite presidential speechwriters alumni association) was called. Before that (and well after that, too, think of the scholarly Adlai Stevenson or the feisty, straight-talking Harry Truman), a leader's authenticity was measured by his words— what else could it possibly mean to give one's word? Even gang members today know that "word" is a pledge of truth.

Not presidents. Not in recent years. It is impossible to admire the eloquence of a Jack Kennedy recalling Americans to their citizenship with the words "Ask not what your country can do for you but what you can do for your country" without thinking of Ted Sorenson or Richard

Goodwin, impossible to recall the ideological animus of a Richard Nixon defending himself against America's "enemies" within without remembering Pat Buchanan or Bill Safire, impossible to embrace the big-screen sentimentality of a Ronald Reagan at the fiftieth anniversary of the Normandy Invasion without thanking Peggy Noonan or David Gergen; and it is impossible to confront the conversational brilliance of Bill Clinton without thinking about. . . . Well, there's the rub, for there was no voice in Bill Clinton's White House other than Bill Clinton's own, with all its natural strengths and all its rhetorical limitations. This is not because Don Baer and Michael Waldman and Ann Lewis and Sid Blumenthal and their many adepts at speechwriting and communications in the White House were not and are not writers, but because, for all his complaints about words and flaccid speechwriting, Bill Clinton had little use for writers. Some might say, cynically (and not wrongly) that Stan Greenberg's focus groups and Mark Penn's and Doug Schoen's polls and Dick Morris's triangulations—the petty pollster's obsession with the pulse of America—is what took the place of speechwriting in this White House. Clinton so often seemed to borrow his speeches from words already on the lips of the American majority (the actual phrases employed to package policies were tried out in focus groups). The pollster pens platitudes to capture the littleness of what is on the American mind rather than crafting words to rally the American spirit to greatness—a mission ordinary Americans may not yet have imagined. The pollster writes in the indicative mood, content with where it finds us; the speechwriter writes in the imperative mood, intent on bestirring us to action. It is often said today (I have said it myself) that the times are too pedestrian and the mind-set far too cynical and antiheroic to lend itself to old-fashioned rhetoricians who, on television's midget screens, would merely look foolishly oversized and dated. True enough, but true in part because politicians and teachers are complicit in the mediocrity and connive in reinforcing complacency and pride in ordinariness.

The polling mode that became a surrogate for leadership in the Clinton White House dictated a mode of speechwriting that could not employ writers, let alone rise to greatness. The speech that captures where America *is* (Clinton's forte) may not be the speech that helps America understand where it needs to go (Clinton's seeming failure of visionary leadership and Reagan's greatest success—however thin and sentimental the vision he offered: he was an actor who recognized a good script when he saw one).

Yet that a president as gifted with words and ideas as Clinton should have failed to leave behind a legacy in writing remains a conundrum that cannot be explained alone by his failure to grasp the full potential of rhetorical leadership. It has to do with a failure of words, but a failure associated with a choice of rhetoric typical of the sibling rather than the father. That is, it is related to what I believe is a key characteristic of Bill Clinton as president: that he felt comfortable as and was elected because he had the personality of America's first "brother president." Historically, the White House has been the provenance of father presidents, who (as historians constantly remind us) have had to play dual roles in considerable tension with one another: the one as chief executive officer of a busy and functioning republic, the other as symbolic father (king) to a people yearning, as all peoples tend to yearn, for the psychological trappings of patriarchal monarchy (matriarchal will also do). Constitutional monarchies traditionally divided the roles between a monarch and a prime minister. Charles de Gaulle's most lasting gift to France was a Fifth Republic in which an independently elected president could be invested with all the paternal authority of the national father while an elected prime minister could actually administer the country (Michel Rocard doing the dirty work of running things and being rewarded for his prudence by being ejected from office while Mitterrand sat in the father's chair receiving the reverence of a grateful nation).

In the United States, the presidency has been an office burdened with the incompatible responsibilities of both roles, and most candidates for the presidency have responded by playing at being good fathers or at least (whatever their actual age) avuncular elders. Even younger executives like Teddy Roosevelt and Jack Kennedy played characters propelled into patriarchy out of season, as Al Pacino was in *The Godfather* when seniority was thrust upon him before his time.

Bill Clinton, however, ran and served as a "brother president." His approach to language supports this point. The brother president is the oral president, who spurns the written word as a fustian medium of fathers. He casts himself self-consciously as the talker-lite, the "don't take yourself too seriously the way dad did" sibling for whom talk is a medium of exchange rather than an expression of authority. It would not occur to him to dress his attendants in Viennese opera costumes as Nixon briefly thought to do, or to address the future in the grandilo-quent tones of epic cinema as Reagan could. He spoke, rather, to the simple present in the voice of the quotidian.

Clinton dreams, of course, of a "legacy," but in every meeting I have been in he is far too busy addressing the present with a thousand mar-velous schemes to assure that today flourishes to actually start "think-ing about tomorrow." He seems always the proud sibling looking sharply to either side, never the distanced father who can look forward and back. He abjures the mysteries of the fathers in favor of a fraternal transparency. Joe Klein notices how Clinton needs to "demystify" the president's mission. And indeed, he has preferred that we see him as just another "jobholder" for a position for which the American people have "hired" him. This reeks at once of baseness and of democracy, and reminds us how closely linked those two ideas are. Oh, how we love this brother president, so like us in his egalitarian ways! Oh, how we revile this brother president, too much like us in his egalitarian ways! Tyrants knew how to make of rulership a secular priesthood, and then wrap it in paternal mysteries that would distance them from those they would rule. The eradication of distance undermines authority. Clinton did it on purpose. Can democracy function without authority? He thought so. Can authority be democratic? The answer is not certain if Cinton is the test.

Clinton opted for the hyperdemocratic, perhaps because he loved equality, perhaps because he possessed only the gifts of the brother. Either way, the mysteries of fathers remained mysterious to him. Imme-diacy was quite simply how he used words, how he governed. Hence he picked a sibling for a running mate (a problem for Gore during the 2000 election because he was not the son aspiring to fatherhood but the lit-tle brother aspiring to—what?—leapfrog his older sibling and become the older brother?). Clinton will *tell* you what kind of underwear he wears (would Bush or Reagan have ever even been asked the sibling's dumb query about boxer shorts or briefs which Clinton answered so easily?). He will lie a little too casually to his brothers and sisters about his private sins, as he could never lie to his father and as a father would never lie casually to his children without paying the severest penalties. And we in turn forgive him like a naughty sibling for sins like our own, knowing that a parent committing the same sins would be held to his own higher patriarchal standards and be tarred and feathered as a moralizing hypocrite (the Republicans ran *their* paternalistic hypocrites right out of the speakership and on out of town).

With lowered expectations, we forgive our brothers, whereas we often murder our erring fathers. Perhaps it is not so odd, after all, that a president with as many embittered enemies as Clinton has nevertheless been spared assassination attempts, which have in America's history been reserved for father figures and patriarchs—even "nice" ones like Reagan and young ones like Kennedy. Nor is it surprising that George Bush Jr. chose the "brother" route in his own presidential candidacy—and not just because the presidential father role was, in his family, quite literally already taken. It works. It plays to the relaxed, unjudgmental characteristics of the postmodern American electorate. Gore, on the other hand, in time pushed aside the younger-brother role bequeathed him by Clinton and reverted to the father type. He had trouble with the role not because he couldn't play it but perhaps because he played it all too arrogantly in a country grown tired of fathers and the natural hypocrisy with which it associated them. When the vice-president sighed in grown-up exasperation at Bush's boyish evasions in the first candidates' debate, sympathy went to Brother Bush, not Father Gore. Oddly, words were not the friends they should have been to Gore. He was, for example, accused of gross exaggeration when in fact he committed only rhetorical flourishes of a kind well known to politicians (and practiced with relative impunity by Clinton).

Gore seems more at ease with words than with the instrument with which he produces them, his own voice—hence his peculiar habit of trying on distinctive styles of speech. He can play casual and easy on Letterman, "do" a sermon that is a pretty fair knockoff of black Baptist preaching, mock himself with vicious acuity each time, and yet still stumble into sing-song pedantry when he actually has to give a for-real speech—as if the imitations were all there were. How much these stylistic shortcomings contributed to his defeat is not clear to me. But for a man as literate as Gore up against a man as word-anxious as Bush, literacy helped far less than it should have.

Now, as far as words go, Brother Clinton did far better than Brother/Father Gore. Yet he preferred speechwriters who were compilers, assemblers, and word managers, was drawn to adept word programmers—living, breathing instantiations of WordPerfect who could put ideas and formulations at his disposal to help him shape his conversational forays into the present tense. The speeches make for vivid conversation, with an air of personalized intimacy that caught the listener up in the president's personal rhetoric. But once his audience was gone from the chamber, little was left to the conversationalist but the detritus of out-of-date anecdotes and instantly stale bons mots. What bestirs listeners for a moment cannot engross readers who come to a speech weeks or years later.

The blame is not all Clinton's. His sibling's style and rhetorical extemporaneousness were dictated as much by the character of the times and the mood of the people who chose him as by the qualities of kinship for which they chose him. Incensed critics from the friendly left like Joe Klein or James MacGregor Burns (who savaged the president for his middle-of-the-road, sibling-centered moderation in his *Dead Center: Clinton-Gore Leadership and the Perils of Moderation*) are at war not with Clinton but with the times that elevated him to the presidency. Burns wants bold, inspirational, confrontational candidates—bringing what he calls "transformative" rather than "transactional" leadership—and is persuaded that Clinton never was such a leader and that neither Al Gore nor George Bush Jr. ever will be. America may indeed need visionary, heroic leadership, but these are unheroic times, and what America wants and voted for in 1992 and 1996 and 2000 as well was ordinary administration by a sibling president who would not stray too far from what the country took itself to be. Much of what America took itself to be—moderate, tolerant, and multicultural—is good for America, and accounts for much of Clinton's success as well as Bush Jr.'s unexpected (if tainted) victory. Burns wants for America (and I also want for America) what America apparently doesn't want for itself. He opts for the inspirationally transformative father, but voters seem to prefer the merely transactional boy Bush and his older sibling Gore. After all, in Bradley and McCain they were offered the choice of mature men and spurned them, though their ambivalence is revealed by their rather high opinion of Lieberman and Cheney, arguably the two most "adult" characters in the 2000 race and the nation's insurance policy against creeping juvenility.

These are television times in which the written word has been trumped by the spoken word, and even text is consumed mainly from endless scrolling lines on computer screens. Can we really expect rhetoric in a period when "chat" is the essence of electronic communication? Can "oratory" seem other than old-fashioned and arch, trumped-up rather than authentic, in the age of hip-hop? The brother president savors authenticity—"Here I am, it's really me"—even at the price of being accused of modesty, whereas the father president is willing to risk alienation or, worse, charges of hypocrisy, in the name of a distancing and impersonal civility—a voice not quite his own but which favors integrity ("Forget me, here is the truth") over authenticity.

The speechwriters themselves reflect the choice, as they narrow the distance between speech and spin. For they are excellent journalists, and perspicacious observers—collectors of data and assemblers of ideas whose object is to capture the flavor and spirit of a series of individual policies. Clinton's speeches did not so much lead the people as show them where they had been. His leadership lay in hindsight—reacting to rather than pointing toward, extrapolating from the map of a journey taken the coordinates for a near destination. Hence the popularity of polling. For all the talk of bridges to the future, Clinton's greatest skill was in walking the byways of the present.

I wanted to think my writerly contributions were solicited for their dramatic structure and narrative vision, but realistically, since the solicitors studiously ignored the architecture and instead pilfered language fragments and single ideas, it seems more likely that I was just another useful source of sound-bites. Each year before the State of the Union Message when Galston or Baer or Waldman would set about soliciting "ideas" and themes for the year's most important speech, I would proudly and a little self-importantly compose my careful small-scale epics. Each year I would warn yet again against the cafeteria list where, in the usual obeisance to each cabinet office, each subject area got its tepid paragraph with its own living and breathing demonstration in the gallery balcony ("This year, the forestry service introduced its new logo on the way to successfully dousing 384 fires, and if you will look up at Hillary you will see sitting next to her Forest Ranger Hector Mendoza, who—[applause] yes Hector! stand up! that's Hector Mendoza who rode his chopper into a smoky maelstrom in Glacier National Forest and helped save over 941 acres of virgin pine . . ."); and each year I would warn against relegating the heart of the speech, a vision of America's future, a new ideological turn, to a couple of bookend paragraphs to open and close a speech otherwise overstuffed with cabinet

secretary wish lists ("And despite your support for the Pacific Fleet's carrier task force, I must note with sorrow that my requests over three pre-
vious years for an increase in spending for the Navy Seal training
station in Okinawa, which still lacks deepwater snorkeling facilities,
have been repeatedly denied, putting the fleet's mission at risk—I call
on you now, have a look at that young woman on Mrs. Clinton's left,
that's Sondra Saylor. She's the Seals' first winner in the annual rapid
deepwater descent prize [wild applause], thank you, Sondra, we all
thank you for your service, now let me ask the women and men in this
august chamber, I want you to imagine how many more fine young ser-
vicewomen and men we could train if we could upgrade our training
facilities..."). And each year I would warn that shorter was better, that
messages about the future got lost as the messengers hung around talking about achievements of the past ("... in the year gone by, our programs added 4,321 police officers to municipal forces, gave 1,899
substitute teachers a leg up to regular teaching careers, were responsible for the seizure of 681 illegal assault weapons, and put 600 federal-
ly subsidized veterinarians into cow country as a preemptive strike
against mad cow disease, which ... well folks, have a look up there in
the balcony, sitting right next to Chelsea you'll see Bessie, one of thousands of heifers in good health who ... [applause] that's right, stand up,
Bessie, and take a bow ...") And each year, I would sit down in rapt
anticipation to watch the president address the joint session of Congress
only to hear those same old wish lists surrounded by two new bookend
paragraphs of whatever was left of the big ideas we'd plumbed in our
seminars delivered over the better part of two hours (it felt as if the word
count went up every year) and punctuated by grand gestures to the balcony where living, breathing, spitting images of the best half dozen
small-bore policy proposals were found sitting, grinning shyly next to
Hillary or Chelsea or whoever was holding down the family section,
while the chamber broke into only partially partisan applause from senators and representatives who *knew* they were on TV and whether they
clapped or didn't clap, it could only be for the benefit of the virtual audience rather than the real-life heroes-for-the-evening to whom their
noisy plaudits were ostensibly being directed.

Yet, though I sighed and groaned and the media elites griped and
criticized, the public hailed the chief. Laundry lists and cafeteria menus

# STATE OF THE UNION

### ADDRESS TO THE 106<sup>th</sup> CONGRESS

### FIRST SESSION

*To Benjamin Barber
with thanks
Bill Clinton*

## *President William J. Clinton*

JANUARY 19, 1999 • WASHINGTON, D.C.

were the means by which most Americans negotiated their way through their own versions of mundanity, and if this older-brother president knew how to do it with efficiency and success and perhaps even a dash of modest élan, more power to him. Lots of small-bore programs met the needs of lots of ordinary people, which was more than most politicians ever did. Conservatives spoke derisively of "little big government," but that strikes me as a compliment. On the speech, the press agreed with me—it was too long on particulars and too short on vision, too fragmented to usher in the future, too pedestrian to memorialize the past—nineteen courses but no coherent menu, no principles of cuisine, the chef gone missing. And yet the public would weigh in with easy praise, leaving us, the experts in rhetoric, fairly flummoxed, not understanding why the American public didn't understand the obvious that we understood so well. I ended up at the conclusion of each State of the Union sounding the way Jim Burns sounds today, mad at my president for refusing to sell grand visions to a people who were looking for a decent pair of specs at a price that wouldn't empty their pocketbooks. They got what they had elected, and he gave them what they had voted for. Heroism isn't necessarily the stuff of democracy, which calls on ordinary citizens to do ordinary things as well as they can. Brecht reminds us that the country we must pity is not the one without heroes but the one that needs heroes.

Could Clinton have pushed the envelope without corrupting its democratic contents? Turned vivid description into something verging on vivid prescription? Made a test for eyeglasses into a recipe for vision? I am not sure. The president got the speechwriters he needed and the speechwriters his constituents deserved. Plain-spoken journalists who put word next to word and paragraph after paragraph until a speech composed of simple and plain words depicting straightforward and useful programs had been laid out end to end like so many matchbooks in a carefully assembled collection. No literary lions were required, no artful Safires or Camelot-dreaming Goodwins or lithe Noonans climbing their computers to the City on the Hill. Nineteen ninety-seven was not 1517 and did not call for nailing up ninety-five theses on some imposing cathedral portal to launch a Protestant Reformation. Clinton had need, rather, of accommodating, empathetic collators, a story collector here and a fact organizer there, a chief writer with one ear open to the ideas and formulas of myriad speech architects who could be counted on to cancel one another out in the end, and the other ear attentively turned to the president: tuned to *his* voice, *his* style. They knew he would in any case make the speech his own. As he did in the year when the writers somehow succeeded in conceiving and then composing a speech that was relatively focused and relatively succinct and relatively list-free, only to discover, on the day of the State of the Union, prompted by Hillary, who in listening to a run-through insisted the voice (however eloquent) was not his, that the president took it upon himself to transform the speech back into a prosaic and meandering and hence endless cafeteria menu, read now, however, in the president's own authentic cadences and with the same sure-fire impact on the public. Michael or Don or someone must have sighed somewhere deep within his writer's soul, but to me staffers confided only that the speech was surely the better for having been appropriated by the president and given the stamp of his own, unique voice.

Probably there is not much room between the extremes. Perhaps a president must either write his own speeches or be a fine actor who can give voice to the poetry of others. Reagan had gifted speechwriters and little on his mind to get in the way of a powerful delivery of their lines. Experienced actor that he was, he preferred reading lines to writing them, and he did it in a fashion that gave credit to his writers and credence to himself: the lines suited the role and were mostly true to his instincts. His synthetic skills created as much authenticity as most presidents could hope to draw from their own earnestness—corrupted as that earnestness might have been by his decades in politics. And his speechwriters, like apt screenwriters, knew their star and wrote to his vocal strengths and rhetorical cadences.

On the other hand, a Jefferson or a Lincoln forges authenticity by giving expression to deep inner beliefs. He *is* what he preaches and, in giving us his rhetoric, discloses something akin to his soul. When the soul is warped, the voice is bent (Nixon?) but quite authentic. When it is well formed, the voice can ascend to heaven—or quake with the terrors of an encroaching hellfire (Lincoln?).

In the end, Clinton's speechwriting and speech-giving proclivities emanated from the same disposition that made him a brother president, a neighbor-statesman, a man for his times but not necessarily for the ages. The brother president is a constant presence in our daily consciousness; the father president lives forever in memory—in the depths of a consciousness beyond the quotidian. Clinton seemed to need to connect in the here and now, and for him politics was rooted in that immediate connectivity. He spoke to us as to a gathered clan of lovers; we all had affairs with him, even the strangers who account for all but the handful of those of us who have met him. To the degree his ardent connectivity was an effective political prompt, he was successful— which is why Newt Gingrich quite correctly warned his colleagues not to visit personally with Clinton prior to confronting him politically. The charm mode, the seduction mode, the inner circle "you are the only person alive" mode, is simply standard operating procedure for the glib talker. Bill Clinton was our "Music Man"—a Harold Hill for our City on the Hill. It was his special gift to us.

Beware presidents bearing gifts, however. The deficit of Clinton's brand of seductive leadership is that the moment you drift out of the charmed orbit and check your bearings by reference to the compass of your principles and beliefs, what seemed a well-defined security of place immediately becomes directional confusion. Back in the safety of your own chosen orthodoxy, the power of this brother president—relying on oral facility and disarming authenticity as well as a degree of emotional extortion—is dispelled. If he wants to do more than bribe you with his love into an insincere consensus, he has to reach over into your sanctuary. For this, he needs a principled logic for which text and conviction rather than a facility for conversation are the prerequisites.

True sermons take shape and endure only on paper. Sermonizing texts and preached convictions seem more like the archaic baggage of fathers, however. The brother doesn't want to preach at his siblings. Elizabeth Drew, who grumbled in her account of the president's first year, *On the Edge,* about the endless talk and absence of "discipline" in the White House decision-making process, complained directly to me about the absence of discipline in the writing—there was not enough there in Clinton's speeches to last into next week, let alone make it into an enduring atlas of ideas. Hard to get to a legacy with nothing but talk—however politically efficacious it is at the moment of utterance. But equally hard for a president so good at talk to trust in speechifying on paper. Drew thought it was because he needed to be liked, encouraged, reinforced all the time (the son-of-an-alcoholic routine), and you can't do that writing a disciplined speech at midnight in the Oval Office nearly as well as when you're jabbering extemporaneously with a group of reporters or Americorps volunteers or cabinet officers in the Rose Garden.

Perhaps the whole point of all those seminars and the generous invitations to outsiders like me to get in on a speechwriting process usually guarded jealously by a small circle of in-house writers was precisely to guarantee that there would be no paper texts. If you want to assure that there will never be a single, coherent text, invite a dozen intellectuals with egos as inflated as their résumés to spend a day together writing one. Democratize the process and annihilate the product! Then the president is left to do what he really wants to do, which is carry a bunch of cards that are an outline of a talk, and wing it. Or avoid making a decision altogether.

Again, critics from Elizabeth Drew to Senator Bentsen and Robert Reich have commented on the sins of indecision bred by so undisciplined and democratic a process as was represented by the endless seminars and the group-speak texts. Waldman wondered aloud whether any of it, fascinating though it was, "would be very helpful." Too many cooks may spoil the soup, but that means the president is the default chef to cook or not cook as he sees fit. President's teleprompter's broken? Fabulous! Do it on the fly! Wrong speech on the lectern? Good deal! You're on your own!

Surely, you say, this is grossly exaggerated. Most of the millions of words uttered by President Clinton over eight years were written down in loving (boring) detail and though not set in stone were read as written by a president too busy to extemporize every time he had to open his mouth. Yet the speeches he has given, even those composed by well-educated NSC staffers proud of their command over language, are fairly pedestrian: "To the people of Bosnia I say," proclaimed the president, in as tired a string of clichés as a diligent speechwriter could be expected to dredge up to an enthralled audience in Sarajevo at the end of 1997, "You have seen what war has wrought; now you know what peace can bring. So seize the chance before you. . . . The world is watching, and the world is with you. But the choice is yours."

The president's best extemporaneous stuff is like good stand-up comedy, deft lines that amuse and affect directly but rarely transfer to print, where the essentials of timing and inflection are lost. When it comes to stand-up, no one, not even Reagan or Kennedy, can match Clinton. For this, he's adored by reporters. But when it comes to the written word, those same reporters are more disdainful. The *Washington Post* journalist E. J. Dionne, who is as sympathetic to the president's Third Way ideology as any reporter in Washington, can write circles around the White House and is understandably impatient with its lack of discipline with the written word. One could do worse than crib from his *Why Americans Hate Politics* and his *Why the Left Isn't Dead.*

One on one (or one on all), however, the president was peerless. I experienced this directly but impersonally at the 1998 White House Correspondents Association annual dinner, which always featured (roasted) the president. For once, I witnessed the president at a distance, as part of a dazzled crowd (though I missed a fair amount of what transpired because I was also the bedazzled guest of Elizabeth Shogren, the LA *Times* White House correspondent).

Shogren was a first-rate reporter and lacked the biases so much of the press seemed to bring to Clinton, whether pro or con. So when she invited me to the correspondents dinner, I was delighted—seeing it as a chance to meet the gifted journalistic matron whose mature voice I knew well from a number of phone interviews. I was, however, unprepared for the prom night apparition who showed up to escort me to the Washington Hilton until I remembered that Clinton's Hollywood connections had made the White House correspondents dinner an event as much about Hollywood as about Washington. True to the president, the dinner was drawing an unusually Hollywood crowd—from Michael Douglas and Sharon Stone to Warren Beatty and Paula Jones, who had apparently abandoned that pretense of aggrieved modesty she had briefly tried on for the media and was vying with Hillary for first-lady attention, courtesy of conservative journalists hoping to embarrass the president.

The Hilton entrance was roped off for these eastern Oscars by police barricades, behind which milled crowds of normally sane Washington secretaries and Hill staffers sharing insights such as "over here babe!" and "oh man oh man oh man," and ogling "starlets" who were in fact demure journalists just like Elizabeth, women who once a year poured themselves into evening wear two sizes too small in order to play their appointed roles.

I spotted Henry Kissinger outside the ballroom. On the few occasions we'd encountered one another over the period that separated the dinner that evening from the Ph.D. orals he nearly failed me on at Harvard thirty-five years earlier, he'd displayed an attitude that prudently mixed disdain with indifference—if he remembered I had been an irritating student decades earlier, he didn't betray it. Time tempers us all, especially when confronted by stunning pulchritude. The dour expression that had settled on Henry's face when he saw me approaching fell away in an instant when he realized the woman he was watching was inexplicably accompanying me. He plunged into an earnest conversation with me (her), and would not be diverted from it by celebrities or autograph seekers.

I think he would have remained rooted to that spot for the entire evening. The president had helped create an atmosphere at this moment in his presidency in which seduction seemed altogether permissible if not quite admirable. Still, I tired of Kissinger's fascination and lured Elizabeth away on the pretext of introducing her to Melanne Verveer across the hall. Not an ideal pretext. For Melanne, who was the president's deputy chief of staff and the first lady's chief of staff and one of my friends and confidantes in the White House, froze. Despite the discretion I'd shown (unlike many of my seminar colleagues over the years), every time I appeared with a reporter or in print, the White House folks who knew about it grew anxious—"Don't spill the beans," Michael Waldman had whispered only half in jest when he saw me later that evening in the ballroom, leaving me to ponder exactly which beans I had that were worth spilling.

George Stephanopoulos sashayed down the corridor, a coterie of admirers nearly jogging by his side to keep up with him, but came to a sufficiently abrupt halt in front of us to send the coterie lurching several paces farther down the hall before it could halt. "Hey, Ben, what's happening? Things okay?"—this while he stared at Elizabeth as if he didn't recognize the sharp-witted reporter he had to know all too well. George had left the White House and was now making less than friendly noises on ABC about his erstwhile mentor. Another jilted seductee of the executive seducer with whom it was easier to have an affair than a friendship?

The speeches at dinner were typical roast fare, except the president's, which was roast fare deluxe. In Hollywood comic mode. Dazzling. Amid a sea of actors, professional talkers, his nemesis Paula Jones, the men and women who, wordsmiths themselves, reported his every word, he held forth. He had all of them rapt, enraptured, amused, happily outraged, the hardest audience in America (though not that night) completely in his hands. He left the second-rate TV comedians sent up to pave the way—to make with the off-color anecdotes and deploy Paula Jones sexual innuendos with all the finesse of World Federation wrestlers—looking like amateurs. This was Clinton the talker at his best. Words to wow an audience, win a following, put out a fire, disarm the critics. We were all disarmed. We were all his. For that night.

In the morning, however, the enemies would reemerge unscathed, the lawyers would still file their briefs, the old fire of battles unwon would be reignited, the legacy would remain not only unwritten but wholly out of sight. That's the impotence of stand-up rhetoric. The inefficacy of mere facility. The brother president had won the evening, but a few hours after the ballroom had emptied out and the last guests had left for the *Vanity Fair* party that was the A-list's post-dinner destination, the morning would dawn and the day that followed would belong again to those for whom the rule of the brother inspired only fratricide, against which neither the rhetoric-lite of the preceding evening nor the half-written speeches of a facile conversationalist could provide adequate protection.

Now, with the president's second term complete and the words multiplying as their impact is diminished (his speech at Gore's nominating convention was both inspired and forgettable), it seems clear that the hole Clinton dug for himself where a legacy should have been is not by any means only a matter of the words that he did or did not say, or that were or were not written for him. But the weakness of his words despite the vigor of his speech nonetheless disclosed a certain ongoing weakness of philosophy and program. He did so many of the right things, yet lacked the capacity to put them in a context where what was right about them stood out, larger than the sum of the legislative pieces by which they were constituted. He transformed the Democrats' ideology, but backed off the language that could have memorialized the transformation in lasting terms. Ironically, he called regularly on the very kinds of writers who might have helped him reach higher rhetorically—Stephen Carter, Chris Edley, and Alan Brinkley were fine craftsmen with words as were other of his willing interlocutors—but though he listened earnestly to their thoughts, he declined to embrace their rhetoric.

Of course, had Clinton been another Ronald Reagan and Michael Waldman some Democratic Peggy Noonan, then Clinton would have had Waldman consult his thesaurus and peruse his history books and plunder Plutarch and Cicero and Lincoln and Churchill and write all the speeches for him (or hire clones to do it under his disciplined direction). Period. And we never would have been called on to write our memos and attend the seminars and edify the president as Skip Gates and Sam Beer and Theda Skocpol and Bob Putnam and so many others had. Only because this anarchically democratic Democratic president was as in love with group talk as he was diffident about solitary writing were any of us there in the first place.

Jerry Brown, formerly known as California's "Governor Moonbeam" and more recently the mayor of Oakland, invited citizens and scholars alike to attend a six-week "Oakland Table" seminar that mused on big-topic themes like the nature of democracy. Even the hard-hitting pragmatist mayor Ed Koch of New York used to invite intellectuals to Gracie Mansion for roundtables. But Clinton still wins the prize: thus Senator Lloyd Bentsen's remark about Clinton's staff as the "meetingest crowd I've ever seen." Certainly the president was the meetingest president anyone had seen in a very long time (at least since the sixties, when meetings were not for getting things done but for the pure participatory sake of meeting). More to the point, he was surely the least writingest president of modern times—brilliantly literate without being even modestly literary. He amazed his speechwriters with his verbal gifts even as he disappointed them by abusing their texts so freely and abandoning them so easily. A speechifying, meetingest man who, in never fully appreciating the written word, deprived himself of its extraordinary power over the course of human events.

# CHAPTER FIVE

# A Blizzard in D.C.

**THE WINTER OF 1995–96** was pretty bleak, and I don't just mean the weather. The toll that the government shutdown in December of 1995 would take had not yet been reckoned and though the Republicans seemed to be getting the worst of it, one couldn't be sure. It was still the Gingrich era, and his compelling '94 electoral triumph, which had not only given the Republicans the House of Representatives but given them a much more conservative cast than they had previously had, continued to be read as a deep historical shift in American politics. The '96 primaries were just getting underway, and the elections threatened to secure the revolution, to enlarge the Republican congressional majority, and perhaps even to oust Clinton after a single term. Perhaps that's why there was still an appetite in the White House for outside counsel from generalists like me. After all, Clinton had already made the concrete decisions that led him away from his "social investment" policy to a deficit reduction strategy that had yet to pay dividends, and had moved from pushing a failed health plan to considering a welfare reform scheme whose benefits were far from clear and which would engender corrosive conflict within the party. This was a period during which Clinton would later be described as stumbling toward a "failed presidency."

The outsiders Galston roped in for the 1996 State of the Union session were certainly not policy specialists on educational financing or the Indonesian economy. Dick Morris seemed to be calling the policy shots openly, so specific policy recommendations were not at issue. We were presumably of use only because we were broad-gauged intellectuals with a passion for the meaning of America, the conditions of justice, and the currents of history. We were modern prophets, women and men who affected to read the story of where we were and how we had gotten here in a way that might predict where we should be heading and what kinds of strategic notions might help us get there. I know that sounds, if not actually pretentious, a little portentous, but that's how it was.

Now, strictly speaking, by the winter of '96 Galston was long gone from the White House. After years of intellectual toil before and after Clinton's '92 victory, he had grown tired of marginalizing his family to compete with twenty-five-year-old indefatigables for the time of the president. If the young upstarts with no families hung around till midnight chomping on pizza and strategizing the issues, how could a senior deputy do other than pretend he had no family and do the same? An evening with his own kid might mean ceding crucial policy decisions to some kid in the White House. Galston had left the administration the preceding summer, determined to reintroduce himself to his family. But he was still roping academic calves for the episodic intellectual rodeos the president continued to demand. In fact, I had the impression he had more influence now that he had left his formal position than he did when slaving at policy papers for the Domestic Policy Council. It was nearly Christmas when White House schedulers apparently noticed that no one had been invited to the January 7 dinner that would again precede the State of the Union speech, and Galston was called in to arrange another seminar.

Galston followed the routine developed over the last several years: we filed written statements in time for the president to look over our collective output while he was vacationing at Renaissance Weekend over New Year's. That gave us only a couple of days. Then, at a dinner in early January, the authors would be given the opportunity to elaborate their views and engage in an exchange with the president, resulting, it was hoped, in an improved State of the Union speech and fresh thinking for the thereafter. Only the cast of characters had been revised. Bob Putnam, Skip Gates, and I were back from a year ago (Stephen Carter had also been invited again but failed to show up).

There were plenty of new faces—Bill ran down the list over the phone. They included a surprising number of my old friends (obviously Bill Galston's as well—the community of political and social theorists is a little incestuous). The communitarian-guru-in-the-making Amitai Etzioni, for example, who had set up shop at George Washington University years earlier and was brilliantly exploiting the Washington scene to advance the interests of the communitarian movement and its journal the *Responsive Community* (on whose editorial board I sat); and the political theorist Jenny Mansbridge, whom I'd known since high school and done time with in graduate school at Harvard and who had written thoughtfully and critically on democracy, participation, and women. Also the Yale Law School philosopher Bruce Ackerman, a boyish and bookish genius who had a flair for making persuasive political points from an unlikely utopian legal philosopher's perch.[1] In another world Ackerman might have been elevated to the Supreme Court (his name was on all the right leftist lists), but his utopian optimism and political naïveté conspired against it in this world. Amy Gutmann had been invited as well. Harvard-trained (the time of the Ivies is not yet over), Princeton-based, Gutmann had committed her career to issues of education and citizenship. Michael Walzer, the editor of *Dissent* magazine and a reclusive member of the social science division of the Institute for Advanced Studies at Princeton (known for its work in mathematics and theoretical physics via Einstein, but also a home for advanced social research), had been invited but for unknown reasons did not attend. And there was Randall Kennedy, a colleague of Gates from Harvard (the law school), and Alan Ehrenhalt, a journalist and cultural critic who had written an original communitarian account of Chicago as it was in the 1950s, called *The Lost City*, which had quickly become a source book for those looking for the key to rekindling the spirit of community in our more atomistic, suburban-sprawl times.

Bill had stirred the bowl vigorously, seeking ingredients different from last year's and so, prospectively, a quite different cake. Which was where the trouble with the weather started. January 7 dawned on a raging blizzard, blown in with unexpected force off the Atlantic, one of

---

[1] Best known for his classic study *Social Justice and the Liberal State* (New Haven: Yale University Press, 1980), he recently proposed a pragmatic version of a utopic scheme to give every American $80,000 as a stake to join our "stakeholder society." See Ackerman and Anne Alstott, *The Stakeholder Society* (New Haven: Yale University Press, 1999).

those collisions between an Arctic high-pressure front dropping down from Canada and an Atlantic low blowing up the coast that can cause havoc at the point of intersection along the shoreline. We had all day to get to D.C., and I had planned an afternoon flight from Newark. Canceled. So were all the other flights. And the Metroliners on Amtrak. The interstates were in terrible condition, and it began to look as if I would actually miss act two of the drama inaugurated the preceding year at Camp David. I decided to get my four-wheel over to Metropark (the key Jersey junction on Amtrak's northeast line) and hang there, hoping some engineer might elude the overseers at Penn Station and be foolishly braving the snow in a runaway diesel engine. After a couple of hours, a "Northeast Direct" (read very local and very indirect) train lumbered into Metropark carrying a standing-room-only complement of passengers dumped from all the other Metroliners and planes that weren't running. I pushed my way on, but could not get into a carriage. I shivered on the platform between cars, my feet planted in snow that had drifted in through cracks and crannies above the couplings. The chilling cost of patriotism.

As the train jostled south along icy tracks, I gradually worked my way into the car. There was scarcely room to stand. A large wheelchair-capable rest room stood empty on my immediate left, its WHEELCHAIR sign intimidating passengers who otherwise would have killed for a seat. I pushed open the sliding door and fell onto the lowered toilet seat. I was immediately joined by three other weary passengers. Every five or ten minutes, we would be rousted from our sanctuary by someone who needed the rest room for more than a rest, and we would push out into the crowded passageway, wind blowing in on us from the platform (the door was jammed open by ice). We gave those using the toilet looks that said it was only on loan and would be reclaimed by us as soon as duties were done. In this undignified but relatively comfortable way, I managed to get to Washington.

The pundits who kid that the only way to the White House is via the toilet were, for once, literally correct. Six hours of frigid slow motion, half a dozen unscheduled stops caused by power failures or ice on the rails, and we rolled into Union Station a little after 5 P.M. Trudging through the snow (the Metro stop nearest the White House is not near the White House, at least not in a blizzard), I was able to stop at the Hotel Washington and shed my ice-crusted (outside) and steaming (inside) travel clothes and climb into a business suit. By the time I had pushed on through another few blocks of snow around the south side of the massive mausoleum that was the Treasury Building and up to the southeast entrance to the White House, the fresh suit was as ice-crusted and steaming and limp as the one I'd left behind.

Stepping into the White House that evening was like passing through a door in one of those decidedly unlinear dreams. On one side, a raging blizzard, snow drifts three feet high, dark, empty streets clogged with abandoned cars, a few bundled bodies hurrying through the driving snow. On the other side, high-walled candlelit salons, servants in livery, President and Mrs. Clinton receiving us as if we were strolling the veranda at a Little Rock governor's ball on some balmy evening in late June. The salon next to the private dining room where we would eat was aglow, lit by a blazing fireplace, myriad candles, and soft chandelier lighting that together created the impression of a very expensive stage set (of course, for all practical purposes the White House *is* a very expensive stage set).

The room was as full and alive as the streets had been empty and silent. Blizzard or no, it was immediately apparent that almost all the invited guests had somehow managed to survive and arrive. For all our cynicism about inside-the-Beltway politics, dinner invitations to the White House (let alone *working* dinner invitations) are still platinum in the social world. With such an invitation in hand, no mere flood, earthquake, or blizzard is likely to stay guests from their appointed round. These were social scientists who studied charts and respected data, and most had anticipated the storm and flown in the day before. A few like me had struggled on the day of the dinner to find trains, buses, dogsleds—whatever it took—to get there. Administration officials and White House staffers drifted in, apparently unfazed by the weather raging outside. The White House really was a cocoon: the "real" world beyond the South Lawn appeared as a virtual extension of television programs broadcast from distant cities. The Oval Office did not respond to cues from the weather channel. Or, rather, as on *The Truman Show*, the weather and its effects had to respond to cues from the Oval Office.

So here we were and there they were, all the regulars. Henry Cisneros was still an insider's insider, a cabinet secretary who was also an intellectual, back for a new debate. Although Bob Reich certainly qualified as an intellectual as well as a Clinton friend, and Donna Shalala was an ex-university president (Hunter College and the University of Wisconsin), Cisneros was the only cabinet secretary who seemed privy to these meetings. Or maybe the rest of them regarded the sessions as a waste of time, though Reich certainly would have found some allies for his lonely battle on behalf of redistributionist radicalism. Don Baer, my dinner companion at Camp David, returned in his new role as director of communications—avowing that he really missed writing speeches but felt sufficiently empowered by his new responsibilities to be glad about the promotion. In the year between dinners, his cordiality had become warmth. Michael Waldman had replaced Don as chief speechwriter and seemed more than pleased to be prominently included in the small company. We found a good deal to talk about, since his brother Steve had written the definitive book on the start-up of the community service initiative.[2] Bruce Reed, the DLC's main man on policy, nodded my way but stayed on the other side of the room.

What a difference a year makes. For the White House it had been a period of trying to repair the damage done by the Gingrich revolution. For me it had brought the modest strengthening of relations first knit at Camp David. Having spent the months following our seminar there firing off memos, consulting on speeches (Michael Waldman had called me about the spring Memphis speech on race and then the July 3 Georgetown University speech), talking intermittently with Don Baer and others, and finally, in September, watching in amazement as the president talked perceptively and publicly about my new book *Jihad vs. McWorld* (at a televised religious breakfast—see chapter 10), I was beginning to feel more like an insider than a visitor. George Stephanopoulos greeted me with a personal zeal I had not seen before (other than in Joe Klein's fictionalized account of him on the pages of *Primary Colors*), and complained with a mischievous smile that he was tired of Clinton pulling out a copy of *Jihad vs. McWorld* at every other meeting and talking urgently about its relevance. "I'm not sure he ever really finishes a book, but he hasn't stopped talking about yours. I wish he'd finish it and move on!"

---

[2] Steven Waldman, *The Bill: How the Adventures of Clinton's National Service Bill Reveal What Is Corrupt, Comical, Cynical—and Noble—about Washington* (New York: Viking, 1995).

President and Mrs. Clinton entered a little after seven and, working the room in a manner appropriate to an intimate dinner party, passed by the little confab George and I were engaged in. As always, Clinton was perfectly attuned to everything going on in the room. With Bob Putnam (a little later) he would instantly reference "Bowling Alone," Bob's account of the decline of social membership and social capital in the last thirty years in America. With me he stopped, grabbed my shoulder, and, as if he had been privy to everything we had said previously, dropped into our conversation midsentence without missing a beat: I was saying to Stephanopoulos, "The Republican social conservatives are Jihadic reactionaries, protesting McWorld . . . ," and then all at once Clinton was saying, "I think the Republicans realize success has come in part because they are able to appeal to 'McWorld,' and at the same time placate Jihad, you know, the Christian Right. They've got both the right-wing cultural critics and the corporations on their side. Both Jihad and McWorld."

"True, true," I responded excitedly. "But this gives them only a temporary advantage. Because Jihad and McWorld represent fractured, oppositional forces, and while they are dialectically connected, in the long run they cannot be embraced simultaneously." The president nodded. "And we've got democracy, a commitment to civil society—the space between Jihad and McWorld," I added.

"We can get beyond McWorld," the president offered. "The Republicans can't." It was true. The fissures produced by the tension between Jihad and McWorld were already cracking the Republican Party. The free-market libertarians (McWorld) and the social conservatives (Jihadic Luddites) had radically distinctive agendas. The business guys want laissez-faire, want the government off their backs; the cultural warriors want activist government enforcing their values agenda on the nation—prohibitions on abortion, government mandated school prayer, entertainment media censorship. They have a hard time working together. George Bush Jr. and Gary Bauer, Robert Dole and Pat Buchanan, Christie Whitman and Bill Bennett.

Decades earlier, Irving Kristol had tried to serve both masters in a little book pointedly called *Two Cheers for Capitalism*; yes, free markets were good—worth, however, a cheer less than the traditional three. Because capitalism could undermine the cultural values on which free societies depended. This was a point Alexis de Tocqueville had made: "A free society more than others requires religious convictions and a common religious culture; otherwise, society flies apart."

Everyone quotes Tocqueville, of course—Gingrich no less than Clinton—but that was because he got so many things right. Because he understood both democracy and the perils of majority tyranny, both the power of public opinion and the risks of its abuse, both the inevitability of egalitarianism and the certainty of its cultural costs. Democrats and Republicans alike celebrated his admiring account of "civil society" in America, but in deferring to the new buzzwords progressives meant the unions and the foundations and the social reform movement, while Republicans meant religion and the family. Republicans wanted civil society to *replace* government; Democrats wanted it to reanimate citizenship and hence relegitimize government. One of our ongoing seminar topics would be the different implications of these two positions on the idea of the civic.

All this, and we had only just had cocktails. The storm had vanished. In the wine-induced calm of robust intellectual debate, we might have been in an Enlightenment salon. Then dinner was announced, breaking up the deepening debate. We moved next door. We were dining in the president's private downstairs dining room, much more intimate that the East Room, where state banquets were held, or the State Dining Room just next door. This inviting chamber had been the president's real family dining room until Kennedy's time, when Jackie had installed a truly private dining room in the upstairs living quarters away from the White House's downstairs public spaces, leaving this as an informal public room for "private" dinners—or a private room for "public" dinners.

No Camp David musical chairs this time. Neat place cards around an elegantly set table. Perhaps two dozen of us packed closely around the modest oval. Nursing my disappointment at the sudden conclusion of a discussion with the president that focused on ideas related to my work, I nosed around the table looking for a place card with my name on it. And found it at center table next to the president, on his left-hand side. We were sharing a cashew nut dish (one for every two guests at the table). Our encounter wasn't over at all: it was threatening to become an affair.

We didn't have long to continue our chat, however, just long enough for me to realize I was sharing a cup of my favorite nuts with the most voracious eater in the room (I'm pretty voracious in my own right, but this was a no-contest competition). Bill Galston wanted the formal discussion to begin with the dinner (it wasn't Camp David, and we didn't have all day), so there would be time neither for private conversation nor even to savor the White House chef's post-nouvelle menu, which included lobster and ticama salad in rice paper, chicken with pumpkin gnocchi and spiced huckleberry sauce, and caramel and roasted dried pears mousse cake with kumquat sauce. Despite the comparisons with Andrew Jackson, and Clinton's reputation for fast-food taste, his kitchen was not exactly populist. More Jeffersonian than Jacksonian. High cuisine is wasted in these surroundings, however. Sitting next to the president of the United States, who wants to exclaim "My, what a yummy meal!"? You want to talk, not taste, listen not eat—savor and digest, yes, but ideas rather than sauces.

The shared cashews, however, really were a problem. Every time I casually reached out with my right hand to take a nut, the president's large left hand shot out like a cobra's head, dropping over the mouth of the cup, blocking my access. I hastily withdrew, and the president palmed a couple of cashews. Talk about a common touch! He would look out across the table, exchange words with someone down at the other end, but leave some sixth sense on guard, a third eye marking my hand in motion and parrying my every thrust with a quicker move of his own. If I got three cashews over ten minutes, that was a lot. Don't go *mano a mano* with Bill Clinton over a dish of nuts.

Galston pushed us into our presentations, which went quickly and smoothly. Whereas last year the fundamental clash between old and New Democrats—between Theda Skocpol and the first lady or Paul Starr and me—had absorbed much of the afternoon, this year the debate began with a certain relative consensus. The list of invitees reflected a more New Democrat take, more communitarian and more civic. Putnam, Mansbridge, Ehrenhalt, Etzioni, Gutmann, and I approached politics from the perspective of education, social trust, and citizenship rather than unions, special interests, and class conflict. We focused on neighborhood and community as well as on the federal government, and we understood civil society as a partner of government in nurturing both volunteers and citizens. Not only were there no ardent New Dealers urging that lines be drawn in the sand (likes James MacGregor Burns in his Rooseveltian attack on Clinton published at the end of Clinton's second term, titled *Dead Center*), there were no pure pols either.[3] No Panetta or Ickes, no Dick Morris surrogates like the media pundit David Gergen (a pal of Don Baer, nominally a Republican, but briefly a member of the administration during this period), no urgent pollsters demanding pragmatism and payoff. The question of which ideology had been settled—if, indeed, it was ever really in dispute inside the White House. The challenge was *how* to talk about the civil society agenda, how to execute on and legislatively enact it.

The opening statements seemed less inspiring than last year's, but then I was in a very different place, less likely to feel inspired. To the newcomers it was a virgin experience. As Putnam talked, I grew impatient. Like him, I'd been around this track. I was probably feeling now what George and other staffers had been feeling at earlier round-tables—exasperated at the president's need for talk about issues they imagined were (or should have been) settled. Why was he looking for intellectual comfort from newcomers, when the good old boys had been over it with him again and again? Had we already been jilted, allowed to look on but replaced by new admirers? There was a hunger in the president that could be satisfied only by new voices, even if they were rehearsing stories he knew very well. Maybe he had heard Aeschylus tell the story of Electra; now he wanted to hear it again from Sophocles or Euripides.

I'd been over this ground again and again in memos and drafts for speeches and idea papers all year long. So had Putnam. But here he was again, reciting in exasperating detail the same statistics on declining social membership and trust, recalling again how the war generation (Tom Brokaw's "heroic generation") had yielded a nation of joiners and givers, active citizens in civil society as well as federal elections, while members of the new generation, reared on passive television, had lost their civic bearings. There was a difference in how the over fifties and the under forties perceived presidential programs and policies. The younger people's mistrust made them suspicious of political speeches. They would never watch a State of the Union. (George S. argued a little, but

---

[3] Burns and Georgia J. Sorenson, *Dead Center: Clinton-Gore Leadership and the Perils of Moderation* (New York: Scribner, 2000). Burns, one of Roosevelt's most distinguished biographers, attacks Clinton as a dull "transactional" leader who fails the test of "transformative leadership" that defines the great presidents.

admitted that his polls also showed greater civic loyalty on the part of the older than the younger generation.). Good stuff, Putnam's always is, but nothing new. The president had heard it, we all had heard it before.

Alan Ehrenhalt's was a fresh voice, but rather than addressing the themes of his book that inspired the invitation, his portrait of Chicago's urban neighborhoods in the fifties and how they had manifested a community spirit sorely lacking today, he took off instead on a neocon-servative rant about authority and its loss.[4] He bemoaned its vanishing, ascribing many of the nation's problems to this steady erosion of authoritative voices. He sounded like Dr. Laura, scolding us in that tone of fifties moral righteousness that drives the young wild. Authority? The great conservative sociologist Robert Nisbet had made a postwar career out of portraying its decline and connecting it to the pathologies of the sixties in a manner that helped give birth to the neoconservatism of Irving Kristol, Peter Berger, Michael Novak, and, in time, William Ben-nett, as well as (in a more virulent form) Pat Buchanan's. But the side of community that was linked to authority was not the side that warmed the hearts of progressive communitarians, least of all Bill Clin-ton's. For antiwar baby boomers who remembered sixties slogans like "Resist illegitimate authority," an appeal to authority was bound to arouse more hostility than sympathy. Bill Clinton was not the man to whom the tragedy of authority's demise could be easily sold. In segue-ing from community to authority, Ehrenhalt not only made clear why liberals worry about communitarians; he blew his chance. The presi-dent liked the book, but this wasn't the book.

Skip Gates moved on, ignoring Ehrenhalt. He made a cool and rea-soned advocacy for the need to focus on the race issue. Maybe too cool and reasoned for the advocacy required. Gates sometimes is just too damned civilized to be ardent (whereas I worry I'm too ardent to be civ-ilized). That is perhaps why, a few years later, Gates would campaign for Al Gore while his colleague the passionate Cornel West would go on the road for Bill Bradley. A little later in the evening, the African-American law school professor Randall Kennedy picked up Gates's line. Less diplo-matic than Gates, he assailed "pigmentocracy" and calculated its costs in crime, drugs, and despair. Yet both Kennedy and Gates paired indict-

4 Ehrenhalt, *The Lost City: Discovering the Forgotten Virtues of Community in the Chicago of the 1950s* (New York: Basic Books, 1995).

ments that were the more scathing for being factual and descriptive; moreover, their remedies were gentle and sensible, turning on traditional liberal approaches involving law and living together. I wish they had given themselves over more to rage to push us from our preoccupation with softer matters. Yes, race matters. And it remains America's most intractable challenge. Yet somehow it never found its way to the center of our debates. Jesse Jackson needed a surrogate at these seminars, but never had one. The African-American scholars present had properly concluded that rage would mean marginalization, but inclusion here came at the price of relevance.

It is true that by now the heavy water on the issue was being carried by Christopher Edley, who was busy behind the scenes with George Stephanopoulos trying to devise a strategy to save affirmative action from the New Democrat reformers set on bringing it to an end.[5] Clinton was saying, "Mend it, don't end it," but New Democrats thought that to mend it was to rend it, and so wanted it ended. They were already on the warpath against "welfare as we know it," and had done little in their rhetoric to combat the new move toward incarceration as the surrogate for education in the war against drugs—a war that targeted crack cocaine and was putting ever greater numbers of black men and women into prison. One out of three young black men found themselves in the criminal justice system—in jail, on trial, or on parole—far more than were in college. In 1980 California had spent two dollars on education for every dollar it spent on prisons. By 1995 it was spending a buck and a quarter on prisons for every dollar spent on education. Texas was embarking on a billion-dollar capital program for prison construction. By the year 2000 America had over two million of its citizens in prison, more by far than any other Western democracy. No wonder more than half of America's black households were headed by a woman. No wonder 20 percent of America's children remained in poverty in this most prosperous economy in history. Some cynics even had the gall to suggest that the low unemployment rates were in part due to the incarceration of millions of poorly educated, otherwise unemployable men.

In retrospect, the most damning thing that might be said of our

5 For an account, see Edley, *Not All Black and White: Affirmative Action, Race, and American Values* (New York: Hill & Wang, 1996).

exchanges over several years was that these dire facts were never front and center on our agenda. We never really faced up to the race question at all. Despite the presence of Stephen Carter, Skip Gates, Randall Kennedy, Patricia Williams and other distinguished black intellectuals at our roundtables and seminars, despite the president's own deep commitment to confronting the persistence of prejudice as manifested in the ongoing church burnings in the South, and despite the "conversation on race" that was to preoccupy the administration for much of the second term and the commission on race headed by John Hope Franklin, there was never much more than talk. And at our seminars we never even talked the talk. Clinton didn't walk the talk, but at least he talked it, which was more than could be said for us! It would be nice to think this was because we were not hypocrites. It felt more like benign neglect. Once again, the invisible American did not make an onstage appearance in our unfolding intellectual drama. Not something we can feel proud of, those of us who boasted we were seizing the opportunity to speak truth to power.

Women, who had been invisible not just as subjects but as participants at our Camp David roundtable, were far better represented this time. My old friend the democratic theorist Jenny Mansbridge started out in a critical vein, but quickly melted, offering further proof of the president's capacity for intellectual seduction (much more important than the other kind, at which he apparently was less gifted). Mansbridge had arrived as a committed advocate of the New Party—another "third party" far more progressive than Perot's Reform Party. She had been working actively to persuade Democrats to abandon their own party (and the president with whom she was dining) in favor of a new liberal option. By the time it was her moment to speak, however, she had already been drawn into the president's warming circle of seduction.

Hence, though she began with what promised to be a peroration on behalf of the New Party, she quite abruptly segued into an apologetic reassurance. "I've penned scores of letters on behalf of the New Party," she said, looking right at the president. But even as she spoke, she seemed to change her mind—or allowed the president's laser eyes to change it for her—blurting out that she would not be sending them. No, she said, she would not be urging Democrats to become apostates after all. "Sorry, Mr. President," she exclaimed, as if she had suddenly perceived in her former plan the seeds of treason. Then she stopped. In truth, it probably did the president good to know that, absent this dinner invitation, an intellectual of Jenny's caliber and political experience (she had written the definitive account of the defeat of the Equal Rights Amendment) had been planning to bail on him and on what before meeting him she had clearly regarded as his failed progressivism. Like Newt Gingrich's on the other side, however, her convictions withered in the hot sun of his presence. When she fell silent, so did we.

No one knew whether to feel pleased at her pledge of renewed loyalty or embarrassed by her candor about her former New Party trespasses. No one really wanted to start a discussion about the New Party either, or to find out if Jenny was merely being diplomatic and would revert to her Third Party politics once she escaped the president's aura, so instead we detoured into a cul-de-sac. Something about the dearth of intellectuals on the left, the refusal of too many good progressives to acknowledge any loyalty whatsoever to the Democratic Party, the precious unwillingness of liberal foundations to match the contributions of philanthropies on the right. The Republicans had their advocates: intellectuals on the right like Irving Kristol and his wife, Gertrude Himmelfarb, and their son, the *Weekly Standard* editor Bill Kristol; literary heroes like Norman Podhoretz and his son John (now an editor at Rupert Murdoch's *New York Post*); and bookish scolds like Bill Bennett and George Will. They had their foundations like the American Enterprise Institute, the Bradley and the Cato and the Heritage foundations.

On the left we were too fractious and narcissistic to declare for a partisan cause, and so ended up speaking only for ourselves, watering down what little political effect we might have had. We had the *Nation*, but though the fresh editorship of Katrina Vanden Heuvel was changing this, it had a fustian old-left feel. Irving Howe's (now Michael Walzer's and Mitchell Cohen's) *Dissent* was too esoteric, a little too Europhile, and it was a quarterly to boot. Then there was the *American Prospect*, at that time still a monthly (now a biweekly) and a magazine that had policy wonk liberalism of an extremely useful, but not exactly commercial, character written all over it. Yes, the Left imagined that it was (we were) refusing to betray the calling of truth seeker in the vain attempt to cultivate worldly power and instruct the "foolish masses" (Julian Benda's term in his *The Betrayal of the Intellectuals*). However, for the most part we were simply too busy serving our own special interests (union politics, feminist politics, gay politics, urban politics, multicultural politics) to unite around a party standard or even to be relevant.

Bruce Ackerman's turn coincided with the serving of the dessert course. He recounted the lessons we might learn from the eras of Reconstruction and then Progressivism—a cycle of revolutionary and conservative moments in American history that he had put at the center of his wonderfully maverick constitutional history of the United States called *We the People*.[6] These lessons could help explain and put into perspective the vogue of the Gingrich revolution, but unfortunately, as Ackerman recited them, he was being upstaged by waiters, who seemed little concerned to honor whatever dignity the proceedings were supposed to have. Their sangfroid obliviousness to the delicate unfolding of Ackerman's argument evidently derived not from a disdain for pontificating academics, however, but from a more essential urgency: even when serving kings and prime ministers, they had a schedule to follow and a timetable to meet and a chef to please. Everyone who has ever worked in a restaurant knows that the pace of service is set by the worries (or whims) of the kitchen rather than by the needs and wishes of customers or the serving habits of waiters. Whatever the state of the ceremony, the state of the speechmaking, or for that matter the state of the union, when it was time for dessert it was time for dessert. Even in the White House. So as Bruce moved to his climactic point, a waiter thrust a dish in front of his nose—"Would you care for mousse, sir?" Bruce, focused beyond all flappability, grinned and nodded and kept talking. I'm not sure the rest of us remained quite so disciplined. I certainly was distracted by the dried-pear mousse cake with kumquat sauce a bustling waiter had deftly placed before me. The president was already working with gusto on his, and my mind was poisoned with the notion that if I didn't get right to it, mine might go the way of the cashews.

As we let the piquant mousse melt in our mouths, Ackerman finished up, summoning us to historical patience in the face of Gingrich's conservative moment. Then it was Amitai Etzioni's turn to regale us with the triumphs of the communitarian movement. These were not altogether distinguishable from the triumphs of Amitai Etzioni. He recalled his service in the Carter White House, where he had first been appalled

6 Ackerman, *We The People* (Cambridge: Harvard University Press, 1991).

by the obsessively individualistic ardor for rights in our political culture. He went on to allow as how Tony Blair had been converted to communitarianism under his tutelage. He was charming with that rumbling European accent that seemed preserved from a distant childhood, but there was (as he knew) no real need to teach this crowd about communitarianism. He had already done that by headquartering his communitarian movement at George Washington University, just a few blocks from the White House. The idea already resonated in an administration of New Democrats rooted in a DLC "credo" that read: "We believe in community. We believe that we can achieve our individual destinies only if we share a commitment to our national destiny." Family and civil society, in this perspective, were not incidental but central to political interests.

Amy Gutmann was next, and I was on deck—it would be after coffee that I would actually come to the plate, I told myself. No more goddamn waiters. Amy stayed with a purely academic discourse about the necessity for civility in politics and a deliberative and hence productive approach to political debate. By doing so and thereby modeling the virtues she was recommending, she made a remarkably persuasive case. Sitting right next to him, a seismograph to his every small move, I sensed the president was taking a kind of small shivering pleasure in her heartfelt comments.

Gutmann finished with simple conviction. Well done. Then Galston turned to me: "You're batting cleanup, Ben. Go." I went, but felt less compelling than I'd been the preceding year at Camp David. I made contact, but it felt like an infield single. At most. I was self-conscious about the pedigree of my argument. Like a man about to tell a new crowd his best old joke and then realizing his wife is in the room rolling her eyes, I felt anything I might say to the dinner roundtable would come as a yawn to the president. He'd heard everything I was likely to say in five different versions in the memos and speeches I'd written for him during the year. Nor were there real antagonists to take on at the table; we were all reading from the same book this year, if occasionally on different pages. The president glanced sideways at me with a "come on, let's go" look. I plunged ahead.

To frame my comments, I recalled how Oliver Stone's newly released movie *Nixon* was calculated to increase the political cynicism of the ahistorical young, just as his *JFK* had done at the beginning of the nineties. Paranoia was becoming a political norm for too many young Americans. Hollywood made big bucks selling cynicism *about* Washington in conspiratorial movies pillorying Beltway bullies and White House wackos, villains all, and then sent big bucks *to* Washington to buy politicians it liked, reinforcing the cynicism bred by its films. We needed to reframe what politics was about, rename politics as the business of ordinary citizens. Government wasn't a "them" or an "it"; it was ours, an extension of civil society, the people's voice. We needed a conception of the political that returned it to the people. We needed a blueprint of the political that tied together the disparate pieces whose linkages had become largely invisible in the fractious privatism of special interests. We needed a vision of the political that disclosed the new interdependence: Americans disdained foreign policy, acting with parochial insouciance in the face of global problems. But that was because we did not help them see that in an era of economic, technological, and ecological interdependence the distinctions between domestic and foreign were increasingly meaningless. We had to make the invisible visible, reveal the hidden connections. We had to show America why it wasn't us against the world, it was us in the world; it wasn't private liberty against public monopoly, it was an intersecting tri-archy of government, civil society, and economics that could function only in partnership. Monopoly and bureaucratic elephantinism were not vices of government alone; they were to be found in the market sector as well.

My five minutes ran out just as my confidence was kicking in. I was

*A typical "seminar" dinner at the White House (January 1998).*
*(Official White House photo.)*

feeling a little more comfortable in my passions, preparing to talk about the danger private monopolies posed to public liberty. Galston signaled me without trying to be subtle. Time. Just as well. I was veering onto dangerous ground. In this White House, men trembled at the thought of being considered antimarket or critical of business, even if it was business as in big and bad business as in oil cartel or Disney/ABC or Microsoft. Though the administration was eventually to mobilize the Justice Department against Bill Gates, it was currently planning the giveaway of digital spectra and the deregulation of the new telecommunications and continued to toe the New Democrat line making a confrontation with business forces a taboo. Hence, the administration's most horrendous piece of legislation (overshadowed by the liberal media's more vociferous outcry against the less insidious Welfare Reform Bill): the 1996 Telecommunications Act, which would undo the mild presence of government in media regulation that the Federal Communications Act of 1934 had introduced in calling radio a public utility worthy of regulation in the public interest. Taboo. Stay away from this stuff! Saved by Bill's bell.

As soon as I skidded to a halt, Galston waved his hand. Floor's open. General discussion. Mr. President? Clinton looked at Hillary: "You go first." She shook her head pleasantly: "No, you." The president leapt in like a professorial moderator in some student debating society. He spent ten minutes summarizing what had been said. Faultlessly. As he portrayed our successive interventions, he reacted to them. It was a masterful performance, though I found myself wishing he had gone before us so we could react to him rather than the other way round. That might have served his needs better.

To Putnam, Clinton offered a visit to the basement single-lane bowling alley, one of the few left in America, where solitary chief executives could escape the pressures of office for a few minutes of release. "Good publicity for you, Bob, good publicity for bowling alone. Maybe it's not such a bad thing after all? What do you think?" Putnam laughed appreciatively. This was political charm at its most personal and effective. A gentle chiding that disguised the obvious flattery with which the president acknowledged Putnam's work. The president turned serious. "Professor Ackerman tracked our cycles of conservatism and change. Well, let me say, Bob Dole came away from the budget discussions with an undeserved reputation for accommodation. Don't kid yourselves. He's been no better than Gingrich's House reactionaries. Maybe worse.

He's been obstinate on the Brady Bill, lousy on the crime bill, no better on a whole series of critical budget items."

Ackerman glowed. Who didn't when basking in the president's gaze? The president went on, taking up Ackerman's reference points one after the other. "You talk about Reconstruction. Tell you this, I'm not in as bad shape as Andrew Johnson." That's what he thought in those idyllic months of his "failed presidency" when he had shoehorned his victory in the budget battle between the disaster of health care and the nightmare of the Lewinsky scandal. If he could only have read the tea leaves drying at that very moment in the bottom of Paula Jones's cup. Andrew Johnson, the only impeached president in history. Fell irony. Only this hint in Clinton's remarks of what was to come: "Not as bad as Johnson, but of course I'm not in as good shape as Lincoln." At least before Mr. Lincoln's encounter with John Wilkes Booth. Clinton turned to me: "Benjamin wrote me last year, a moving letter about Lincoln that's relevant here." Now I was glowing. I'd written him to suggest some text for a speech and referred to Lincoln's ability to turn hard political decisions into matters of moral passion, and he was sharing from memory what I'd written with the dinner company.

Brimming with confidence, Clinton finished with a peroration that was a summation of his first term, a veritable State of the Presidency improvised on the way to thinking about his State of the Union. "I think I'm in better shape than I've been for a long time. Though we have accomplished less than we hoped, we have accomplished more of what I actually promised than any one of our last five presidents. Of course, I don't get the credit." (Why is there always a slight whine in Clinton's rhetoric, even when he is narrating real achievements?) "The percent of GNP we spent on government is smaller than anytime since 1933. And I got our party to vote with me on more issues than any other recent president—don't get credit for that either."

"We have two problems . . ." He turned serious. From listing accomplishments with gusto to acknowledging challenges with somber earnestness—that affecting pathos he inspired (manipulated?) by clenching down on his lip, though he did not actually bite it at this moment: ". . . severe problems. The breathtaking rise in inequality and the absence of any corporate responsibility for this." (He violated the taboo!) "And the problem of juveniles—crime, race, teen pregnancy, drugs. Gingrich's congressional freshmen have made government the problem, except for defense and the paving of our highways. They make government out as a substitute for responsibility. Well, the shutdown helped show people all the local things government does. But they still don't see. One woman, she complained to me, 'Don't let the government mess with my Medicare.' Like she thought it was a private program government might undermine!"

It was true. Government in America has been turned into an "it," an evil "*them*" in far-away capital cities. As if congresspersons drop in from Mars. "Government's part of the problem, not part of the solution," Reagan had said, and Americans had believed him, pushing away the democratic institutions that alone empowered them to take on the real problems. In 2000 George Bush Jr. was still scolding the Democrats for not realizing that taxes "belong to the people, not to the government," as if the government did not belong to the people. Too many Americans still mistake the community programs that benefit them (transportation, child care, job training, Head Start) as local or private-sector projects that have nothing to do with their taxes. Just telling people the facts doesn't work. That's what the president was saying.

"We can't just boast about the economy, even though it's in good shape, because people don't see themselves as more secure." He had that right. The administration boasts about 25 million new jobs, but how many of them are outsourced? How many are consultancies and unpensioned perma-temp jobs that can be shed as quickly as they were created? How many will survive the next major economic downturn? Or will there never be another one? All these doubts seemed to lie just below the surface of the president's remarks. "Our best polls come from the over-fifty population; the young are much more cynical—this confirms your generational divide Bob [Putnam]. Well, Medicare and Medicaid are real programs, serving real people—the older generation. But education and welfare are more like ideas. The programs aren't there or don't sell. We need to talk more about what the ideas mean."

The president was talking about "ideas" here as abstractions. I wasn't sure when he urged us to focus on what ideas "mean" whether he wanted us to focus more on the real programs, or to get back to the real meaning of the ideas themselves to clarify the significance of the programs. Certainly the problem in his first term had been more with the ideas than with the programs: the programs always seemed clear enough, but the essential ideas—the vision—that the programs were intended to implement were fuzzy.

Take education: the federal education budget is less than 5 percent of the nation's education budget, so how can the federal government have much of an impact? The real challenge for the president is to remind Americans of what public education means: it is our national institution for civic integration, it is how a disparate nation of immigrants forges citizens, it is where the children of the tribes learn to trust one another and work together. It is not only education for the public but education in what it means to be a public, to constitute a citizenry. The defense of public education against privatization and vouchers cannot turn merely on technical arguments about budgets or standards or efficiency; it has to rise from deeply felt American principles a president has a special responsibility to enunciate (something Al Gore actually did in his acceptance speech at the 2000 Democratic convention in LA).

The same is true for welfare, which the president wanted so badly to reform. If the idea of welfare feels to most Americans like giving over the hard-earned dollars of disciplined workers to a bunch of nonworking deadbeats, no welfare program, however much it is reformed, can be sustained. The seed for the Democrats' abandonment of "welfare as we know it" was already planted by the New Democrats' surrender to this basically Republican "idea"—the idea that welfare and its reallocation of resources is about envy, and the transfer of private goods from the industrious to the lazy. It was this essential idea that had to be debated if welfare reform was to be more than an excuse for a war on the poor; it was ideas, not programs, that were the key to presidential leadership.

As I rehearsed these critical arguments in my head, the president was winding down. "Well, at least we've stopped shooting ourselves in the foot," he said a little wearily. "*I've* stopped shooting *myself* in the foot." He spoke in all candor. Even as he was busy shooting himself in the groin. He was proud that he had stopped being his own worst enemy, just as he was becoming his own worst enemy, doing what no enemy could do. "There is a commonsense center out there." (And how! That center would save him from himself.) "And if we still have trouble getting our message out, you almost have to pity the poor Republicans. There they are in every primary, trying to get their message out. And what do they get? For every twenty seconds of their voice they get on the air, they get six minutes of commentary." He was getting a little soft and fuzzy. Feeling good. "For all these problems, I'm more optimistic about America in the global setting than I was when I took this job. Yes, we have to continue to lead without there being missiles leveled against us. Here Dole deserves credit." Five minutes earlier he was reviling his challenger down the road for his legislative intransigence. The president was really going for a soft landing. "He deserves credit, he's remained an internationalist. There's no other alternative."

The president was done. And hadn't left much for us to do. Perhaps he, too, was a little tired of the seminar, a little winded with all the words, the same words, blowing back and forth across the table. But it wasn't quite over. The vice-president had waited patiently, but wanted his say. Now he jumped in, speaking in his characteristic fashion, a little too intensively, too extensively, arousing interest but just a little off focus, trying to get in *his* issues—they would be technology and reinventing government—and still seem to be on subject. His issues might have helped us invest our old ideological quarrels with some substance; as it was, though, they felt a little beside the point, a little ponderous, and Gore, more self-aware than he needed to be, was aware of it.

"I know I've spoken too long, I didn't intend to go so long"—it hadn't been that long, until he said so, and then it seemed that long, but he kept talking, only to interrupt himself again—"I've exceeded my time, I should stop."

As an astute politician with a rare command of both facts and ideas, Gore was remarkably ill at ease. Never has someone quite so capable of command seemed quite so self-conscious, never has a warrior by nature aroused such doubts when he wasn't actually in combat. This was in part the effect of the vice-presidency. Lyndon Johnson, one of the most intimidating presidents of the last half century, had seemed repressed, even timid, in service to John Kennedy (of course, unlike Gore, he despised his younger rival, who had beaten him to the number one post). Yet the vice-presidency also played to Gore's weaknesses. Al Gore was the kind of man who, had he inherited a kingdom, might have made a blessed and much praised prince. That he had to compete for office against self-satisfied and ingratiating politicos was an unkind but necessary condition of democratic politics, where what it takes to win elections is not always a very useful predicate for what it takes to govern. I suspect Gore would have been a far better president than he was a candidate for the presidency.

At the end of this particular long evening, he was being truer to the truth than to the moment. Gore wanted us to reflect on technology, on how it changed things. Traditional democracy had rooted itself in the technology of print; what would the new technology do to it? (Nothing good, despite its preference for horizontal interactivity and the elimination of middlemen, I said to him after dinner; technology tends to reflect the culture into which it is introduced as much as it determines that culture.) "Think about it," he lectured us quietly. "Gingrich's contract was first published in *TV Guide*."

The reference to the Republican contract appeared to egg the president back into action. He was clearly still focused on "ideas." Though the vice-president wasn't through, the president jumped in. "Look, in '92 I focused on principles and ideas. That was good. Then in '93 and '94 I got diverted to policies and their specifics and that hurt us." Exactly what I'd been thinking about a few minutes earlier: ideas preceded programs, which to be successful had to connect to some thematic, even visionary, spine that held them together coherently. Yet even as he said it, he was passing everything through that emperor of incrementalism, Dick Morris, who was now doing front and center what last year he had been doing back channel—showing Clinton how he could fashion a hundred tiny policy specifics without ever having to call on or inspire a single medium-sized idea. There seemed to be at least three Bill Clintons weathering the winter storm in our company. The relaxed great-ideas president intellectually at home among thinkers and scholars—sitting alongside the worried politician pragmatist ready to jettison all his principles to secure one real program—and then off to the side the addicted lover left lonely by the austere zealotry of his other two selves and willing to jeopardize all they had achieved for a little all too human comfort. Bill Clinton was Walt Whitman, he was many, embracing the North and the South, the East and the West. And almost making it work.

My mind was spinning: the trouble with the old Great Society Democrats was that they watered down ideas by making what should have been a grand vision seem plain parochial. Galston let me take the floor again. I tried to specify my argument with examples: the magnificent New Deal idea of jobs and social security as part of the human birthright had by the end of the Great Society somehow been transformed into special-interest group claims by "private" unions. The encompassing idea of spaceship Earth with its fragile ecosphere, to which we all owed a public responsibility, came to look like the private logic of privileged hikers and campers who joined the Sierra Club to secure support for their leisure-time activities—a bunch of upscale nature lovers who disdained ordinary jobholders and the less pristine leisure-time activities like snowmobiling in which those vulgarians chose to engage. Where President Reagan had taken small, obviously private interests such as shareholder profitability and lower business taxes and turned them into large public goods (the logic of supply-side economics), Democrats too often took large public goods and turned them into what looked like the special privileges of narrow elites. I finished with a political gesture: "That's how we lost the majority to Gingrich. That's why, yes, Mr. President, you're right (though this wasn't exactly what he had said), that's why we need more than small-bore programs, we need big ideas that can integrate and forge a vision from those programs and policies." That's what I said to the president, trying to turn his ambiguous nod to ideas into a critique of the Dick Morris approach. The Clinton of big ideas seemed reinforced, gesticulating enthusiastically as I talked. But the other two Clintons would control the next couple of years, robbing him of his reputation and, to some degree, of his legacy.

It got heavy. We were tiring, and the words hung in the air. Through the high windows, beyond the reflection of the chandeliers and candles flickering in the glass, the storm was subsiding. For the first time that day, the air was nearly still, leaving the flakes falling vertically in Christmas card perfection. In the brief silence Amy Gutmann jumped in. A simple energy. A simple phrase. "Maybe the idea we have to convey is, 'Don't just balance the budget, balance the burdens.' " Nice. Should have made the State of the Union speech, but it didn't. The president reentered the conversation one last time, finally addressing the contentious issue of global markets. "We need to face the new burdens of the global economy too. We need security there. We have to address the dislocations of global business by providing the dislocated with permanent security."

Elizabeth Drew had written in her critical assessment of the first term that the president had made security an issue only for a year, during '94, and then had abandoned it. Nothing stayed abandoned in this White House. "Permanent security means reward for effort, access to

education and training, permanent non–job based health care, trans-
ferable pensions—and all with an international accent. But this means
a role for government." The trouble is, government in the international arena cannot play a role because while the economy has superseded
national sovereignty, politics has not; and until it does, providing any
kind of security for workers and citizens will be problematic.

The president knew as much even as he spoke. He was on the defensive. Gingrich had made all his inroads by attacking government, and
Clinton was a New Democrat willing to admit government needed a lot
of fixing. He kept coming back to the need for government, but always
ambivalently. "Saving government from its own excesses," was how
Michael Waldman described Clinton's intentions. Yet he would soon be
reembracing the very Gingrich ideology he was assailing tonight. This
was the exasperating thing about Clinton: the talk and the walk took
place in different chambers in the large house of his brain. In proclaiming the "end of the era of big government" in his upcoming State of the
Union speech, he would reinforce the libertarian prejudices against
government for which Americans already had rather too much sympathy. But Gingrich got under Clinton's skin much as Clinton got under
Gingrich's: they were nemeses who needed one another. The president
couldn't resist alluding to him again. "The Speaker, he's said, the trouble with us is that we look like 'intelligent troglodytes,' that's what he's
charged us with being. We hang on to the old truths of the New Deal
that once worked and once were necessary; but those truths are now
standing in the way of the path of change. So we've resisted the necessary changes, the new path of decentralization and privatization and
getting individuals to take responsibility."

The president had passed effortlessly from an intelligent defense of
government to an intelligent attack on government. From LBJ to Newt.
I remembered our first Camp David meeting. We shouldn't worry, faced
with two opposing strategies; he "would do both."

I stumbled back into the conversation one last time, at its very tail
end, wanting to seem relevant, hoping to find a way to make the impossible dualism credible to myself: the Democratic forked tongue saying,
"We need government/we mustn't be needy of government." Galston
and Hillary were whispering; probably she wanted things wound up. I
hurried through something about civil society, how it joined the worlds
of public government and private responsibility, empowering us with-

out disempowering government. We didn't have to make the polarized choice between big bad government and user-friendly private markets that Newt was offering. We were not required either to embrace an antiquarian past of welfare statism or to sell out to a Darwinist future of every man for himself. Civil society, friend of liberty but friend also to public goods. Theater of voluntary action but nursery of political citizenship. A middle way (a third way?) preserving the virtues of private liberty without sacrificing the benefits of public government. A way around Newt's stark dualism.

I think it sounds better here (if it sounds okay here) than it sounded at the end of the night. Good idea, but too much, too late. Like a fresh salad served after the mousse and stilton and porto had all been relished and consumed. Particularly since I myself didn't quite believe what I was saying, although I certainly wanted very much to believe it. With a kind of collective burp we adjourned. Hillary asked who needed help getting to wherever we were going—the first sign that the storm was in somebody's consciousness inside the White House. There were Jeep Cherokees available. The president quipped, "If you can't get home, you can stay here: it's your house anyway, I'm just a guest." If I'd been more prescient (and opportunistic) I might have tested the offer. Was the Lincoln Bedroom available to refugees from inclement weather?

It was nearly eleven. We'd been at it for three hours and forty minutes. On the way out, I stopped to chat with Bruce Reed and Don Baer. Don asked, "You will be able to come down and talk to us, won't you?" Of course I would. To Clinton I said, more directly, "You know, I've said to Don and Bruce, and I want to say to you, I am ready to do anything I can to help with this agenda." The president beamed, nodded vigorously, and then—I suppose I sounded ingratiating—responded vaguely, murmuring something about how Bruce would of course be working on the "big issues" and, well . . .

Stopping myself from blurting out "Yes? And "well . . . what!?'" I reached for the petition. I had prepared a petition on an egregious case concerning a good friend, Dr. Preston King, an African-American who had been badly treated by a draft board in the South in the 1960s and who had fled the country, with a federal warrant out for his arrest. For thirty years he had pursued an exemplary career as a successful political theorist in England, his views those of a classical progressive liber-

al—no radical Black Panther/Weather Underground overtones. And
for thirty years he had been left in forced exile by a country that insisted it would arrest him if he set foot on its soil. My petition requested a
full and unconditional pardon. (Earlier attempts in other administrations had been rebuffed by the Justice Department on the grounds that
the Department *never* pardons people wanted on federal warrants. They
have to "come in" first, and then maybe a deal is possible.) Preston King,
believing that culpability lay with the government rather than with
him, understandably refused this kind of a deal. But even as I told the
president I had an appeal, I felt guilty, felt I was using an invitation to
offer counsel to pursue a political agenda (however noble). I mumbled
that I would give the document to Bruce Reed. I suppose it was foolish
to expect a politician himself deeply vulnerable on the draft issue to go
to bat for a draft resister from the same epoch. Bruce took the petition
with a look of steely noncommittal. My guilt deepened. In subsequent
years, as from time to time I inquired about the case, my fears deepened.
Despite prodding from me and then many others, nothing happened. A
host of supporters took up the petition, including Preston's daughter,
who had been elected to the British Parliament in the Blair landslide,
but by then I had become the in-house pessimist. Not going to happen.
The Justice Department never forgives outstanding federal warrants.
Case closed.

Well, not quite. To my delight and the president's credit, Preston King
finally received retroactive justice (which is not quite the same thing as
full justice). In February 2000 the president issued a full pardon, and
King was able to return to America. The occasion, sadly, was his brother's funeral. But the slate had been wiped clean, and an American citizen and an African-American intellectual of the first order had
returned home. I comfort myself that if, in my several years of informal
consultation with the president, I did little more than kid myself that I
was having some marginal influence, I had in concert with many others who had worked tirelessly on Preston's case at least this one solid
accomplishment: the release of an innocent American from the
bondage of a case that was an affront to the dignity and liberty of every
American. A small counterweight in the scales of justice in which the
Marc Rich pardon weighed so heavily?

Leaving the White House that night, plunging into the dark night and
drifting snowbanks, I felt less buoyant than I had a year earlier. The sec-

ond time is never the same as the first. Not in any affair. I felt manically proud to have been invited to return to another State of the Union preparatory dinner, gratified to be fussed over by staffers. Yet, at the same time, it was frustrating, exasperating, maddening. The line taken by the tough pols impatient with the endless talk resonated. Why replay the tapes? Why still another debate? Running in the 2000 Democratic primary against Senator Bradley, Al Gore expressed what he must often have felt at these tables: "The presidency is not an academic exercise. It's not a seminar on some grand theory. It's not a place from which to ponder problems." Why, then, was I still standing in line to get five minutes of the president's ear when I'd had that ten times over in the course of the intervening year? I'd written memos, contributed to speeches, consulted with staffers, pondered strategic issues with speechwriters. Where was the *action*? As Gore insisted against Bradley's effort to play Adlai Stevenson, surely "the presidency is a day by day fight for real people."[7]

Crossing Pennsylvania Avenue in the deep silence of an urban snowstorm's aftermath, I caught myself. Enough carping. Having had what every public intellectual who ever dreamed of power could possibly want—the presidential ear, his praise, his respect, even his affection—surely I had enough. Yet, somehow when it's Bill Clinton haunting your thoughts, enough is never enough.

[7] Quoted in Robert Pear, "Gore Matches Bradley Efforts," *New York Times*, February 28, 2000.

# CHAPTER SIX

# The Community Service President

IN A PRESIDENCY criticized for being something less than what the innate brilliance of the president promised, in a presidency where even fans ended up feeling vaguely disappointed, as if they'd gotten only a two-star meal at what they figured would be a three-star restaurant, Bill Clinton had one unmitigated success. Typical of the "little" programs old Democrats criticized as demeaning to the grand new vision the progressive Democratic Party was supposed to have, it nonetheless affected many lives and embodied the very best of Clinton's vision of a New Democrat governance. It was a program in which citizens were empowered as partners of government and in which government teamed with civil society voluntary associations and the private sector to pursue together civic ends that no single partner could achieve alone.

In the quite remarkable service program called Americorps, what would become the heart of the Corporation for National Service's menu of service programs aimed at making both citizens and government stronger, Clinton called on memories going back to his meeting with President Kennedy. He delivered on promises about national service made throughout his presidential campaign to establish what was indeed the signature program of his presidency. Other programs drew more media attention: there were great "failures" (the health policy debacle) and more pressworthy ambitions (the Middle East peace process). Because neither watching Americans nor the media from which they too often (but not always) take their cue are much interested in "civic news," Americorps was largely forgotten by the end of the second term, with all that term's far more newsworthy scandals. Yet Americorps was Clinton at his most earnest, at his most instinctive, at his very best.

It was this Clinton I first met nearly two years before my journey to Camp David, in January 1995, when my spectatorship was transformed into engagement. On the day the White House called, it was February 24, 1993, and Americorps was still in an early phase of gestation.

The call saying Clinton was coming to Rutgers University came on a Wednesday morning, just six months after the New York convention where I'd watched Clinton dance on the stage at Madison Square Garden and then (or so I thought) retired back into academia to play the enthralled spectator to his administration.

The White House had decided that Rutgers and the service learning program I ran at the Walt Whitman Center for the Culture and Politics of Democracy would make an appropriate backdrop for the president's speech announcing his new service program—which Susan Stroud said would become the signature project for Clinton's citizen-minded administration.

Susan was a friend and colleague with whom I'd worked when she was the director of Campus Compact, a national organization of college presidents interested in developing community service on the nation's college campuses. Now she was serving Eli Siegal (who would become Americorps' first CEO) and President Clinton in helping to formulate a vision for a new national service program, a priority of the early days of the president's first term. Not just a continuation of the Reagan-Bush Points of Light Foundation, which had nourished private philanthropic impulses, but a new service approach focusing on civic responsibility and real government/civil society partnerships. The kind of citizenship and service that irritated conservatives who thought service should be a substitute for government.

Less than twenty-four hours earlier, Stroud had opened a noncommittal "exploratory" discussion with me. Rutgers was one of several venues being considered for a presidential visit. What could we offer? A couple of hours later on Tuesday afternoon, consulting my overwrought imagination, I faxed a two-page summary of what I hoped were enticements: of course we'd be the ideal venue! We were a major public university with a new and innovative program that promised every student a service learning experience that was tied directly to the curriculum as well as to civic ideals; and, hang on, we could also offer a set of real on-the-ground service projects the president could visit— where he could chat with Rutgers students in service and community members working with and benefiting from the program, great photo ops rooted in the real thing; oh yes, we didn't just offer photo ops but guaranteed strong press coverage in what was, after all, the greater New York metropolitan region (Rutgers is twenty-nine miles from New York); moreover (an event venue was a big issue), I could get the Rutgers Athletic Center ("the RAC") decked out and, cross my heart and hope to die, fill it with ten thousand enthusiastic, I mean screaming teens and beaming college students for the main event, the president's speech (I had no idea how I was going to do that); and (an even more extravagant and unfounded promise) I had already secured the full cooperation of the university administration. (Actually, I had not been able to reach the university's president, Francis Lawrence, at all before I sent my fax.) As worthy a bill of particulars as one could imagine! "Imagine" was the term, since the offerings were made up from scratch for Susan's benefit. I'd figure out later what we could actually do. Rather Clintonesque, I later realized.

So began, in a frenzy of dreamlike promises and hysterical activity trying to make good on them, my actual involvement with William Jefferson Clinton. I thought (and for a while, he thought) community service might be his most representative program. I had been thinking for thirty years about democracy, citizenship, and service, so this was not really a random crossroads I was traversing in encountering the president. When I was seventeen, I had spent a year in Switzerland, where at twenty every male citizen was constrained to do national service (Switzerland's vaunted "armed neutrality"), and (for an American) had written with unusual affection about the Swiss system of national military service in my first book, *The Death of Communal Liberty* (1974). Later among the practical suggestions I made for a more participatory system in *Strong Democracy* (1984), I'd proposed a system of national civilian service. With President Bloustein, I had helped launch Rutgers's model service learning program. How could Clinton's inspired commitment to citizen service not be an inspiration to me?

President Clinton had, moreover, put a spin on service that differentiated it from much of what had come before and allowed it to stand for New Democrat ideology in a way that made Republicans nervous. One crucial difference between his approach and traditional efforts was that Clinton wanted to see service as an expression of civic responsibility, as a way station on the road to full citizenship by young people much too alienated from government as well as from the communities in which they lived. Service was not so much a discretionary function of the altruist—"Noblesse oblige, fellas: we're fantastically well off, so let's give our less fortunate neighbors a hand up!"—as an imperative of civic education. You serve your neighbor because your own liberty can thrive only when the communities to which you belong also thrive. Altruists may have obligations imposed on them by morals, but citizens have responsibilities that define their civic engagement in community. After years in which service was understood as part of a privatized, philanthropic ethic, Clinton had reembraced the tradition of service as an experiential learning ground for citizenship—exactly the tradition I had celebrated and elaborated on in the books on democracy that had helped to ground my own academic reputation. Clinton later told me he had read *Strong Democracy* while he was still governor of Arkansas (was there anything on politics he hadn't read?), but Arkansas's "education governor" didn't need instruction from anyone in the role service learning could play in civic education.

That was why service so quickly became a defining issue for his leadership in the first term: he was creating a "community service presidency" that celebrated New Democratic partnerships between public and private and that focused on the responsibility of citizens (New Democrat emphasis) without giving up on the responsibility of government (traditional Democratic emphasis). Moreover, he was doing something even harder than creating a new, signature program: he was revising, renaming, and reorienting a program that, under the "Points of Light" banner, had been critically important to both Presidents Reagan and Bush. He was trying to rebrand someone else's program by giving it a contrary ideological spin that turned an essentially anti-government commitment to devolving state responsibilities to private philanthropies back into a citizenship program aimed at relegitimizing the state as a civic educator. The idea was no longer to get young people to volunteer for private service *instead* of acting as responsible citizens, but to make service a learning venue *for* active citizenship.

The struggle between these two understandings of service persists today. Clinton spent much of his first term fighting to create his new vision for service; his failure to do so marked the limits of his leadership. In the beginning, he probably did little more than underscore service as voluntarism and may in the end have actually limited its chances for expansion by having it so closely identified with him as a "signature project." But none of this was yet obvious in 1993.

Back then, a convergence of commitments—Rutgers's practical program of service learning, the administration's still theoretical commitment to national service—occasioned a presidential visit to Rutgers that, merely by virtue of the president's iconic status, gave our service learning program a mighty push forward. However, the more immediate result of Clinton's decision to visit us was simply chaos. Hardly eight hours after Susan's call, while the university was just beginning to react to the news of the president's imminent visit (by cosmic bureaucratic timekeeping, it takes about a week in academia to do the work of an hour in the real world), I was chatting amiably with Steve, the first of several members of the presidential advance team who had already arrived on campus and would set the terms for and prepare the president's visit. It was a rather peculiar and one-sided conversation over coffee in a neighborhood hotel next to the university.

"Who will be handling press and communications?" Steve queried. I ventured something along the lines of "Well, there's a press office, but well, I guess I will, I'll try to oversee it . . . ."

"You? Really? How about security?"

"Oh, security," I responded in my most casual manner. "That would be the university police . . . er . . . let me give them a call. I'm not sure. I'll look into it."

"You will? Security too? How about the venue? You told Susan you can get ten thousand to fill the gym?"

"I did? I mean I did, sure, eight, nine, maybe ten thousand. The RAC—great new facility, the New Jersey Nets played there for a while before their Meadowlands arena was finished."

"Ten thousand?"

"Don't worry, Steve. We'll fill it up. I'll get right on it."

"You? How?"

"Students, lots of students," I volunteered, thinking as I said it that our students would be in class Monday morning and there were hardly that many at Rutgers and Douglas Colleges together, and it was almost the weekend, pretty late to be getting out publicity. Steve was looking at me hard. I couldn't keep saying I would do it. He knew if press and security and attendance all depended on me there would be more pickpockets than audience members and no one to report what happened anyway.

"All kinds of students," I said, hopefully. "You know. High school. College. Kids from our programs."

"You'll take care of that?"

"I'll try . . ." (his face darkened again) "I mean, I will, you can count on it." This wasn't like the memo to Susan. Whatever I said I'd do, I actually had to do. Or someone had to do. But I was scheduled to go to Smith College in Northampton, Massachusetts, the next day to fulfill a long-standing lecture commitment. First things first. I was an academic and I couldn't (wouldn't) bail.

For the first twenty-four hours of these weighty (and comical) negotiations, I felt like a solitary dreamer ambling through a reverie about an imagined presidential encounter. I was the hero of the French film *La Belle Américaine* (a fin-tailed American beauty of a convertible) who parleys his fancy borrowed car into a relationship with the French prime minister, giving geopolitical advice from his nine-year-old's school atlas over the phone and becoming an intimate counselor completely by accident and for no good reason at all. On the other hand, this was the real president, not the movies, and I had to get real. By the end of Wednesday evening, I'd identified at least a few bridges to reality: Rutgers did sport a police department with arms-bearing cops (security), a vice-president for administration and a university relations office, both of whom knew what they were doing (logistics), a press office that didn't know what it was doing (publicity . . . maybe), and a university president who was perhaps even hungrier for exposure than his visitor from D.C. (protocol). We'd evened up the odds of our initial relationship (staff of the Executive Office of the United States of America, maybe 3,451, vs. staff of the Whitman Center, maybe 3) with the university's infrastructure, people who could actually do the kinds of things I had been elaborating on with such metaphysical inventiveness.

The frenzied hours between my return from Northampton late Thursday afternoon and the president's arrival on Monday passed in a blur. I would never again engage in this kind of nitty-gritty operational planning (lucky for the White House and lucky for me), but it was a heady experience at the time: ever-longer meetings involving more and more people focusing on ever-expanding crises involving more and more dilemmas: Ohmygod, the signs we spent two days making are too small! Oygewalt, President Lawrence is insisting President Clinton have lunch at Lawrence's house, but the schedule can't possibly accommodate a luncheon! Ohforchrissakes, there aren't enough tickets to Clinton's afternoon reception following the RAC event for all the board of governor members and state politicos standing in line to get them! And where are they all going to park? Dammit, the Rutgers administration is pushing all my service people off of the list to get all its patronage people on the list! Ohshit, the White House wants a bona fide student to introduce the president; it's Saturday, how the hell am I gonna find a warm body that can talk, let alone the perfect candidate they're insisting on!? (Besides, this means *I* can't introduce him!)

Things worked out. Nakia Tomlinson, a beautiful African-American freshman dancer and service volunteer would introduce the president, and she *was* the perfect candidate and the president was thrilled; the too small signs got remade, bigger and better, and the advance PR people loved them. Lunch at Lawrence's was nixed. And we managed to get ten thousand young adults (well, kids, including the college students) and pack them in neat and colorful rows into the Rutgers Athletic Center. We even got the parking straightened out. It was, to be sure, the sort of thing the White House did awfully well under any circumstances. The president arrived in the morning, toured our community service program in the company of a rampaging press corps (just the way the White House likes it), and then returned to the RAC for the big event.

The RAC event was a huge success. Ten thousand kids cheered and chanted and sang, the Rutgers band knocked out pop tunes usually heard at basketball and football games, MTV covered the thing start to finish and got a prize interview with Clinton, and colleagues to whom I had handed out tickets like some mortar-board Mayor Daley grinned at me from front-section seats, while the president and his party beamed and waved from a stage whose backdrop was a teeming swarm of delirious community service kids from the university's CASE program and the neighborhoods they served, decked out in chicken yellow T-shirts we'd had made up with the Whitman Center service logo on them.

I had already had a taste of the Clinton machine's extraordinary way with media events—no wonder he'd won the election!—earlier that morning when fastidious advance staffers had calculated camera angles and distributed mini-bleachers and arranged podium seating placements with a cunning sense of television marketing that made for a perfect event later on, right up to and through the MTV interview with a relaxed Clinton that followed the speech and assured nationwide exposure to the target audience of fifteen- to twenty-five-year-olds. The plans for this party came from the same playbook the Clinton Democratic Party had called on to design its nomination extravaganza at Madison Square Garden. Nobody could match Clinton on this kind of stuff.

The speech itself was not quite a rouser, being geared to what the White House clearly regarded as a mildly academic audience (nineteen-year-old sophomores majoring in MTV count as an academic audience in the raw world of retail American politics). After umpteen acknowledgments of the folks on the platform and the folks in the audience and the folks who had started the service idea and the folks who were fighting for it in the Congress, the speech got moving, managing rather neatly to combine political philosophy, persuasion, and policy. There was the part about the service ethic as a civic ethic, an effective little lecture on citizenship; there was the rhetoric of persuasion aimed at inspiration, the Kennedy-like call to think of and do for community and country rather than just for self; and there was the concrete proposal for a Corporation for National and Community Service that would facilitate service among the young and the old right in their local communities, with the government as first facilitator but not itself in the service business.[1]

Nakia had introduced Clinton with charming freshness—so truly perfect a choice that Clinton had gushed, "I wish I could take you with me everywhere, we'd make a great duo there, let's give her another hand, I thought she was great!" He prefaced his remarks with a compliment to "Professor Benjamin Barber's leadership and service." It was a small thing, I knew, a protocol item probably inserted by Susan Stroud into the speech as prelude to a dozen other compliments to state politicians and historical figures in the service movement. The president

---

[1] The speechwriter Michael Waldman's brother, Steve, wrote a wonderful book on the bureaucratic and Capitol Hill politics of the Corporation for National Service called *The Bill* (I don't think he intended the double entendre). It does not, however, capture the intellectual debate about the meaning of service or the intellectual sources of that debate.

thanks a score of people every time he opens his mouth to give a speech—that's politics. Nonetheless, there was something seductive about hearing my name on the lips of the president of the United States speaking before a crowd of ten thousand. I realized even as I savored them that these silly sentiments were the first small signs of vanity aroused, a suddenly acquired taste for reputation and power that would masquerade as a desire to serve. But how could I not embrace the moment?

At the reception later, I had the chance to stand toe to toe with Clinton and talk. Yes, he knew who I was, was grateful for all the planning and hard work. Yes, he'd read *Strong Democracy*, Hillary had too. Yes, he was pleased to have *this* copy I was pressing into his hands, even though he had read it before, and no, don't worry, the Secret Service guy (who promptly grabbed it from Clinton's hands as if it might conceal a thin plastique explosive device) would just scan and check it out, and make sure it was put back in his own hands when he was back in Washington. Yes, Susan Stroud would . . . and no, Eli Siegal's hadn't . . . and thank you, Ben, it was a great day.

And then the press of a hundred reception guests forced him to move on. Yet he had made it seem special, different from everyone else, made me feel appreciated not just for the work and planning for this event but for a lifetime of work and planning on behalf of democracy. Poised to move on, working the crowd, he stopped and gave my wife, Leah, a warm grin and shook her hand and said something flattering. Then he was grabbing the hand of one of my staffers I'd presented, moving on as he was always moving on. Like a rolling stone. No moss growing on this chief executive. He was there big-time, filling all the space, and then he was gone, a sad and swollen hollow left behind to remind you of how much room he had taken up.

His imprint lasted days, weeks, more. Even where he never had a chance to go, the expectation of a possible visit left its mark. Though Clinton never came close to our Whitman Center offices in Hickman Hall, our dingy elevators had been redecorated, our halls repainted, broken tiles replaced. For months I dined off of the patronage I'd been able to hand out. Best of all, our service learning program, merely tolerated up until then by the higher reaches of the Rutgers administration, finally received the impetus it needed to achieve a permanent institutional home at the university. It no longer suffered the orphan's fate and was embraced by officials who had formerly spurned it. Thus does presidential power do its work indirectly. Clinton had struck a mighty blow for "strong democracy." I even found the Whitman Center manager I'd long sought when Senator Bradley pursued me around the reception hall to let me know that Erika Gabrielson, his favorite legislative aide, wanted to segue to the nonprofit sector. She knew and admired my writing (as he did, he added, all flattery and butter), and she wanted to come to work for me. Gabrielson did, and breathed new life into the Whitman Center and its service programs—and was with me a year later on my first trip to the White House for a Roosevelt Room conference on service, citizenship, and civil society.

If Clinton's Rutgers visit served as the public launch for his service program, it was also the private launch for my involvement with the White House. Much of that engagement, beyond the annual seminars and the broader strategic questions that defined them and the speech-writing associated with them, focused on my obsessive concern with assuring that Clinton's service program would not merely replicate the Reagan/Bush approach. Their take on volunteerism privatized service, individualized the servers ("heroes," "points of light"), and reduced a potential "citizen education program" to a "government isn't necessary" program. It said, "Let the philanthropies and the philanthropic take over the social welfare functions of government. Let discretionary charity replace the civic obligations democracies normally assume to meet the needs of their citizens." This privatizing attitude would reemerge in the George W. Bush administration in 2001, although the Corporation for National Service was one Clinton program the new President would not dismantle.

Clinton's dedication to service came from other wellsprings—from sources steeped in civic spirit, where service entailed learning social responsibility and, far from being a surrogate for government, was a way to engage young people in citizenship, helping them to see that democracy meant that citizens themselves had social obligations that were as important as the obligations of governmental bureaucracies. It was a matter not of private persons doing the work of public government but of public citizens with a direct responsibility for democracy taking on some of the chores of public institutions with an indirect (delegated) responsibility for democracy. It was a way to devolve democracy, not destroy it.

At the autumn 1994 South Lawn White House launch for Americorps, to which I was invited—and which did become the signature-program of the fully funded Corporation for National Service—the link between service and citizenship seemed secure. The first wave of corps recruits, who had been through a rigorous summer program of "training," were on hand, and the focus was on their spirit of engagement, their willingness to serve their country. Although they would serve in local programs under the auspices of state "commissions" for community service (I was appointed to the New Jersey commission by a reluctant Governor Whitman), they stood as symbols of a national government wedded to bringing young people back into the orbit of democracy. They were "freshmen" in the same school of democracy in which Peace Corps veterans were alumni.

It was well known that Peace Corps alumni had continued to dedicate themselves to civil society and public service. I had urged the administration to dub its first summer's retreat for new Americorps members (at San Francisco's closed naval base at the Presidio) "A summer of service for a lifetime of citizenship." The Peace Corps never managed to eradicate poverty in Asia or disease in Africa or illiteracy in Latin America, but it did forge a community of Americans who remained dedicated citizens throughout their lives. Surveys suggest that Peace Corps alumni compose a remarkably civic and politically active segment of an otherwise privatized and cynical citizenry. On the other hand, it is also evident that there is not a necessary correlation between a young person's commitment to community service and her interest in politics. Community service volunteers do not necessarily vote in greater numbers than their completely passive peers.

The young people standing with Clinton and Gore on the temporary stage erected under a tent on the South Lawn were rocking a little uncertainly to a band that was playing Beach Boys–style music more appropriate to Clinton's youth than to the age of the kids in Americorps shirts, who probably were listening to grundge or heavy metal on their own. Still, they looked exactly like Peace Corps volunteers resurrected from the long-ago sixties, and they promised a new generation of equally dedicated citizens.

Under this tent, at my first official White House event, still more of a stranger than a familiar to the administration, I first met Al From, the president of the Democratic Leadership Council, whose policy positions were reflected so strongly in the seminars in which I would soon take part. This part of his program I could buy into without reservation. The White House contingent that was working on service in D.C. and that had been at Rutgers was well represented here, along with a smattering of cabinet officers like my colleague and friend Donna Shalala from Hunter College and the University of Wisconsin, now Health and Human Services secretary, who presumably was there to give expression to the idea that Americorps would contribute to America's health and welfare in significant ways—even though it wouldn't and couldn't and even though that wasn't really the point of a service program aimed at enhancing citizenship and strengthening civic responsibility among the young.

There was little question even at this rambunctious civic circus that the civic approach Clinton was inaugurating ran against the American grain of voluntarism, and would remain under pressure even at the Corporation for National Service, especially when the administration headed over to Capitol Hill to seek funding in a Republican Congress. Hence, a few years later, when the corporation—having passed the leadership torch from Eli Siegal to Harris Wofford of Pennsylvania—began to involve itself in the Philadelphia service summit that was the brainchild of General Colin Powell, the tightly wound civic ideology I had considered secure quickly unraveled. The late nineties version of service reverted to the late eighties version of service I had thought the president's program had superseded and eclipsed. With George W. Bush as president and Colin Powell in the cabinet, the battle won would be lost all over again.

Congress had never really bought into Clinton's spin: after all, it had been decades since the military had gone recruiting wearing its civic hat. After the Vietnam War the emphasis had shifted to the seductions of "career opportunities" and continuing education. Serving your country curried little favor among youthful cynics for whom the "country" meant a pack of lying politicians, greedy bureaucrats, and bankrupt foreign interests. Hence, slogans like "Be the best you can!" and the absurd "I am an army of one" that pandered to a flaccid narcissism. As a consequence, Congress focused not on Americorps as a citizen builder or the impact of service on the servers, but on the impact service might have on communities and neighborhoods that would no longer be codependents of a corrupt federal government. The measure of Americorps' success would be service program "outcomes"—meals served, homeless sheltered, graffiti cleaned, refuse picked up, waterways cleaned up. This both avoided the civic sentimentality Congress was peculiarly unwilling to indulge in (you might think representatives to the sovereign legislative body of the American Republic would be happy to indulge) and met the new "accountability" standards being deployed by evaluating the service program in terms of something that could actually be measured.

Social scientists have always preferred to measure the measurable, even if the things that get measured are not really of interest. Following them, Congress recognized that while the impact on service volunteers promised by the citizen education approach might be vital to its foundational philosophy, measuring such a subtle, gradual, and qualitative impact would always be hard. How do you set quantitative measures for an enhanced civic competence or a heightened sense of civic responsibility? A poll taken by students at Harvard's Institute for Politics in 2000 suggests that the gulf in perception between politics and community service is as wide as ever, with 60 percent of 800 randomly chosen respondents saying they had done community service, while only 16 percent had joined a political or issues-related organization, and only 7 percent had volunteered or planned to volunteer for a political campaign.[2] But though the "civic competence" test we developed at the Whitman Center at Rutgers measuring the impact of service learning on college students found changes in affect and attitude difficult to assess, what evidence we gathered did indicate that when service learning was intense, enduring, and rooted in classroom reflection, it *was* likely to have real impact on citizenship.[3]

Meals served and beaches raked, however, are easier to measure and fit more neatly on the charts than subtle changes in civic affect, and serve the privatized philanthropic ideology Republicans favored at the same time. On the way to meeting these congressional criteria, then, the Corporation for National Service (responsible for the Americorps program) itself seemed to shift from a citizen education approach to an

[2] David S. Broder, "The 30 Million Missing Voters," *Washington Post Weekly Edition*, July 24, 2000.

[3] "Civic Assessment Instrument Report" (Walt Whitman Center, Rutgers University, 1998).

outcomes approach. By the time Wofford began to think about Colin Powell's idea for a service summit under the title "A Presidents' Summit on the American Future," the impulse to distinguish the administration's citizen service ideology from the private everyday-heroes philanthropic approach (front and center in the eighties and forcefully reasserted by Powell) had thus grown pretty faint.

I met with Wofford a good half year prior to the summit and came away impressed with the new chairman's sincerity and dedication to service though a little worried about his own ideological position (was he moving back from civic training to a more privatized volunteerism approach?) and uncertain about his political instincts. It seemed to me that Powell, well advised by the architects of the Reagan/Bush Points of Light program (like my friend Ray Chambers), was set not only to steal President Clinton's thunder on service but to shift the emphasis boldly back to the antigovernmental service ethos of the earlier period. The Corporation for National Service seemed in danger of ceding the war to Powell before a single battle had been fought, in part because it was perhaps less impressed than I was by what I saw as the political as well as the ideological peril.

In fairness, the issues are subtle and not readily understood by either politicians or the public. Privatization and antigovernment rhetoric has reached so far down into both political parties and the subconscious psyches of the American people that warning bells no longer ring, even when the *res publica*—those "things of the public" that constitute the commonwealth or the "republic"—are under assault. Certainly almost all Americans agree that voluntarism is a good thing. But they most certainly do not agree on what voluntarism is or how it is relates to government—which they like a good deal less than they like voluntarism. Most supporters of voluntarism share a healthy conviction that free societies are rooted in an engaged citizenry committed to ongoing neighborhood voluntary activity, and that was presumably the common ground on which Powell hoped to build for the summit in Philadelphia. Alexis de Tocqueville had insisted that the spirit of democracy was local, and participatory democrats like me would argue that democracy is bottom up not top down, and thus depends on the education and involvement of citizens in community self-governance.

But whether self-governance is understood as a road to a stronger national democracy or as part of an assault on all democratic governance depends very much on whether Americans want to enhance trust and confidence in democracy locally and nationally, or sap it still further, pretending that the market sector can somehow directly solve all our social problems. In fact, concealed in the enthusiasm for voluntarism are several conflicting views about the place of voluntary activity in the American way of democracy. So while the language of voluntarism may suggest a welcome bridging language that could transcend narrow partisan difference and help "repair the breach" separating citizens from their government—this was how the Powell campaign was playing it—it also disguised salient political differences.

Not so surprisingly, these differences tracked more traditional ideological cleavages that divide progressives and conservatives over the role of government in securing American liberty, and about which President Clinton, pursuing an ideology that would get beyond traditional nineteenth-century ideological and class cleavages (no more class war!), was understandably suspicious. Nonetheless, the differences abided. Conservatives often saw voluntarism as replacing a government that "doesn't work" rather then as a road to better government. Voluntary activity, "private" and largely apolitical, would entail a beneficent transfer of responsibility from public officials and democratic institutions to the private sector, where charity and philanthropy could take up the slack.

For progressives, however, voluntary service activity represented a strengthening of democracy, a devolution of power not to individuals and private corporations but to local democratic institutions and self-governing communities. It was a way to share responsibility and build partnerships between citizens and their elected officials, a way to pull down rather than put up walls between government and the rest of us. The privatized Points of Light approach to voluntarism had been a welcome invitation to Americans to become more involved in their communities. For some, however, this seemed to be a message calling on "heroic" school principals and self-sacrificing pastors, one by one and one on one, to solve all the intractable problems government had supposedly failed to solve. That was both deeply impractical and a stealth attack on democratic governance. In place of democracy's national citizens, a nation of private volunteers.

Now, casting voluntarism as less a recipe than a surrogate for good citizenship might be a way to underscore the alleged bankruptcy of the welfare state and such traditional public institutions as public schools and federal welfare agencies. Far from "repairing the breach," though, it widened the gulf between Americans and their government and taught a lesson not just about the benefits of self-sufficiency but about the futility of organized social cooperation. It pushed for private, individual, and market strategies and left volunteers with their distrust of government and their distaste for the governors largely intact. What it did for voluntarism was admirable, but what it did for (and to) citizenship was far less clear, as the Harvard survey noted earlier made clear.

In any case, the primary social experiment President Clinton had fashioned to embody his new service ideology—the Corporation for National and Community Service—was aimed at transforming the earlier ethic of private voluntarism into an ethic of citizenship. Clinton had absorbed the lesson of Putnam's "Bowling Alone" and was persuaded that the decline in social capital and social trust represented by the erosion of group civic and social activities was perilous to citizenship: he was now making his own presidential case against "serving alone" and in private as an individual volunteer, and for "serving together" as a citizen volunteer among others working in teams under the aegis of democratic government—both federal and state.

His approach involved crucial innovations aimed at expanding purely private visions of voluntarism. The first innovation was to link service explicitly to education by making credits for higher educational expenses the primary reward for those who enlisted in Americorps. We are not born citizens, but must learn the skills and arts of liberty (thus the "liberal arts") in what Tocqueville called an ongoing "apprenticeship of liberty" (the "most arduous of all apprenticeships," he wrote). We have to be educated for service, and service itself is an education for citizenship. Putting the two together was not just a convenience but an expression of the essential connection between learning and service (thus the corporation's higher education program called "Learn and Serve"). Critics were forever complaining that the education voucher approach meant that the president was "paying" for voluntarism, an obvious oxymoron, but that criticism was valid only if he was trying to fashion "volunteers" rather than citizens. But since citizens were the goal and citizen education the means, then tying service to education was not only sensible but a crucial symbol of the program's essential civic meaning.

The second innovation was to make the service volunteers of the corporation's several programs part of a partnership between the federal government, the states, and local communities. Service volunteers would sign on to a national program, but serve in regional and local programs coordinated by autonomous state commissions in cooperation with private-sector charities and civic associations. Americorps volunteers would be neither emissaries of the federal government nor independent local volunteers: they would be human bridges spanning federal and local, public and private, the civic and the personal. Their service would be at once local and national, empowering them as responsible citizens even as it benefited the communities in which they labored. Moreover, the practice matched the theory, winning over many of its severest initial critics in the towns, cities, and rural districts where Americorps teams served out their year of community involvement.

Convincing and effective as this philosophy was during the first term, by the time plans got under way for the service summit in Philadelphia, it was clear to me that the citizen service approach was no longer prominent in the corporation's thinking. There was also a certain obliviousness bordering on naïveté to the politics being played out by those jousting for position at the summit, which was in theory being denominated as a "Presidents' Summit"—involving Ford, Carter, Bush, and Clinton, and hence allegedly transpartisan—but which was fast becoming a platform for Powell, the Republicans, and their Points of Light brand of voluntarism (planning for the conference had begun prior to the 1996 election). Clinton's signature program was in danger of being stolen out from under his nose by a summit meeting that should have been its culminating triumph. But since the Clinton Third Way approach was to bridge old left-right dualisms, the myth that the summit was to be bipartisan or even transpartisan was all too easy to buy into. And so the integrity of Clinton's vision of service as a road to citizenship was day by day eroded at its core.

When I had first met with Harris Wofford and two other people involved in planning the summit over lunch six weeks before the 1996 election, he announced the spring conference as if it were primarily a Clinton initiative that would be controlled by the White House; Colin Powell might be fronting the meeting, but the Corporation would dominate the planning. It wasn't clear to me how that was going to happen, however, since our luncheon was almost immediately taken over by the old Bush/Reagan "volunteerism" approach in the person of Gregg Petersmeyer, a good friend of Ray Chambers, who with Chambers had been a kingpin in the design of Bush's Points of Light program and who appeared to be the key player in the Colin Powell game plan. If Petersmeyer was quarterbacking, Wofford—though CEO of Clinton's Corporation for National Service—would at best end up blocking for him, and Clinton could find himself on the sidelines. The mind-set at the Corporation was still civic, but Wofford—judiciously nonconfrontational— seemed to want to avoid taking on Powell or even Petersmeyer. He was a gentleman diplomat—exactly right for the service activities he was running—but perhaps too gentlemanly for the politics of the summit.

After lunch, Wofford pulled together a senior Corporation staff meeting to which I was to make a presentation. I again hammered at the civic mission of national service and the need for civic training and citizen education as an integral part of preparation for service. Wofford's deputy Susan Stroud beamed, Wofford nodded, and the staff exuded assent from every pore. But our afternoon session was interrupted by a fire alarm that sent us all out into the hot September afternoon (had Petersmeyer pulled the alarm?), and we never got around to the politics of how to turn Clinton's civic approach into an offensive to make Powell's upcoming summit something other than an ad for the Reagan/Bush approach to service.

At loose ends on the street (the building was vacated for a bomb search), I took my leave from Wofford and wandered in the late afternoon over to the White House, looking for Don Baer. After hearing out my complaints sympathetically, Baer made it clear that the larger election agenda was absorbing everyone's attention and that there was likely to be little focus on the summit. By then I had been unceremoniously ousted from the New Jersey Commission on National Service, where I had spent two years harassing Republican Governor Christie Whitman's other appointees about the civic character of service (they were mostly a points-of-light gang of practical, on-the-ground service folk who did good works but disdained government).[4] As I had waxed elo-

---

4 "Your term of office expired on June 15, 1996," read my brief letter from the appointments director of a governor who never met with her commission a single time in the period I served. She must have loathed my continuing affair with the Clinton administration and my dogged didacticism on behalf of the citizenship approach to service.

quent in its defense back in Jersey, however, the ideology I defended was losing ground in Washington. Don couldn't do anything about the absence of focus in the White House on service, but he did invite me to make my pitch.

By the spring of 1997, with the president reelected and gearing up for a second term, there was more receptivity for that pitch. I spent a good deal of the spring selling service as a crucial form of citizenship education geared not just to reinventing government but to relegitimizing it. I made my case in multiple memos and in-house visits to anyone in the administration who would listen. I was helped by the growing realization even among staffers uninterested in service that Powell's initiative for the upcoming Philadelphia summit was now getting major media coverage and that Bush and Powell, not Clinton, were being seen as its protagonists and heroes. This was no longer a matter of the policy on service (low priority); it was a matter of the president's reputation (high priority). Powell was doing all the heavy organizational lifting, and his voluntarist voice was the voice being heard. *Newsweek* was running a weekly column on service summit news, including commitments by private corporations to participate in one or another service program. From the Corporation, silence—at least as far as the public was concerned. Service, the president's first and most beloved legislative child, was being kidnapped and then made over into a critic of its parents. I bombarded the White House with my warning memos, pressing hard on the need to "repossess the spirit of the Service Summit." With the Philadelphia gathering only weeks off, Baer invited me to talk to a key group of staffers in the Communications Office (maybe just to turn off my memo spigot).

"Ben's a good friend of ours," Don improvised in way of introduction. "He's been helping for a long time as a friend of the president. He's the guru of all this service stuff. When you want to hear about citizenship, civil society, and service, you rub his tummy, and it just comes out. Thank God he's here." To live up to Don's flattery, I waded into a fairly grand peroration at whose heart was still another version of the service-is-citizenship argument. It emphasized that while outcomes might be politically important in selling the Hill on funding, the ideological core of the program was that it created lifetime citizens who would contribute for decades to the civic health of the nation. I concluded with an entreaty—I made it my slogan—"Take back the summit!" From the looks on the bureaucratic faces around the room, it must have sounded like some fervent feminist plea to take back the night. But it also carried a political warning that no one missed.

The communications meeting was followed by an interagency executive branch gathering hosted by Steve Silverman (the cabinet secretary) at which those in each cabinet office responsible for service-related programs met to be harangued by me in much the same manner. To the Interior Department rep I would plead, "Let's make Earth Day (April 22) a celebration of environmental service!" To the Labor Department rep, "Let's make Take Your Daughter to Work Day (April 24) a celebration of women as service volunteers!" To a Forestry Service rep, "Let's make Arbor Day (April 25) a celebration of community tree planting!" Relevance, relevance! It was almost comical, but the politics of it was plain enough: turn every nominal "federal" remembrance day into another event that will lead in to the Philadelphia summit; take every relevant service aspect of every relevant cabinet office and hang multicolored bunting over it so the public will understand the relationship between service and governance. Use the president's April 5 Saturday radio address to focus again on Americorps and the ideals of citizenship for which it stands.

I had already proposed for the radio speech words to this effect:

"We may be born free, but we have to acquire the civic skills that put flesh on liberty's bones. Voluntarism is a school of citizenship. Community service is a tutorial in democracy. . . . As we approach National Volunteers Week [the occasion for the radio speech], let us think of it as National Service Week, National Citizens Week, National Democracy Week. And remember that what we honor for a week is in reality a lifelong commitment to liberty and justice for all."

This was typical: I was trying to ratchet up the civic idealism quotient, to ask more of Americans, to expect more of their citizenship. It seemed a plausible tactic, because Americans tend (at least we imagine they do) to rise to the level of their better angels when called upon to do so—the response to Kennedy's "Ask not what your country can do for you . . ."—and to sink to the level of their pettiest demons when allowed to do so (as, say, in reality television's *Survivor* program).

I was never busier with White House affairs, never more engaged in the nitty-gritty, than during this period following the president's reelection in 1996 and the Philadelphia summit in the spring of 1997. I didn't see the president, but felt close to him because I was carrying his banner in a battle of words and images that went to the quick of all he stood for. They weren't going to steal his programs of citizenship to make war on democratic government and do the privatizing work of laissez-faire liberalism—not if I had anything to do with it. If that meant rallying his own staffers to the cause by reminding them what the cause was, I was ready. If it meant being partisan and obnoxious in a period when Dick Morris's heavy hand on behalf of politics-lite was still being felt (though Morris had self-destructed the preceding summer around what turned out to be a deadly combination of private toe-nibbling and public arrogance), so be it. I wasn't working at being partisan; I was only trying to argue for the president's vision of service as powerfully distinctive from what the Powell people had sold to *Newsweek* and other media—and that argument was inevitably a partisan one.

With a meanness and rage closely connected to their Whitewater campaign (and later the sexual trials), Clinton's worst Republican adversaries had turned on his best program, one they had the best reasons to appreciate because it aimed explicitly at lessening the dependency of Americans on bureaucratic welfare programs, at encouraging citizenship and patriotism, and at strengthening the self-sufficiency of America's communities. In their impatience to bring him down, they were acting as partisan enemies of his least partisan program. The less noxious adversaries preparing the summit in Philadelphia were not trying to kill service, but they were trying to redefine it down, turning it back into another privatization program. If the summit was a chip in their poker game, how else but in partisan anger could Clinton's interests there be defended?

I had concluded you had to be a fool or a hater to use the service program as a way to get at Clinton. He was, at his best, the community service president. Tens of thousands (should have been millions) of young people had already worn the T-shirts, and by the end of his term several hundred thousand would walk the service talk and make real their patriotic commitment to an America where citizens help one another get things done. America would be—will be—the better for it for decades to come. Not because of the homeless the kids sheltered or the meals they prepared or the swamps they drained or the urban parks they cleaned up, but because they had shed their all-American anarchistic coats with heavy winter linings of me-me-me-radical-individualism and put on metaphorical *sweatshirts* inscribed with the simple word "citizen." They knew that the good things that happened to them and their communities happened because a bunch of "me's" had become a coherent "we" in which the individual "me's" were not repressed or assimilated but made to feel real and whole. That was Americorps, a war on hate and ignorance and selfishness and bigotry. That was Americorps, the best of Clinton, and the program that had to be represented at the summit, where, after all, the president was not one of several ex-'s on display, but the sitting chief executive of the United States, who had inaugurated the most extensive service program in the nation's history.

The summit itself came off pretty well. A balance had been struck in which Clinton's core ideas were again visible and in which his speech was more than just another presidential monologue among several. If Colin Powell was still the quarterback, Clinton had reappeared as the coach and general manager. If it was not quite his event, his agenda was no longer a tool of other people's schemes or a potential casualty of their ambitions.

As for me, I had come full circle: from playing host to the president at Rutgers four years earlier, where the national service initiative had been announced, to playing a crazed cheerleader and hyperactive catalyst for a Philadelphia service summit where the president's service agenda achieved renewed momentum. I'd lobbied White House friends and harangued White House strangers, I'd challenged the Corporation's ambivalence and worked to repoliticize the planning process, I'd written summit weekend op-eds (notably for the *Philadephia Inquirer*'s special service summit editions) and met with a couple of editors and editorial boards in Philadelphia and Los Angeles to reinforce the message. At every relevant moment I'd offered my versions of the relevant speeches to reflect the philosophy I was defending in my memos.

Service had been my way into the charmed circle; now perhaps it would provide a graceful exit. For if the summit allowed the president to sing a siren song for service to the listening nation, it sounded to me like a swan song for my service to him. It was time to move on. Or so I was thinking right up to the final night of the summit, when I found myself sitting with Ann Lewis and Melanne Verveer and a bunch of White House friends listening to the band and waiting for the president to speak. And then, as I heard a door swing shut somewhere in the back of my restless consciousness, another suddenly popped open.

# CHAPTER SEVEN

# Chairman of the NEH (Not!)

**CAMPAIGNING FOR THE NEH CHAIRMANSHIP** while pretending not to was my induction by fire into real inside-the-Beltway Washington politics. It was also the closest I came to trading in my status as a some-time outsider for the uncertain benefits of insidership. I had persuaded myself that my voice was more likely to be heard from afar as a visitor than from close in as a turf warrior with an executive appointment, and the work I had just done in preparation for the service summit was strong evidence on behalf of that conviction. But the National Endowment for the Humanities position was the exception to the rule—the only one that interested me intrinsically because it intersected with my academic career and was in tune with my commitment to the arts and humanities as the lifeblood of democracy. The NEH comprised a fiefdom I actually knew something about (not that ignorance or incompetence are insuperable barriers to office-holding in Washington). From the time Bill Bennett had occupied the chairmanship (on his way to being education secretary and then drug czar in the Reagan years), I had looked upon the NEH job with a certain covetousness, a position I could actually fill. Its bully pulpit feature was especially enticing. Bill Bennett and then Lynne Cheney (wife of the new vice-president in 2001) had used it as a launching pad for the cultural wars with great effect, exploiting culture's D.C. podium (ironically) to do battle with culture's liberal Washington and New York stalwarts. The budget (under $100 million) was by Washington standards negligible, but exactly because the NEH lacked real fiscal power words acquired a certain default priority. And words were, of course, my specialty.

For years Clinton had responded to my vague intimations of my availability, how I was ready to "help" in more direct ways, with puzzled looks and muttered responses along the lines of "How do you mean . . . ?" Too proud, too fearful, simply to blurt out "Gimme a job!" and not really wanting one anyway, I had danced around, as vague as he was. But sitting in the cavernous Philadelphia convention hall in the staffer section at the final evening of the Presidents' Summit on Service in the spring of 1997, feeling a little like a staffer because of all the work I'd done on this event, a casual conversation had abruptly opened a door and offered a new opportunity. Melanne Verveer (deputy chief of staff) and Ann Lewis (now occupying Don Baer's job overseeing communications) were sitting just behind me, and our conversation turned to the current chair's impending retirement from the endowment. That would be Sheldon Hackney. It was at this instant that the sound of a door swinging shut was replaced by the swoosh of a door popping open.

Sheldon Hackney, formerly president of the University of Pennsylvania (where I'd held my first teaching job in the late sixties), had all of the virtues and a few too many of the vices of an academic. He was deliberate (both prudent and slow) to a fault, and (like me and most other academics) he probably overestimated the impact of ideas. His earnest idealism blunted his capacity to respond quickly or interact decisively and, once in the chairmanship, left him outside of the inner circle of talk at the White House. Although he was a person of genuine integrity and compelling vision, it was as if in trying to avoid Bill Bennett's noisy cultural-warfare approach, he ended up in a temple of silence.

Since our original meeting in Prague, where I gave a keynote address to the first annual meeting of a new international civil society group called CIVICUS, I had become one of an informal group spending the occasional day at Hackney's offices in the renovated Old Post Office Building with him and some senior staffers along with other carefully chosen visitors. At these leisurely sessions, mini-versions of the president's seminars, we'd spend more time than any of us could really afford chewing over the Endowment's mission and Hackney's signature project, the Conversation with America, which was intended to get Americans talking about what it meant to be an American. But what did that mean? What should the conversation really get America conversing about? Clinton himself was a consummate talker and had tried to turn a good deal of policy wrangling (race, the Middle East) into marathon official conversations, so Hackney was certainly on the right track. His particular target subject was diversity: how being an American was about being a member of a diversified, multicultural society. Yet how could diversity and multiculturalism be sold to an America that seemed to resist exactly what it was becoming (diverse and multicultural)? Who ought the participants in the conversations to be? Eloquent elites (the choir to whom one did not really need to preach) or ordinary folks (unlikely to be persuaded and not much interested in talk in any case)?

In assembling the cast of characters, we too often could think only of our own names and others among the usual suspects and more often than not we ourselves ended up as key participants in the well-meant but forgettable forums that marked the Conversation with America's unnoticed journey through the American talk landscape. Jerry Springer, we were not. Dominated as this landscape was by a media with almost no interest in serious talk, we generally conversed on an island enveloped by silence other than the sound of our own voices. Hackney's tribute to American diversity would presumably have struck the country at large as one great yawn, had it struck it at all. Hackney represented well his president's fondness for seminars and talk that seemed ultimately to have little impact on policy and action.

With this unremarkable history running through my mind, I felt emboldened to give a jocularly aggressive response to Melanne's and Ann's comments about Hackney's impending retirement. Affecting a casualness I did not feel, I asked, "Who are you considering?" Lewis was casual in response. "Don't know. We aren't really clear. Do you have ideas? Names?" There it was: a casual moment offering an anything but casual opportunity. Though protecting myself by maintaining the half-joking tone, I more or less blurted out, "How about me?"

Melanne stared hard at me for a moment, as if taking the measure of my gumption. "Would you really be interested?" Now I was staring, taking the measure of her seriousness. The spontaneous gambit had turned earnest. "Well, yes. Yes, I am. I mean if the President thought I could serve him usefully . . . I think I could do it." And then I was off. I couldn't stop talking, talking about Bennett, about Cheney, about

Hackney's strengths and the shortcomings in his tolerantly bland and academic approach (badly repaying his kindnesses to me), talking about the need for strong rhetoric on behalf of the president's larger mission, talking about the role of the humanities as an emblem of democracy's critical independence and high-mindedness—talking far more than I needed to or should have. All they wanted to know was whether I was interested.

When I finally coasted to a stop, Melanne remained silent, staring again. I'd blown it. Jabbering on when a single yes would have sufficed. But Melanne and Ann, both generous and easy people, declined to judge me. Instead, Ann invited me to ride back to the hotel through the rain in one of the Secret Service vans dedicated to staffers. Relieved, I took her up on it. Back at the hotel where the president was staying, canvas porticos had been erected to protect him from curious onlookers and (presumably) potential assassins, and under their protective cover Ann wished me good night. Unasked, I volunteered again that, yes, I was serious, and then I caught myself and shut up before I fell into another talking jag. Ann nodded. She and Melanne would take it up with potential allies like Don Baer, Ellen Lovell, and Eli Siegal. If all went well, I'd hear something from others. Maybe even Bob Nash, who ran the Personnel Office. She said.

So began a nail-biting spring and summer of low-key campaigning and endless waiting. "No," my friends would insist, "you can't afford to be high-profile, you certainly don't want to appear to be campaigning for the post. That would only awaken the sleeping dogs who might oppose you. Gore doesn't seem to have a candidate, but he really should and alerted to your campaign, he might be inspired to find one just so he'd have his own horse in the race!" Then again, I needed a campaign and as Ellen Lovell told me, "We can't run it for you," so I really did have to call people, e-mail them, write anyone who might be helpful, actually everyone with any connections to anyone, get *them* to call or write— but, of course, they shouldn't appear to be campaigning for me either. I didn't have the presence in Washington to make do without a campaign, but I was far too liberal and had far too much of a paper record to slide into the nomination unnoticed. I'd written fourteen books and hundreds of articles, I was a "participatory democrat" who had criticized representative government (some nutty antifederalist?), who had favored the Swiss system of direct participation in governance through referenda and initiatives (I'd testified in Congress in 1979 on behalf of a bill to introduce a national referendum and initiative process, what kind of nut was I anyway?), who had been an antiwar protester and a friend of disarmament back in the sixties (was the administration about to appoint Jerry Rubin to the NEH?). No, this wouldn't be easy.

I was lucky in my friends. Mike Levy was again counseling me. Having come from the academy (his Ph.D. was from Rutgers), he knew the distrust that serious, prolonged scholarship could breed in our anti-intellectual nation. Selling someone with a paper record as long as mine would be daunting. Lani Guinier, with a far shorter academic history, had watched her nomination for attorney general go down the drain because a couple of her essays had been subjected to what might generously be called misunderstanding and what in fact amounted to wholesale distortion. Maybe the president could have saved her—he was intelligent enough to explain her position—but that would have used up political capital he didn't feel he could spare, so she was hung out to dry, in her case, after her apparent victory as the administration's nominee.

No wonder Mike figured it would be a delicate, if not impossible, campaign. He not only had his doctorate from Rutgers; he was a political theorist and scholar at Texas A&M before he had gone to work for Senator Lloyd Bentsen. He was ideally positioned: he knew academia and knew politics. He was trusted on the Hill—after all, he'd been deputy secretary of the treasury for political affairs under Bentsen, meaning that he represented Treasury to the Hill. He could write a brief vouchsafing the integrity of my views. Meanwhile, the White House would set some of those teeming twenty-somethings who seemed to dominate the executive staff to canvassing my work, searching like sharp-eyed lawyers for potential red flags (literally) in the oeuvre that might get me in trouble. Indeed, I would be asked to dredge up evidence on myself: What might I have written that could be misinterpreted, get me into trouble? "We're just anticipating" was the line, and it was obviously meant as good lawyering: figure out how I might be vulnerable to the other side before the other side figured it out, and be ready for them on the firing line. But it felt as if I was being readied for some benign Stalin-style confession of sins that would facilitate my being quickly ditched, should a hint of trouble be uncovered.

I hoped I had some friends in the right places. Henry Cisneros, for example, whom I'd known prior to his service to Clinton at the Housing Department and (as a regular participant in debates) in the White House. Though he was then at Univision (he has since moved on), he told me he continued to speak to Clinton and Gore once a month or so, and would put in a word. Eli Siegal had left the Corporation for National Service (where he'd been both its architect and its first CEO) but was back helping develop the president's proposals for a school-to-work program. Ever since our meeting at the president's Rutgers visit in '94, he had been a generous friend, and he now responded to my call with enthusiasm: "The president needs you!" he told me, and volunteered to gather intelligence and offer support. Elaine Kamarck, also gone from the administration to take a job at Harvard's Kennedy School, responded warmly and said she'd find out if Gore had a candidate of his own (she was close to Gore then and was later a leading policy adviser to his presidential campaign). Joe Duffey, who was chairing the USIS, was even more forthcoming: "The NEH needs some intellectual capital; I'll do all I can."

Friends and allies were obviously necessary, but my problem would

*The author and the President after the Princeton University speech, spring 1997.*
*(Official White House photo.)*

not in any case be a lack of supporters: rather, it kept coming back to the
written record. I worried that sharp-eyed senatorial aides would zero in
on subtle leftist echoes in my work likely to pass unnoticed by the untutored readers in the White House Personnel Office during their superfi-
cial trek through academic underbrush they could not possibly be
expected to understand. I could only nervously recall how a particularly foolish "great man" of political science had read one of my first books
on participatory democracy in Switzerland and written a letter to the
president of the American Political Science Association (James MacGregor Burns, the eminent historian who recently wrote a book critical of
Clinton) to protest my appointment as program chair of the association's
Bicentennial Year Annual Meeting in 1976. In his letter of protest he
had complained bitterly about a photograph of a Swiss citizen preparing
to vote directly in one of those famous Swiss *Landesgemeinden* (participatory cantonal assemblies). "Why, the man is holding a cross behind his
back!" my fatuous critic exclaimed. "You can't possibly have Barber as
your program chair! He's clearly attacking the separation of church and
state!" I'd been flabbergasted. I had scarcely noticed the cross, trying
only to portray the solemn patriotism of the Swiss engaged in a primeval
act of citizenship. If a supposedly brilliant political scientist had found
this seeming constitutional waywardness on my part in a photo, what
might callow enemies cum sleuths discover in thousands upon thousands of additional pages of dense academic prose?

When interviewed by White House personnel about my work, I'd
always start by saying how I prided myself on my patriotism. Yes, I have
been a critic, I'd say, but I've never taken the anti-American line. On the
contrary, I have boasted about an America defined by its openness to
self-criticism. This is our civic virtue, our adherence to a form of "constitutional patriotism" that includes the right, even the duty, to critique
the Constitution. Not only is that the essence of patriotism; it is the
essence of the open society and the humanities in service to the open
society that, if I was appointed, it would be my job to represent, I would
say. And then look into the eyes of my interlocutor, hoping for support,
but usually finding only circumspect doubt, as in "Is this guy for real?"

I survived the initial interrogation of my academic work—I think.
Probably only because in the end no one could take the trouble to seriously read everything—or read anything at all with any real seriousness. (My White House readers were twenty-somethings like my

students at the university, and this kind of reading must have seemed an unmitigated burden to them.) So by the middle of the summer of '97 it began to look as if I was not only a survivor but a serious candidate, maybe even among the frontrunners. By the middle of July, Irv Milotsky from the *New York Times* Washington Bureau called, asking about my chances for the NEH job. Uncertain about the protocol, I called Bob Nash at the White House, got a deputy named Patsy Thomason, who allowed as how she had no idea who I was. "Sorry, but I'm not even remotely filled in." Oh God. I filled her in. She suggested I avoid all press calls. Probably bad advice, but I had from the beginning avoided press inquiries about anything I did with the White House, and decided not to change the policy now. I had my secretary at the Whitman Center tell the *Times* I wasn't available for comment and wouldn't be.

These were odd times for me. The minutiae in which my "campaign" played out are not especially interesting, but they suggest how quickly a personal relationship with a president can become a typically Kafkaesque relationship with a bureaucracy, a relationship paralyzed by political inertia just as soon as the personal becomes "professional." I was spoiled by access, given an illusory sense of self-importance by intimacy, but it now became clear what the difference between insiders and outsiders really was. Outsiders were nicely, even solicitously, treated because they were discretionary assistants on tap because the president had some use for them. Job seekers, on the other hand, were irksome supplicants who were trying to get something from the president. The very books I'd written that had attracted the president's attention were attracting the Personnel Office's suspicion.

No wonder that in my new "client of potential White House largesse" status, the White House was not available to me for comment on my status. An early July call from Marcia Scott at the Personnel Office had begun with a jolly and oddly disconnected invitation: "I'd love to talk to you," Marcia had said, with no reference to the NEH at all, as if she were a fan angling for a talk over tea. The conversation, when I got to Washington, turned out to be formal—with Ellen Lovell and Bob Nash. They assured me, despite what I might have heard about the appointment process, that it would be smooth and fast—however it came out. No more than ten days. So after ten days, I called Marcia, full of hope. A youthful assistant picked up the phone and replied gaily, "Marcia? Oh, Marcia just left for Europe. She'll be gone for two weeks. Can I help you?" I didn't think so. Actually, the Appointments Office was in chaos, with holdups at the Joint Chiefs of Staff as well as the empty ambassadorships in Mexico City and Paris preoccupying the principals. I interpreted it all as a reflection on the weakness of my own candidacy, but I came later to realize that when appointments have to go through the bureaucracy and then be embraced by the Senate, it isn't really about the president anymore. My intimate affair at special dinners with him had turned into a prom party for hundreds in anticipation of which thousands were lined up in hopes of being invited.

My candidacy seemed stalled. Then in August I found out why. The *Chronicle of Higher Education* ran an article headlined "Two Scholars Are Said to Be Finalists for Top Humanities-Endowment Post," naming Bill Ferris of Mississippi and me as the candidates. Two? I stupidly hadn't even thought about other possible candidates. But I was also exultant. Maybe I had a rival, but I had apparently run the bureaucracy's gauntlet and come through unscathed. I was the other candidate. Maybe the president was still rooting for me, nudging the lethargic bureaucrats.

My joy was marred by the reality of a competitor, however. Where had he come from, this all too serious contender with excellent qualifications? Now it came down to the politics. Me and Ferris. At this level the résumé and credentials were moot. Still I tried to read them to my advantage: I was a Clinton intimate, a scholar whose work bridged the social sciences and humanities, a champion of the arts and humanities as handmaidens of a democratic America, the author of a widely circulated essay on the role of the arts and humanities in a democracy, in a publication assembled by the president's own prestigious Commission on the Arts and Humanities (chaired by my friend John Brademas, a brainy former congressman who had been president of New York University and had also volunteered to put in a word) as well as a recent book called *Jihad vs. McWorld,* which the president himself had displayed at a religious breakfast a year earlier. My rival was a guitar-playing musicologist from Mississippi who had written a short and quite delicious book on the Delta Blues (but the president hadn't waved it around at a religious breakfast, I consoled myself), a fine folklorist but someone without Washington experience or a direct connection to the White House. But the two résumés were not really the point—other than how they played to the politics. It wasn't Barber vs. Ferris but New

Jersey vs. Mississippi (Trent Lott country), a hyperactive, too vociferous liberal whose mile-long record was a potential minefield in Senate hearings vs. a modest, studious, and charming southerner whose folklorist background was devoid of provocative or indeed any discernible politics at all. So this was the politics. Once I got my mind around them, it was clear I never really had a chance.

A Mississippi constituent of Trent Lott whom Lott knew and liked, Bill Ferris was an independent and sported no ardent Democratic history that would alienate Republicans. Lott had a simple message for the White House that, at least as it was recounted to me, went something like this: "You know how we feel about the NEH, not our favorite program. You appoint that Barber guy, well, you'll have to fight for confirmation, and then if you prevail, he'll have to fight for every cent he wants for the humanities, just the way you'll have to fight to preserve the endowment. On the other hand, you give me Ferris, he's a Mississippi boy who isn't looking to pick a fight; he'll be an excellent chairman, and he'll waltz through the nomination process. And once appointed, no fuss and bother, he'll get what he needs, no arguments, no politics, the endowment will be safe." This, as I understand it, is roughly what happened. Not the precise words, but the gist.

This is not, however, how it was put to me at the time. Perhaps the White House just didn't want to say it was playing smart politics. The president wasn't one for earnest conversations that could turn into earnest confrontations. Don Baer, my most consistent friend inside the White House other than Galston, was retiring that summer, and he either didn't know much or wasn't talking. Anyway, he was leaving. The exodus had started, and he wanted a little peace. Time for family, for making some money. Autonomy again. There was a White House farewell party for him in August, and he asked me to come. I called him and then called Melanne, too, with the same plea. I really want to be there for Don's farewell, I said. But I know we're reaching the critical stage in the NEH thing, and I don't want Don's farewell to also be my own. Please don't embarrass me by getting me down there on the pretense of my friendship with Don, and then kissing me off.

Not to worry. They'd never do that. "Of course not, Ben. Never." That from both Don and Melanne. By this time, with four years of experience in Washington, I should have known, should at the crucial moment have recalled Bertolt Brecht's little ode to political cynicism I cite regularly in lectures: "The Leaders talk of peace; the mobilization orders are already written out." The White House talks of Barber; Ferris is already appointed.

Don's farewell was extremely well attended: the president, vice-president, and first lady along with almost the entire senior staff, including Erskine Bowles and Rahm Emanuel, and among my friends, Ann Lewis, Joe Duffey, Bill Galston, and Melanne. It was a truly touching occasion. From the few I'd attended, I knew the mood was usually jocular—a good-natured roast of someone who, if he was lucky, was loved and hated in equal parts. The roasting was pretty hot—prolonged jokes and clever, coarse, even vicious routines that were only thinly disguised with bonhomie. But Don had been a grown-up in a kindergarten of staffers, an even-keeled straight shooter with a balding pate and a tolerant demeanor to prove he was an adult. He had elicited the affection and admiration of nearly everyone. He'd been friends with the progressives, yet had been closely associated not only with the New Democrats but with David Gergen and Dick Morris—more closely than the progressives normally would have tolerated. I certainly wished he'd been less keen on Morris and Gergen (though Gergen was another adult who steadied a rocky White House boat in tumultuous times before the 1996 election).

Morris ally or not, however, Baer had also championed ideas and ideals and, after Galston had introduced me to the White House, had been responsible for my ongoing role in speechwriting and long-term strategizing. We'd sat together in his tiny office in the rabbit warren that was communications in the basement of the West Wing a great many times, and he'd never shrunk from debating my odd rhetorical strategies and my unconventional policy recommendations with me. We shared a conviction that service and community responsibility had to play a key role in the set of ideas that framed policy, and were both partial to civil society strategies that put some of the responsibilities for the health of society on citizens and their voluntary associations (as long as they did not displace government). Don seemed to have only friends in a White House where it was easy to have only enemies. So after the lame staff gibes and friendly roast-style jokes, after the younger of his two kids inspired raucous mirth by removing first the obviously unfamiliar toddler's tie and then the rest of his clothes, the mood turned serious: the speeches from Gore, Hillary, and the president were heartfelt.

I took it all in through two filters—one, my affection for Don, which left me feeling cozily warm and oddly proud (yes, I was on the outside, but this was my guy); the other, an anxiety ignited by brief comments made to me before the ceremonies began by Melanne and Bill Galston, comments that filled me with foreboding. I'd crossed Galston's path almost immediately upon arrival, and he who was normally amiable had been awkward and cool when I'd mumbled something to him about how thrilled I was to be a finalist for the NEH. "That's nice, if it's true," he said, and moved quickly on. I had been warned—I thought. (Actually, Bill later told me he was simply not in the loop on this and what I took as a warning was simply a profession of ignorance.)

I had also been greeted warmly by both the vice-president and Mrs. Clinton, but neither had alluded to my candidacy. Hillary had talked at length about the Millennial Commission work I was doing in Paris and New Jersey without disclosing a hint of the more pertinent affair. Discretion? Or embarrassment? Then Melanne had struck fear in my heart: right before the festivities began, she said, "We have to talk." As in "We have to talk, you're fired." Or "We have to talk, I'm filing for divorce." Or "We have to talk, your candidacy is dead." "Can you come by my office after?" is all she actually said.

If I didn't already know I was in trouble by the time I took my leave from Don and worried my way to her office, I certainly knew by the solicitude with which a staffer ushered me into Melanne's antecham-ber, as if I was being whisked into a surgeon's office to be told a relative had not survived the operation. Melanne was direct, genuine. She'd been my champion, she said. So had the president. He and many others around her saw me not just as a friend, a supporter, an adviser; no, I had been—this was the president's term, she said—a soul mate, who shared his deepest convictions. "But . . . ," she rushed on, intent on finishing before I could interrupt, "but we can't put you on the line. You're too controversial, too vulnerable to right-wing attack. You know, the Chris-tian Right, maybe."

I interrupted anyway, not ready to hear the end of the story. I knew it was futile, post hoc, but I couldn't stop myself from arguing. I have my friends on the other side of the aisle, I said weakly. I've been friend-ly with the Straussians (a group of conservative political theorists trained by Leo Strauss and Allan Bloom of the University of Chicago who had important students, friends, and allies in high places in the

Republican Party), and we respect one another. She looked puzzled: "The Straussians?" Bill Bennett, I volunteered. Bill Kristol, Irving's son, at the *Weekly Standard*. Norman Podhoretz's boy, John (now an editor at Murdoch's *New York Post*), who baby-sat my kids in the early seventies. (This was really grasping at straws!) I tried to make it relevant: "I think they like my line on civic virtue and civil society. Social responsibility. You know."

Melanne nodded wearily. "I know, Ben, I know. I've been making the arguments for months. But they are worried you'll draw fire."

Who were "they"? The officious politicos like Bowles who seemed to carry the smallness of the banished Dick Morris in their souls and were turning the second term into an exercise in fear and avoidance? How much of the politics of caution was necessary now? I started to say something about the need for boldness. I was incensed. This was the very scenario I had implored her to avoid: Don's farewell party as my farewell party. Melanne, suddenly impatient, cut me off. I wasn't getting it.

"It's done, Ben."

"The decision?" I asked, deflating like a ruptured tire.

"It's been made."

I went completely flat. Having discharged her distasteful duty and dispatched me, she moved quickly to rally me. "But Ben," her tone was much softer now, almost motherly, "the president told me he wanted *me* to talk to you, not just anyone. He doesn't usually have specific messages, but this time is different: he asked me to say he doesn't want this to be the end."

The end of what? My White House connection? A job? My affair with the president?

Melanne went on reading her tender script: "He wants to find a way to use you . . ." I must have winced, because she interrupted herself. "No, I don't mean *that* way—to use you in his administration. He is an admirer. More."

She knows what I'm thinking and adds quickly, "It's just the NEH isn't right. Washington can swallow you and your family up—if the Right gets on your case. But something else, yes; people are always leaving. There are many different possibilities."

I stared, taken aback by this new tack.

"Maybe something inside the White House," she continued. "You should talk with Sid Blumenthal. Something that wouldn't require congressional approval."

I finally spoke up, thanking her but mumbling something about how I'm fifty-eight, how fifteen years ago I might have taken something on the Domestic Policy Council, a deputy assistant to the president for whatever, but look how overqualified and underused Bill Galston was. I don't want that at my age.

She was now the one who couldn't stop talking, trying to alleviate her embarrassment. "There are lots of posts out there, Ben. With your reputation, all you need is a post. A deputy secretary can be heard." But being too well heard is my problem, I'm thinking to myself, isn't that why I was so controversial? And besides (still to myself), don't deputy secretaries require congressional approval? She persisted, drifting to the foreign arena—"You know, lots of developing nations are experimenting with democracy and need help." My God, was she going to offer the embassy in Sierra Leone or Kuwait? Now it was my turn to impose closure.

"I'm not looking for a job, Melanne. I have a job I love. Teaching. Writing. That's what brought me here to begin with. The NEH was something special. Yes, I would do a lot for this president. But he doesn't have to find me a job for the sake of a job. Really."

Melanne seemed relieved. Wishing me farewell and the very best, she added, sincerely, "Look, Ben, if you want to write the president and discuss this, talk about how you feel, your desire to serve, and how . . . you can be sure it will get on his desk—without being intercepted."

I thought, yes, I will write him. Should write him. I'm not quite cured. I want to argue, explain to him why he should have appointed me. Maybe, somehow, show him he still should. At this moment I believed what I'd been told, even though later on I would become convinced that Ferris's Trent Lott connection was the overriding factor in the appointment. But now it was time to go. Melanne had spent forty-five minutes with me, an eternity in a bustling, high-pressured White House. This really was a beyond-the-Beltway kindness, if in the service of the brutal politics of everyday Washington.

I jumped a cab to National Airport for the flight back to Bradley Field in Hartford (I came in from my summer cottage in the Berkshires for this crash-and-burn mission). But the elfin gods of politics are attentive, always looking for an angle. I was ready to let go, but they were appar-

ently not. I had moved seats on the near-empty commuter flight to
Hartford to avoid the bumpy back of the plane, only to end up in a seat
next to Ralph Nader, who was on his way to his own Connecticut retreat
in Windsor. We had crossed paths several times and, though we were
hardly close friends, were political familiars with sufficiently common
convictions to talk like allies. He seemed to know something about the
nomination controversy and asked the right questions to provoke me. I
found myself talking, then jabbering and finally venting, imprudently
telling him (as I couldn't tell Melanne) how, well, how screwed I was
feeling. Then I became sheepish. I was playing the very jilted-lover role
I'd abjured, and I didn't like how I sounded, petty and vengeful and self-
absorbed. But Nader was all over me. "This is another appointments
debacle! You're no exception, Ben. Think about the attorney general
mess. And you know how bad they've been on judicial nominations?
Not just Peter Edelman, I mean Clinton won't put people on the federal
bench President Bush would have willingly appointed. The Republicans
have a lock on the process. You gotta go public."

I didn't want to go public.

"So what are you gonna say when the press call? I mean you're free
now; you can say what you believe." Nader was implacable. You're
playing too softly for the D.C. game, he insisted. You're too cooperative,
too gentle. Bill Weld's got the right idea (Weld was the ex-governor of
Massachusetts who was refusing to be brushed off on a possible Mexican ambassadorship)—don't take no for an answer!

"Come on, Ben, where's civility, where's playing by the rules, where's
discretion gotten you?" Nader looked at me hard, as if I were some pick-
up-truck test driver refusing to spill the beans about those inflammable
gas tanks out of misplaced company loyalty.

I had only a night to think about it as things turned out. The *New York
Times* called the next day. I had anticipated a hiatus. Nader's diatribe
had, however, driven me in the other direction. I asked myself what I
would have done if the president had asked my advice about what to do
with me. "Be objective, Ben, what should I do? You or Ferris?" Startling
myself, I realized I would have had to counsel the wisdom of the decision he actually took.

"What's that, Mr. President, you're thinking of taking a chance on a
guy who is a known leftie, and one with a long written record no one

has fully vetted? A Vietnam protester, never served in the military? With *your* record on Vietnam, Mr. President? When Trent Lott is offering peace and an easy confirmation, not to speak of a clear funding track at maybe double the current rate, if you just give him his Mississippi guy for the job—a guy, by the way, who is a charming fellow southerner and a fine academic folklorist (nothing to be ashamed of in front of the academic community) who plays a mean guitar and can do the job just fine? So what's to decide, Mr. President?"

This was at least one way to look at it. Yes, there was another way, and even a man freed of my resentment could still make a case for it. Yeah, you might say, there was nothing to decide for President Clinton. Unless he wanted to use the NEH to stand up for something he believed in, unless he wanted to fight for something he cared about (but then, how often did this president really fight for anything?). Unless he thought giving away a few bucks to scholars wasn't worth forgoing public argument on behalf of the indispensable role of the arts and humanities in a civilized, democratic society (but then, who cared about a civilized, democratic society?). Unless he wanted to make the NEH an ally of the National Endowment of the Arts to make common cause against the enemies who had put it under siege (but when had Clinton passed up a triangulating, centrist move to stand up for something he really believed in?). Unless he wanted to weave a vision of what it means to live in a society where democracy is as much a way of life as a form of government and requires the vital contributions a flourishing arts and humanities can make (but could it be said he had such a vision?).

Clinton would say his end game was compelled by a bitter irony: that to defend what the endowment stood for would precisely be to put it at risk. The critics would tolerate a puny NEH on a "Don't ask, don't tell" basis where it kept its ideology in the closet, but if it outed its message, it was out of business. Perhaps what I really wanted to tell the president (and would tell him in my letter) was that it was better to let the NEH go out of business: the bribe in dollars isn't big enough to warrant the sell-out, isn't generous enough to pay for your silence on what the arts and humanities stand for.

Still—here came the irrefutable and definitive counter-counterargument—it wasn't really my call to make. From the beginning of my affair with Clinton, it had been obvious to me that he was the elected official, that his was both the power and the accountability. This was the decisive point. The only relevant voice here was the president's. While I could (and in time would) write him my mind and let my loyal friends bitch to me that he'd missed his chance to put in a firebrand who would have done him and the humanities proud, in my gut I knew that though he owed the country everything, he owed me nothing. What he owed America was his best judgment, and though it might disappoint my hopes, if he reckoned it would be imprudent to trade away a sure thing (a decent man in the chairmanship, a guaranteed nomination, a funded program) for a quicksilver chance at maybe getting a fervent spokesman for his vision, but one who would draw fire, it was his to reckon. If he preferred a quiet sure thing who also bought him a moment of peace with Lott to a risky noisemaker who might cost him political capital, so be it. He had been elected to make precisely these judgments. You could certainly say Clinton was vindicated when years later in the first weeks of Governor George W. Bush's presidency, Ferris was invited to stay on under a Republican administration, Trent Lott still singing his praises. Ferris is a man, who, when asked by the press whether he was a Republican or a Democrat, could answer "I'm an educator." That's politics on a much higher level than I was capable of. And if you think I'm being too political in excusing Clinton, take your idealism, and run for office. It's called democracy, and, in theory, I fancied myself one of democracy's philosopher laureates.

By the time I reached my cottage, I'd reached my decision. Or rather realized there had never been any decision to make but this one. I might pout a little here, vent a little there, but it was over. I got ready to steal back from the few weeks remaining of summer a real vacation. When the *Times* called, the very next day, I played dumb. "I understand you have a story to tell," the reporter said as bluntly as he could. Nader hadn't waited even twenty-four hours.

"Who told you that?"

"Ralph Nader."

More dumb stuff. "Really? What story was that?"

"About how you got hung out to dry."

Ralph must have recounted, gleefully, my whole private venting. "He told you that story?"

"Yeah, well, sort of. But it isn't a story unless you want to confirm it."

I had vented for private relief. My public story was the real story: the overriding logic of the president's ultimate democratic accountability.

"The president's the guy who was elected," I said. "No one ever promised me anything."

"You weren't told you would get the nomination?"

"No, of course not." That was the truth. "I was a candidate is all. I don't see that you have a story."

He was disappointed. "You sure? Sounds to me like Lani Guinier all over again."

"I guess it is . . . in the sense that I'm another candidate who didn't get the nod some people maybe expected and I was hoping for. Unlike me, she got further and the turnaround was much more painful and embarrassing. But still, I never really quite understood their rage, all those disappointed on her behalf. I know Lani and admire and like her. She would have been marvelous. But none of us are owed a post. Not even after our names are public, or a nomination is tendered. It's all at the pleasure of the president, right up to the swearing in. And after. He's the only elected official in the whole executive branch other than the guy waiting for him to drop dead; everyone else serves exclusively at his discretion. The president has to balance a hundred interests and make a decision about what will further his aims and strengthen his governance based on the information of the moment." The reporter listened to my little lecture in disappointed silence.

This wasn't about falling on my sword. I was focused, for my own good too, on what the stakes really were and for whom. If I hadn't fully grasped it before this minute, I grasped it now. The buck stopped with Clinton. Nothing noble in this view of things, just a kind of realism— the utility of an education in political science. Or maybe it was just that I was fifty-eight when it happened, not thirty-eight. I've been on the losing end of a lot of destiny's deals, and on the winning end of a few as well. Fortune plays its role, and you can't fight fortune. I'm a rebel and resister when it makes a difference, but when the struggle ends and the loss is clear, continued resistance curdles into resentment and feeds on those who carry it, without changing the outcome an iota. I would be damned if I'd play another of the president's jilted lovers, stewing in the poison of their indignant jealousies and simmering resentments.

I moved on. I did stop to write the president the note Melanne promised me she would hand on to him. I guess to this extent I succumbed to the temptations of a lover's spite. I gave Clinton an only slightly masked piece of my mind. Why I believed I could have served, why it might not be so smart to protect the NEH and NEA by burying them in anonymity. Out of danger, they would also be out of hearing; beyond controversy, they would be beyond relevance. Besides, the ideologues wouldn't be satisfied with Lott's compromise. The enemies of the arts and the humanities would be propitiated only by total victory—the institutional death of the two offending endowments.

Just as my heart's disappointment raised its voice, however, I turned the brief over to my political science head. By using my personal grievance as an excuse to address the larger question that had troubled me throughout Clinton's two terms, I raised the stakes and took my own fate out of the equation. I wrote,

> Prudence is of course part of political wisdom. Lincoln tacked on the issue of slavery to hold the Union together and he suspended habeas corpus when he thought national security was at stake. . . . But prudence followed too slavishly becomes imprudence. . . . That is why I am skeptical about Dick Morris's philosophy of governance. He misses something elementary about leadership when he urges that you tack across the wind of public opinion in order to reach your principled destination. While tacking is oft times a necessity, your leadership and your democratic passion have blessed you with the tools not only to select the destination, but also to influence the direction in which public opinion's prevailing winds blow. You don't have always to tack to the polls, your extraordinary eloquence and capacity to mould opinion can change how the polls read and where the wind blows.
>
> Dylan said "the answer is blowin' in the wind," but what he did for America was to show how speech (and song) can change the wind's direction. I would have liked to help change the direction of the prevailing winds on the question of the humanities and the arts in America. I wanted to challenge the foolish and shortsighted notions that they are indolent luxuries of a free society that need no spirited public support; that a consumerist, profit-mongering market sector will take good care of them; that our democracy does not need their civic nurturing to flourish; that liberty grows independently of culture.
>
> In the end, Mr. President, I just don't believe the NEH and NEA are worth saving if the only way to save them is to render them nearly

invisible—to bury the spirited defense of democracy and culture that alone justifies the two Endowments' existence.

Writing the letter closed out my summer romance with the NEH. Upon reading it, I had to acknowledge it gave added weight to the president's decision to look elsewhere for a chairman. Too confrontational. A lawyer with this rambunctious a message might just get his client hung! And so, I figured, ended my long-term affair with the president. Whatever mild regret he might feel when he thought about it (if he ever did think about it) would probably be best assuaged by dropping my name from the lists. No more seminars, no more invites, no more flattery. It was over. And I was immensely relieved.

# CHAPTER EIGHT

## Hollywood East—A Dinner at the White House

**I WAS WRONG** of course. It is never really over with President Clinton. He was inevitably drawn to fans who became critics, anxious to justify and defend his being, himself seduced by those about to break the bonds of his seduction. Just a few weeks after my fateful conversation with Melanne following Don's farewell party, an invitation arrived out of the blue to attend a fall White House formal dinner. The arts and humanities awards. Exactly the kind of dinner for which, had I become NEH chair, I'd have been preparing the guest list. Ferris would certainly be there. Well, so would I (damn it!). The invitation included my wife, Leah, who in the years of my active but wholly nonsocial White House work had never accompanied me to Washington. She wanted to go. I wanted to go. If the letter I wrote thinking it would bring closure hadn't, maybe this would. Or not.

I went curious, the novelist in me aroused. Could it really be that it wasn't over? I'd been in the White House dozens of times, in the formal rooms perhaps on half a dozen occasions, but this time was different. I was more like, well, an outsider again. And all the dinners I'd attended were working affairs with a handful of visitors, a bunch of staffers, and the president around a single table. This was a state affair—the East Room decked out in finery for the reception, the State Dining Room hosting a feast for a couple of hundred guests, with dozens of tables set for eight, leaving only the narrowest of paths for guests to negotiate;

and the guests, dressed for the Waldorf Astoria—or was it the Hollywood Bowl?

And then there were the stars. The honorees and their guests. Staffers were clearly in attendance on this night not because duty called but because they had competed for and won a scarce ticket to the kind of glamour-fest that all America adored and that the Clintons themselves so obviously relished. The president is famous for his cultivation of that other version of the meretricious—not the shallow glory of Washington's power brokers but the hollow glory of Hollywood's beauty brokers. And if the difference between the two is no longer easily discernible, and not just because of Ronald Reagan and Barbra Streisand and Sonny Bono and (of course) Cher, those who actually live in Washington continue to yearn for what monied lobbyists cannot purchase and popular sovereignty cannot command. Hence, the two celebrity constellations crisscross the country, passing in the air, to seek out one another's glory and confirm one another's reputations—often on television, the medium that belongs to neither but is desperately courted by both. Warren Beatty and Clint Eastwood toy with politics on both flanks of the American center, while those actually in the center reach out to flatter them. Candidates for office go on bended knee to the gilded Canossa that is Hollywood to do obeisance to its celluloid (and now digital) popes.

The president's ongoing flirtation with Hollywood has both burnished and tarnished his own reputation, diminishing his legacy but perhaps setting him up for a post-presidential career that will be a surrogate for the legacy he may fail to leave behind. The yearning to go west where the stars are brighter contributes to Clinton's unfortunate image as a slick operator infatuated with celebrity (although late-night television's Bill Maher has noted rather wickedly that the antonym for slick may not be earnest but plain dumb—George Bush Jr. take note). Slick or smart, in his infatuation with Hollywood, the president is more or less a typical American (perhaps his most admired trait). He certainly does not need Hollywood Hills' pickings to find women and men mired in self-importance and superficiality, with so many ensconced just a few blocks away up at the other end of Pennsylvania Avenue.

With the NEH matter out of the way, and this promising to be my last White House soiree, I was determined to enjoy my night with the stars, this commingling of glory, celebrity, and fatuousness that the awards dinner would inevitably yield (the actual awards had been meted out earlier in the day, leaving the evening for fun and entertainment). It wasn't so different from the White House correspondents dinner, except this one was in the White House and its stars were New York bohemians, artists, and intellectuals unlikely to be at either a correspondents bash or a White House state dinner—let alone a working wonk seminar.

Trying without much success to match my wife's glamour (she wore a bare shoulder/bare back gown that slinked down her dancer's body a little more provocatively than I had been imagining when I urged her to put it on), for the first time I pulled on my tux for a White House affair. I was glad I had. Glamour *was* in the air, and Leah was not alone in her easy sexiness. Arriving at the east gate, we were immediately picked up and escorted into the basement parlor rooms under the massive public rooms of the White House, where the guests were being gathered together and prepared for a still-grander entrance upstairs. Vartan Gregorian, the ubiquitous chairman of the New York Public Library, later president of Brown University and then of the Carnegie Endowment, caught my eye, and we began an only slightly ponderous conversation about our common commitment to civil society until, sensing how much more appropriate it would be, we dropped the big ideas and fell to gossiping. André Schiffrin, the publisher, was chatting with his author, the award winner Studs Terkel, and nodded to me. We'd met, but we didn't really know each other. The White House is a club, however, and to be there at all is to be pleased to acknowledge everyone else—after all, aren't we all wonderful merely by virtue of having been invited? I was about to greet Joe Duffey when a uniformed lackey who seemed to have materialized from Louis XIV's court presented himself, took Leah's hand on his arm, and escorted us to the East Room, where we were announced, court style, "Professor Benjamin Barber and his wife, Leah Kreutzer Barber." Whew.

The few staffers lucky enough to have scored tickets looked ravishing, their everyday, "She isn't wearing Sears Roebuck, is she?" gear replaced by "Isn't that Armani?" outfits to keep up with the guests from the other coast. Take Ellen Lovell, for example, one of my favorites at the White House and another example of why the first lady's staff has always seemed to me to outshine the president's (Melanne Verveer was another). Ellen had her hair swept up in a romantic swirl that highlighted a face whose beauty, because it was usually submerged in high-pressure business and crisis-induced tautness, seemed tonight quite foreign to her everyday self. Though I knew her well, I stared at her as if she might be a Beverly Hills starlet, and she had to remind me who she was. "Oh, Ellen, I didn't . . . I mean I thought . . ." I stumbled into silence, realizing there was no appropriate way to say she was too striking to be recognized.

Sid Blumenthal saved me from my rising blush, ambling over to greet me, full of the same boyish arrogance he had displayed at a Bard College conference we shared years ago when he gave a brilliant dinner talk on the '92 election (was he already campaigning for a job?) at which, however, his self-congratulatory demeanor occluded to a degree the brilliance for which his audience would have liked to congratulate him. I moved quickly to congratulate him now on his new job before he could do it for me, and he responded with a flood of words about how much he liked the job, how he could be both a loyalist and a critic, how his true calling was politics (true, true). He really did seem perfect for the job, and would prove to be so in the coming crises. Meanwhile, he probed gently—trying to figure out my White House connections?—but then turned tactfully to a more academic train of thought, asking about my current writing and insisting I must stop to see him on my next trip to the White House. I ended up dropping in on him as regularly and easily as I had earlier on Don Baer. Then he idled over to the next guest, leaving me to introduce Leah to Joe Duffey and Sheldon Hackney, whose job I'd so futilely coveted. Both, along with everyone else, seemed eager only to reassure and flatter me. (But then, they always seemed eager to reassure and flatter everyone.) John Brademas and Ellen Lovell both whispered in my ear, like king's messengers, that the king had offered award speeches that morning pilfered from "familiar" materials, my essay for the Brademas Presidential Committee on the Arts and Humanities, where I had been arguing that the arts and humanities were democracy's vital core and needed to be funded for democracy's sake rather than their own. Melanne Verveer gently buoyed me up on a tide of little compliments.

Leah was bored with the politicos, but spotted Edward Villella, the great dancer, and they managed to flirt discreetly—her admiration arousing his interest. Our peregrinations in the East Room were interrupted by the descent of the king and queen into our midst. This being a formal evening, it was immediately clear there would be no informal chatting. A reception line was forming, and the first couple were on automatic pilot, greeting guests with pro forma smiles, directing their tired gaze at the waiting cameras, both of them seeming a little haggard, as if they had just awakened from prescient dreams that revealed what the next twelve months would bring. I would have skipped the line, except that Leah might not otherwise have had a chance to meet the president (or re-meet him: she'd been introduced years ago at Rutgers, on that first, fateful meeting around the service program). When we made our way into his presence, the sun had gone out. No glowing orb of the kind I'd experienced at Camp David. He greeted me numbly, with only a familiar "hello, Ben" to distinguish me from the many notable strangers on the guest list. His eyes were glazed over, his face beet red (an afternoon on a sun-burnt golf course? Simple exhaustion? A call from Monica?) How many photo ops would there be? The photos came out looking far more animated than the president actually was. Hillary was warmer, but still managed time only for a quick hello/goodbye hug. And that was that, I thought. That really was the end of the affair. Peering into the rest of the evening, I foresaw dinner in an anonymous room of two hundred and back out onto Pennsylvania Avenue and: The End.

The surprises were not over, however. Searching the seating charts to find our tables, Clinton again startled me: he would not leave me alone. I was seated at his table, along with the actor Jason Robards, the singer Betty Carter, the actress Angela Lansbury, Mrs. Leonard Slatkin, the maestro's wife (the maestro was in Japan), and Senator John McCain. What the hell was I doing there? In a room of dozens of tables and two hundred people or more? I couldn't figure it out: Grand gesture? Abject apology? A reward for my discretion? Simple kindness? Or mere serendipity? (No, nothing happened serendipitously in this White House!) Perhaps I *was* his soul mate? Why else have me so close at each of the few meals we shared? It wasn't that we did those buddy things presidents do with certain intimates with whom they can drop all public pretense. On the contrary, I always felt a little formal, and the president, for all his charm, always seemed just a hair tentative with me. During this evening's repast, we talked casually but not intimately, ramblingly but certainly not intently. The NEH never came up. Maybe he had forgotten. Or never even known, maybe staffers had done all the decision-making on this one. The whole thing was in my imagination: a president larger than life insinuating himself into my conjectures and dreams when he probably could scarcely keep my name straight. The mouse in the shadow of the elephant imagines all that heft is conceived exclusively to eclipse him; the elephant doesn't even know the mouse is there.

Yet though I had enough perspective to know it was mostly my imagination, I couldn't stop asking myself: Why? Was I some providential parent to whom a place of honor had to go, even if attention was focused elsewhere? Was I making too much of accidents that would be invisible to those arranging the dinner? (Really? Barber's been at his side at all the dinners? How'd that happen?) Well, there was no point in thinking about it. It simply was. Leah had settled in comfortably at a table with Robert Pinsky, the unassuming and deeply gifted poet laureate of the United States, whom she'd long admired and with whom she found an immediate rapport (didn't hurt that he was a Rutgers graduate), and she also had my friends Joe Duffey and John Brademas by her side.

Calming the inner commotion that being seated with Clinton had stirred up in me, I realized how pleased I was to be with Robards and Lansbury. I grew up in a theater family, married a choreographer and theater movement director, and misspent a certain part of my youth convincing myself that philosophers not only belonged (like Machiavelli, Voltaire, Rousseau, and Sartre) in the theater but could philosophize effectively only under the spell of Dionysus. I worked episodically in the theater, writing plays that were produced off Broadway and in regional theaters, and directed occasionally. These were more than coincidences of biography, however.

Politics and theater share a deep kinship that is founded on the performance aspects of political leadership and the constituency character of live audiences: more than one rebellion has begun with an audience being whipped into a political frenzy, which is why tyrants generally close or take over the theaters first when they embark on the road to censorship and political dominion over other domains of life. It is not just, in today's epoch of ubiquitous screens, that theater folk like Ronald Reagan and Václav Havel and John Paul II become politicians, popes, and presidents—or even demagogues (Austria's Jörg Haider or our own David Duke)—benefiting from screen personalities and cosmetic makeovers; it is that the histories of theater and of the state have been forever intertwined. The birth of tragedy in a religious ceremony involving a priest and a congregation (chorus) in ancient Athens tracked the birth of monarchy and its transformation into democracy (a tribune representing the tribe). Dramatic poets like Sophocles and Aristophanes were democracy's first champions against the aristocratic pretensions of philosophers like Plato, who thought the people too base to govern themselves and banned poets from his republic for thinking otherwise. The French revolutionaries made civic pageants and revolutionary festivals a powerful instrument of the transformation of their nation, just as Ibsen, Shaw, and Brecht made the stage a venue for rebellion against Victorian and bourgeois social conventions.

There was no reason, then, to regard as anything but natural a table at which an actor like Robards, who before his death at the end of 2000 had regularly portrayed fictional presidents and other politicians, sat with a charismatic real-life president, who has been the principal player in what is either our era's leading tragedy or its most entertaining farce. I not only felt at home but felt appropriately addressed right down to my own familial roots. My father, Philip W. Barber, had worked with the renowned theater group called the "47 Workshop" at Harvard, and when the workshop's creator, Professor Baker, moved to Yale in 1931 had followed him there along with the Radcliffe poet and playwright Doris Frankel. She later (and a little reluctantly) would become my mother. With Baker they had helped found what became the Yale Drama School. During that heady era's twin commitments to radical politics and innovative theater, my father had helped conceive the "Living Newspaper," a dramatic enactment of current news geared to radical politics. My father wasn't himself particularly political, but his work as the first director of the Federal Theater in New York immersed him in progressivism: he staged the Depression classic *One Third of a Nation* (Roosevelt's one-third of Americans who lived in poverty and went to bed hungry every night), and with my mother had been active in the founding of another highly political institution, the Group Theater.

While my father worked under Hallie Flanagan at the Federal Theater (both were Iowans and Grinnelleans), my mother was writing for Broadway (*Don't Throw Glass Houses* and, after the war, *Love Me Long*, with Shirley Booth). My mother was even less obviously political than my father, but spent much of her career helping to conceive and write those amazing sagas of everyday politics called soap operas, replete with Monica-and-Hillary–style sub-plots before Clinton was born: on radio, she created *Ma Perkins* and wrote *Just Plain Bill* and *Helen Trent*.

Later, for television, she was a headwriter on *All My Children* and *General Hospital,* kept at it through her seventies (she died at eighty-four, just before I met Clinton, surrounded by her dusty scripts for *Playhouse Ninety* and *Hallmark Playhouse* in an apartment on Manhattan's Riverside Drive). She was a lifelong Democrat who did more for democracy's popular culture than most politicians ever can.

I asked Jason Robards how much he identified with the political parts he often played; like most efficient and talented actors he professed to be practicing his craft, and nothing more. Like the performer in the German film *Mephisto,* about a favorite player of Hitler forced into impersonating the soul of the Third Reich at Nuremberg-style pageants, most serious stage artists like Robards will say, "I am just an actor, only an actor." But we see more in them and ask more of them. We don't think twice when Barbra Streisand embraces Clinton and makes political statements on his behalf, or when Charlton Heston waves a long gun for the National Rifle Association. Warren Beatty's flirtation with a presidential bid after portraying a senator more honest, more flamboyant, and more cynical than any we will encounter in real life (in *Bulworth*) was greeted with more warmth and interest than derision by the media. There is not a candidate running who does not connive to get on Leno's or Letterman's show—or who is not pressured to do so by staff spin masters.

So perhaps my own split personality with respect to theater and politics was not so strange after all. As a kid growing up in Greenwich Village, I was admiring Harry Truman and Adlai Stevenson and attending Broadway openings with Doris and trailing along after Phil to his cousin Meredith Willson's *The Music Man* (which Meredith's sister Dixie insisted *she* had written and Meredith had stolen from her sans credit). As a young man I was pursuing a Ph.D. in government at Harvard *and* pursuing my political ideals by opposing the war in Vietnam and campaigning against secret military research in the academy *and* writing a one-act play about political justice and a musical about Richard Nixon when he was a fraternity boy college kid (both later produced off-off-Broadway in New York). When I was running as a McCarthy delegate and later visiting friends in the Carter White House, I was writing or directing for Gene Frankel, John Duffy, and Lyn Austin, and working at Ellen Stewart's Café La Mama with my wife staging our version of *Kaspar Hauser* (a play about political socialization and mind control disguised as the story of a feral child). I ran a playwrights' group at the Manhattan Theater Club (co-founded by Philip Barber years earlier) when Nikos Pschacharopoulos was its artistic director, and in 1988 used my theater skills to help render *Strong Democracy* as television, working with Canada's splendid journalist and television personality Patrick Watson. The result was Watson's monumental ten-part series *The Struggle for Democracy*.

I owed to theater much of what I brought to politics and to politics much of what I brought to the theater. Lansbury, Robards, Clinton, and McCain did not constitute a table of anomaly; they were natural intimates with ur-affinities they were probably not aware of. Shakespeare's dismissal of men as mere players strutting and fretting their hour on the stage is also consoling, uniting the small and the large, the petty and the grand, in the subtext of imperfect and impermanent performance. Players all, the politicians and the performers are one.

There was a less serious and far more entertaining side to my occasional life in the theater as well. It wasn't all Greek tragedy and revolutionary pageants and Marxist guerrilla theater. As we sat there in the State Dining Room—a president with stellar performance skills, a maverick ex-POW with authentic charisma, and two commanding actors, I could not help remembering my own, less than towering confrontations with equally commanding actors. I once fired Jill Clayburgh and I took over Meryl Streep's role in a film. Perhaps because I'm related to the Marx brothers. True.

My grandfather, Benjamin Frankel, was a businessman who married into the Rubinstein family. Of the four Rubinstein girls, Rose married my grandfather, Blanche married the manager of the Ritz Hotel in Paris, and Tess and Edna married into the Marxes. That makes Groucho my second cousin several times removed (and then some), at least by marriage . . . I think. I guess I'm genetically autonomous, though I share something with the Marx brothers' kids. Still, I feel there's a little of Groucho in me, and there is certainly something of him in my ten-year-old-daughter, Nellie (even though she's partial to Harpo).

I think I told the president and especially his guests about my noble lineage that evening—adding (as I always do to soften the impact of the Marx brothers connection, mainly for the president's benefit, because the Marx brothers would be the trump card with Jason and Angela) that I was *also* related to the Roosevelts on my father's side, according to my father, who indulged in genealogical sleuthing to fill the empty parts of his living soul. He's dead, so you'll have to take my word for it.

Actually, of my table companions, McCain seemed the most amused by my Groucho story. In a certain way, the senator was both the wryest and the most impressive figure at the table, because he made no effort at all to impress. He was simply *there*. I suspect that weighty sense of "thereness"—born of wartime burdens and the kind of unwilled heroism associated with surviving imprisonment without yielding dignity—had a lot to do with his later successes in the presidential campaign of 2000. Dining with a couple of actors, a professor, and the president cannot seem too daunting after having bombs exploding under your plane while it sits on an aircraft carrier (the *Forrestal* tragedy in 1967), and then spending five years in a Hanoi hellhole as a much abused prisoner of war. Long before he ran for the presidency, McCain exuded on that evening the same sense of slightly self-mocking fortitude that made him so endearing to so many Americans, including a slew of crossover Democrats in 2000. No wonder partisan adversaries who couldn't abide his ideology couldn't resist his candidacy.

He was presumably being coddled and courted on this evening to elicit some interest from him in the arts (vain hope!) and perhaps attenuate the force of his opposition to arts funding. I made him my audience for my theater stories, because to the actors it was just shop talk and the president seemed too distracted to focus in. Having recalled my Groucho connection, I meandered on to recall Meryl Streep and Jill Clayburgh and the comedies I shared with them. But that's for another book in which I will reappear as a playwright. The politics of the theater is sometimes even more comical than the theater of politics.

These diversions aside, our conversation over the awards dinner was less riveting than its cast of characters might have suggested it would be, more languid and undirected than at the working seminars even in their social phase. The president, weary throughout the meal, seemed almost to be avoiding extensive exchange with the actors (perhaps because they were New York stage actors rather than the kind of celluloid celebrities for whom he was a magnet). He spent some time working a tired charm on McCain, who was immune to it, and then meandered into a more general conversation about historical White House decor. Realizing he was sounding like a tour guide, he shifted to who was reading what recently. I pushed Stephen Ambrose's gripping

account of the Lewis and Clark expedition at him (the president immediately exclaimed, "Oh, you mean *Undaunted Courage,* loved it!"). The
president was reading a biography of Ulysses Grant, and Robards
recalled the movie in which he'd played the great and drunken Civil
War general, who became a small and drunken president. That prompted a New York–style foray into recent films in which the entire company could participate. The president had just seen *L.A. Confidential* on the
White House screen, but much preferred the Japanese dance film about
which the New York critics were raving. He supplied the names of the
key actors in the film as if he were a longtime reader of *Silver Screen* and
talked about Bogart and Bacall and about Tom Cruise and Natalie Port-
man with equal ease. Theater was high culture, not his thing, but he
was a thoroughly modern man who knew his movies.

In the company of these visiting actors, at a social dinner, I could
hardly breach the NEH affair with the president. Yet it was heavy
enough on my mind to interfere with my pleasure in the evening. The
closest to personal I came in the light palaver with Clinton was a question about Chelsea's departure for Stanford. I ventured something to
the effect, "You always say, Mr. President, that this is a big public house
and that it belongs to us, but it's your home; how's it feel without her?"

It's a hard adjustment, he answered, tentative. He often goes into her
room at night, he said, and sits on her bed for fifteen or twenty minutes.
Just sits. I imagine him alone in her room, contemplating the large hole
left in the big public house by her absence. "But she calls a lot, so it isn't
so bad," he quickly added, rousing himself from the doldrums into
which my question had pushed him.

I rescued myself by asking him to read us the menu and comment on
it. His flagging energies again catalyzed by my query, he was soon talking about the new chef, whom he liked, and the dessert chef, whom he
adored—"He never makes the same dessert twice unless we ask him
to," he chirped, gay now, like a kid. I reminded him of the Oprah desserts
from Camp David back at our first-term seminar there. He nodded, muttered "dietetic" disapprovingly, and returned to enthusing about this
evening's menu. The cuisine struck me as a bit precious, overly complex, the essential ingredients failing to meld as they must have in the
new chef's imagination as he worked just a little too hard to please his
new boss with something different.

McCain was beginning to enjoy himself, grabbing the president's arm, saying how pleased he was to have been invited, even if he couldn't promise his vote for arts funding. Members of the Marine Band appeared rather abruptly, imitating strolling musicians wandering among the tables, making further conversation all but impossible. These uniformed gypsies elicited from their violins sounds that intoxicated and irritated at the same time. The image of a court again intruded into the picture of a democratic pageant I kept trying to draw for myself. Why did this most accessible of all presidents seem in this grand salon so regal and unapproachable, so tired with the cares of kingship?

My renewed reverie was broken by the stirring of the president in his chair. My God, he was getting up: no time to whisper something about the NEH, no time to inquire if he got the letter, no time even to thank him for the grand gesture of a seat by his side. He was up, nodding pleasantly, "I'm supposed to play the pied piper now, lead you off to the entertainment." Then he was gone, his exit path circling the room so as to intersect as many tables as possible, where he might stop and play host over and over again.

Nadja Salerno-Sonnenberg was waiting to play across the lobby in the East Room, quietly compressing her maniacal energy so that it could explode in a riot of magical musical inflections and diversionary grimaces once the president and first lady were again seated—their presence commanding a performance and decorating the first row, along which the award winners were primly arranged. NEA Chairwoman Jane Alexander seemed to be dozing, while Hillary was fighting the same infectious dropsy with half the room. The wine was taking its toll. But the president had bottomed out earlier and, refreshed, was listening intently. Leah observed in a discreet whisper that whenever the president was down, Hillary seemed up (as in the reception line) and (as now) vice versa. Another way in which they played off of each other's weaknesses?

With the brief musical interlude over, we were again ushered into the great hallway—I had never been so ushered around a familiar place as this evening—where the Marine Band had again transformed itself, this time doing a fair imitation of the Jimmy Dorsey orchestra. Good liquors and bad coffee were served up with an opportunity for dancing. And, for those who could hear despite the raucous band, talk. Leah introduced me to Tom Lee, a Boston investor whose wife, wearing jewels that made Liz Taylor look like a nun, had also been seated at Pinsky's table.

He was pleased to share with us the good news that, having been instrumental in funding some part of the evening, he would be staying in the Lincoln Bedroom. So, I thought, the Lincoln bedroom *was* for sale. But, I quickly consoled myself, if it was in the name of funding a dinner for artists whom too many politicians would just as soon shun (and defund), then perhaps it was a commercial transaction that benefited rather than imperiled our democracy.

The president seemed to have departed, leaving his guests to the revels that, in the retelling, would provide high entertainment for their grandkids in the long decades hereafter.

I was ready to go, finally at the end of the end of the affair. But Leah wanted to dance, and I danced—how could we not? The Marine Band playing the White House was not some Kansas City Hilton lounge lizard act. More a once-in-a-lifetime thing. The slow fox-trot called up two centuries of profane populist dancing on these hallowed populist floors. We kissed, for history and for ourselves, and stepped off the floor. As we gathered ourselves to make a quiet departure, the president reappeared. There he was, still aloft on the second wind that had breezed in on him during Sonnenberg's short concert.

The president was always the last one at the party. And now with Hillary asleep and only Chelsea's empty room awaiting him upstairs, where would he go? I pressed Leah to leave, but she insisted he was glancing our way—we should wait. Then he caught my eye, he was striding over, upon us in an instant. Dropping his huge arms on our shoulders, with those fingers too elongated even for his huge hands clasping us warmly, he pulled us together like a couple of scrawny kids; he was exuding intimacy. A man completely different from the one who had sat by me at dinner in his official stupor, making officially stupefying conversation, was now literally taking us in his arms. His presence was a silent bidding for me to talk, confess, release. I mumbled something about the summer, how hard it had been with the NEH, and then I stumbled to a halt, worried that if I started in for real, as I had with Melanne after Don's party, I might not be able to stop.

He wasn't going to leave it alone. He pulled us closer, mumbling back, something about how he couldn't leave me "to the dogs." I hoped he didn't mind my "tough letter, kind of abrasive." No, he didn't mind, "I'm glad you wrote it, *glad.*" He was glad and I was grateful, and then I was rattling on about his amazing numbers, talking about him not me, telling him, my God, the media assault's left him unscathed, but how hard it must be to hold to principles of any kind under the avalanche of criticism.

"Yes, it's been hard," he allowed. I rushed ahead, hardly waiting for him to finish. We'd gone in an instant from how hard it had been for me to how hard it was for him. He has the narcissist's gift of making conversation about him feel like conversation about you. At this point in the evening, I liked it better that way; it was easier to address *his* hardships. "Give the American people credit," I said. "Their constancy. Amazing really."

"No," he said, his voice lowering into a pout, "the people aren't, the people don't." He was mad at them too, didn't want to give them any credit: "They get pushed around by the media and, by God, there has never been a time in Washington when there have been so many thugs in this town." Now he was venting. Only he was wrong about the people, I said. Plenty of thugs in D.C., yeah. Plenty of jackals in the media. But the American people, "they did well by you." And would. Right to the end of his second term. Constancy would be their signature, at least until he rode out of office on a duststorm of controversial pardons and renewed financial scandals. This seemed to me to be a comforting truth the president needed to recognize. But the Monica scandal hadn't yet broken, and at this point Clinton was feeling from the public an unearned animosity that only later would become a less than fully earned loyalty.

The unexpected moment was ending. The president reclaimed his hands and arms, leaving our shoulders feeling naked. Another hug for me, a handshake for Leah, I heard myself saying (I couldn't believe I was saying it again, as if the summer had never happened!) "Well, maybe sometime, I'll be able . . . figure out . . . I mean . . . to serve . . . ," and then I trailed off, and he echoed my incoherence, nodding, "yes, maybe we will, maybe we will." And as I wondered who "we" was and what it was we will do, off he went, taking his light with him, leaving us in the relative dark of his absence, and the approaching midnight. Leah would now understand what I meant when I spoke of the pool of luminosity that surrounded him when he (it) was on.

We headed for the exit, passing Melanne Verveer, who whispered, "I trust we'll be talking?" and I whispered back, yes, we'll be talking, wondering to myself why and about what, and realizing it was still a long way from over. As if he caught my drift, the president, working his own way out of the room, turned and nodded, his eyes signaling he hadn't forgotten. He reached out casually across a couple of guests and touched Leah's bare shoulder as if to leave on us an impression of his sincerity, a mark that would tell us he remembered our moment and would take it upstairs with him to Chelsea's empty room in this empty nest of a White House. And so, good night, Mr. President, good night, I said.

We were ushered out as we had been ushered in by the same uniformed escorts and their gorgeous accompanying hostesses, who looked like Sioux City ingenues on prom night. Half past midnight, we fell out the east gate and by the Secret Service booths glowing dark purple in the night, and then we were back in the real world. I turned to my wife, my sweetheart, to tell her that finally, yes, I could say it: it was over. Except I couldn't say it.

# CHAPTER NINE

# A Guest from the Harding Era

NINETEEN NINETY-EIGHT WAS a better year for me than for the president. It is not hard to see why. The year was better for almost anyone who could still draw breath than for the president. It was a good year for me in terms of my odd relationship to the White House because despite the unsettling denouement of the NEH search, and what I had thought was the closure represented by the "now we're even" invitation to the awards dinner—here I was, once again being invited to consider the State of the Union Message in the company of the president. I'd survived what other onetime favorites of this president had not: his (quite modest and probably entirely inadvertent) "betrayal." Having refused to play the jilted lover, I was being treated as a still constant if casual friend. January 8, another State of the Union White House dinner seminar on long-term democratic ideology, and I was still there. Just a few weeks before all hell broke loose, intellectuals were still coming and going, philosophies of government were still being debated, ideas were still in play.

Our dinner took place in the calm preceding the president's stormy winter travails in connection with the sex and lies scandal that would plague the balance of his presidency and lead to his impeachment. No snow this year, but the weather gods were not altogether indifferent; they managed an unseasonable tropical dampness that on the day of our meeting produced a shroud of fog that enveloped much of the East Coast. There was a limpness in the White House, as if the peculiar winter humidity was emanating from its innards. The official greeters were flat, and the four-man band playing us into the Red Room, where drinks were being served, was more dutiful than cheerful.

Richard Rorty, perhaps America's best-known philosopher, certainly its most idiosyncratic thinker, was at the door. His presence was a surprise because his pragmatist philosophical inclinations had been inflected in recent years by a postmodernist mood that in essence denied politics its civic rationality. Rorty was a small-*d* democrat, but he had little faith that government reflected the will of its citizens. (My fear was it reflected that will all too accurately!) Although Rorty was certainly a liberal (well to the left of the president), he had devoted considerable intellectual energy to demonstrating that liberalism was a practice impossible to ground in foundational logic. Democracy could no more be justified in some ultimate metaphysic of natural law or divine providence than any form of government. Having him there was sort of like inviting one of those trick-disclosing skeptics to a magic show. I was curious to see how Rorty would perform in this highly politicized setting. He was far more shy here than in academic settings, rather nicer, and without apparent political instincts. In this, his behavior and his philosophy were equally bereft of a grounded politics. Michael Sandel, a communitarian colleague from Harvard, arrived early as well. Sandel had actually appeared on a shortlist for the Supreme Court, though he was strictly a political philosopher and it was hard to imagine exactly why. He was one of those consummate Harvard dons who by never slipping his graduate student earnestness won lifetime tenure in the conservative shadows of Harvard Yard. He was clever and bright and had a well-deserved reputation that soared on Harvard's high-flying wings.

The oddness of the guest list grew with Michael Lind's arrival. Lind had been a conservative intellectual historian and a well-known magazine editor with an affinity for Teddy Roosevelt's old-fashioned muscular nationalism. In the last couple of years, he had crossed over to become a more progressive intellectual historian, without abandoning his affection for T.R. He struck me as a prudent opportunist: smart enough to be opportunistic and too smart to allow himself to be defined by opportunism. The room was acquiring a decidedly communitarian collectivist character, but too abstract and clever by half. This really was going to be an academic seminar, with any pretense of political relevance blown away by the character of the guests. As the years went on, and the practical utility of our seminars became ever more suspect, their academic R&R character grew more pronounced. If our conversation wasn't really going to make much difference, the president seemed to say, let's be sure to have lots of fun!

The arrival of Sam Beer provided the crown on which the lesser jewels in attendance could set themselves. He also anchored the Harvard team. Harvard, a major player in the Kennedy administration and hence by default in the Johnson administration, was again prominent in Clinton's Yale-denominated but in fact Harvard-inclined administration.

It is a small mystery why, in an otherwise democratic nation egalitarian enough to prescribe in Article I, Section 9, of its Constitution that "no title of nobility shall be granted," Harvard and Yale continue to enjoy the reputation of aristocratic institutions empowered to play a special role in American political life. There are historical reasons rooted in longevity and class that explain the prominence nonpareil of England's "Oxbridge." After all, Oxford and Cambridge were for much of Britain's history the only two significant universities and the exclusive tutors to its governing class). But it is harder to grasp America's fascination with and subservience to the self-generated hegemony of "Yarvard." At our meeting that evening, Sam Beer, Michael Sandel, Cass Sunstein, and I were Harvard connected, while among those with whom I shared earlier meetings, Harvard Ph.D.'s/sometime teachers/faculty members included Alan Brinkley, Theda Skocpol, Amy Gutmann, Robert Putnam, Skip Gates, Randall Kennedy, and Jenny Mansbridge, among others—out of all proportion to a statistical academic cross section, and by no means justified by an absence of competitors elsewhere. Our dinners featured Harvard, Yale, Harvard, Princeton, Harvard, Rutgers and Harvard, Harvard, Harvard. Richard Rorty was the exception—a University of Virginia professor with a Ph.D. from Yale. Yet the tyranny of Harvard over Washington is an old story. In a famous anecdote, President Charles Eliot of Harvard is said to have had his secretary place a call to President Teddy Roosevelt in Washington. When eventually Roosevelt picks up the phone, the secretary in Harvard Yard says, "Mr. Roosevelt? The President is on the line."

I had some sense of this Harvard mystique as a graduate student, because while I felt as a New Yorker as if I was doing time in Cambridge, and counted the months until I could escape—I spent the three years it took to write my doctoral dissertation in Switzerland and England—many of my friends took themselves to be in paradise, and saw the end of their studies as a fall from grace. For some, to this day, the "return" to Harvard trumps every other career move. I know Europhile bohemians in love with New York who have said they will never leave, who have uprooted and rushed back to Harvard within a month of the call. As Hegel once waited for his "call" from Berlin—which finally came toward the end of his life and brought him to imperial Prussia's capital city—American academics await the shepherd's horn from Harvard. Skip Gates has assembled many of America's most prominent African-American scholars in Cambridge by waving the crimson banner of Harvard. Jenny Mansbridge and Seyla Benhabib are among the new feminists who were both content and celebrated elsewhere, but who returned to Harvard when invited to do so (Seyla later betrayed Harvard, but only for the blandishments of Yale).

I am always a little surprised when I speak publicly to find that my hosts almost always pick back forty years through the detritus of my c.v. to note my graduate school affiliation with Harvard. I spent the bulk of my time at Harvard looking for women at places like Wellesley, Wheaten College, and Boston University (where I found my first wife), working in the peace movement and scheming to get to New York on weekends (where the girls were far more enticing), and the bulk of my career afterwards at a public university. Certainly I had the good fortune to study with some extraordinary teachers like John Fairbank and Edwin Reischauer, Henry Kissinger and V. O. Key, Stanley Hoffmann and Sam Beer. My thesis adviser was Louis Hartz, who—before an illness drove him mad—taught me the meaning of American liberalism (not the L word, but the Lockean consensualism that drives every politician to the center of the road). Hartz mapped the centrist nation through which Clinton would eventually make his journey.

However, there were equally extraordinary teachers at Berkeley (Sheldon Wolin and John Schaar) and the New School for Social Research (Hannah Arendt and Peter Berger) and the University of Chicago (Leo Strauss and Friedrich von Hayek). Today, the democratization of higher education has meant that the University of North Carolina at Chapel Hill and the University of Texas at Austin and UCLA and the University of Washington at Seattle and Michigan and Rutgers and the University of Maryland also have faculties as celebrated as their basketball teams and Nobel Prize winners to go with their NCAA winners. Yet Harvard dominates every conversation and trumps every list, and at the White House it once again felt like dinner at the Harvard Club— or better at a Harvard/Yale Club mixer of the kind the two New York clubs run for their myriad young M.B.A.'s and LL.B.'s who alone can afford the pricey membership.

The distortions this bias introduces into American life are well known. David Halberstam's "best and brightest"—all those wunder-kinder whose rational calculations about Vietnam were at odds with history, culture, and destiny and nearly destroyed American stability in the sixties—were Harvard Yard deans and dons with too little real understanding of the world beyond the Charles River. Our own White House discussions over the years in which I took part were too often an extension of academic quarrels that failed to join the real political issues. That is perhaps why it was so easy for Morris and Ickes and Panetta and Stephanopoulos to ignore the bright ideas we floated to the earnestly listening president. This was more than just the fragility of eggheads in a you-gotta-break-some-eggs-to-make-an-omelette world. This was not about the isolation of academics from the real world (a problem in its own right) but about the isolation of Harvard from the academic world. The sense of being a chosen tribe. Of taking ourselves so seriously that it didn't matter whether anyone else paid us heed at all. Circles within circles within circles. Harvard's frame of reference some-time didn't seem to extend much beyond Harvard Yard.

Sam Beer provided the occasion for this diversion on American aca-demic elitism, but to his credit he was the exception to the rule of Harvard's self-importance. For though he was a Cambridge man, he had deep Boston ties, and Boston was a completely other kettle of clams than Cambridge. He was connected to the Irish as well as to the Brahmins, to the Kennedys and the Democratic Party. He could stalk the inner corridors of power and at one and the same time show a charming tolerance for peacenik lefties like me. Refusing to be defined by Harvard, he defined it at its best.

He was ageless then and ageless now. He looked little different at the White House that evening in a dapper, perfectly tailored linen suit from when I first encountered him back in the very early sixties while conspiring with Marty Peretz about some peace demonstration or other. Except for the leg. Marty and I were lunching at Waldorf's, one

of those greasy spoon cafeterias on Mass. Avenue that were the preferred meeting places of graduate students, when an extraordinarily
handsome man strode in—on crutches. No malapropism there; he
was *striding* on crutches, a leg dangling in a full cast. His yellow hair
was tinged with just enough gray to suggest elegance rather than age,
and his full mustache, an obvious English affectation, looked altogether unaffected.

Who's that? I blurted out to Marty, thinking this apparition bore a
resemblance to Errol Flynn after a fall from the mast of a pirate ship.

That, Marty informed me, is Professor Beer, teaches British politics,
knows the Kennedys, been here forever.

What'd he do to the leg? I asked, putting aside Errol Flynn and
conjuring up an academic dandy who must have fallen in his bathtub
trying to climb in with his mistress.

Broke it skydiving, said Marty.

Now, this was thirty years or more before "extreme sports" had
become fashionable with twenty-somethings, and Beer was already
fifty-something. And skydiving. Here on a foggy Washington evening in

*Left to right: Michael Lind, Sam Beer, President Clinton, Benjamin Barber, at the
White House, 1998. (Official White House photo.)*

the Red Room, nearly forty years later, was the same Sam Beer, without the cast but looking just a little older than he had then, certainly still capable of jumping from an airplane.

If I had been president, I would have dumped the rest of us and had dinner with Beer (Beer did end up seated to the president's right). He knew the history of the Democratic Party and the history of Britain's Labour Party better than anyone in the country, and—Rorty's very opposite—had an excellent grasp of the politics of reality (what some call realpolitik). He had been a true Teddy Roosevelt nationalist before the arriviste Michael Lind was born, a federalist on the model of Madison and Hamilton. His politics were old-fashioned enough to make him a pre–New Dealer, and thus still relevant to the post–New Deal New Democrat politics of today. A phrase like "working families" (a Clinton favorite and an early Gore 2000 campaign buzz phrase) would sit well with Sam.

He would frame the evening's discussion for us by what he said and who he was: his pitch was for a rehabilitation of government that began with the idea of a robust American nation. This was not a particularly "Harvard" line, and Beer had few academic "disciples." He was a student of Britain and of comparative politics, a supporter of national government, and a pragmatic realist who probably influenced more political party operatives and working policy-makers than scholars. At this moment in the history of the Democratic Party, where government had been discredited and making an argument for it was problematic, he reverted to the idea of the nation as a resilient ideal around which those who believed in the utility of government could rally those who did not. For the idea of the nation, when coupled with democracy and civic engagement, called upon patriotism and national vigor and did an end run around cynicism about governmental inefficiency and dependency-breeding welfare bureaucracies. Beer's forceful arguments for this historical commitment to the civic nation was prescient. Like many of the more successful ideas of the Clinton era, it was aggressively nonpartisan. It became a key idea in John McCain's presidential campaign a few years later and was taken up by other Republican critics of the Christian Right and neo-isolationism like Bill Kristol and his colleagues at the *Weekly Standard*.

The charms of Beer's non-Harvard populism had been obvious to me even when I was a student. Beer shared the office suite of my doctoral adviser at Harvard (Louis Hartz), and when Louis became ill—deranged—Beer stood up to a university that seemed initially reluctant to offer Hartz financial and moral support. I am sure there were many forces at work, but I credit Beer with bringing the Harvard administration to its senses and arranging an exit strategy for Hartz that honored his contributions, protected his privacy, and secured his family.

On a far smaller scale, Beer had shown me the same generous consideration. He had taken the time early in my career to write me the occasional note to congratulate me on a review of Alasdair MacIntyre I'd contributed to the *New Republic* (in the days before its publisher Marty Peretz, my once co-conspirator in the peace movement, took a hard turn to the right) or an essay in *Harper's* on leadership. This felt to a younger scholar the way an encouraging note from Laurence Olivier might feel to an aspiring actor playing a dubious role.

Beer's advanced agelessness was everywhere acknowledged (only the very aged can be called ageless), but he still had the capacity to surprise on this count. We were chatting before dinner with the president, and I was boasting a little, telling Beer how I'd been here before a number of times, when the president cut me off gently, yes, yes, Ben's been coming to these things for five years, but how about you Sam? I know you haven't been here during my tenure. But surely this isn't your first visit to the White House?

"No, no," said Sam politely, "no, I've been here before. Let's see, the first time, that must have been the time my dad brought me to meet, uh, must have been . . . [he paused with an actor's craftiness] . . . Warren Harding. 1921."

Nineteen twenty-one. Ageless Sam looked sixty but was in fact eighty-seven. He had been ten on that visit, he allowed, and his dad had "wanted him to meet a president," though, his dad later said, it might have been better to wait a few years, since Harding "didn't count as much of a president." Clinton's mother would scarcely have been born back then. Sam Beer came to us that night not from Harvard but from Harding, not from academia but out of the pages of the nation's political history.

The cocktail hour was getting on. The guests had all arrived, with participating staffers drifting in to fill the room. Some had arrived late with the president (he had been delayed at a meeting trying to deal with the Indonesian fiscal crisis, the one where the baht was sold out by currency speculators in a move that helped initiate the Asian financial crisis). Ann Lewis had taken Don Baer's place in communications—loyal, politically astute, but less interested in ideas than Don, more adept at selling the president's old ideas than at helping him engender new ones. Yet, though less enamored of philosophizing, she remained supportive of my self-appointed role as a provider of ideas. Sid Blumenthal was doing Bill Galston's work that evening—though Bill himself was there, oddly as an "outsider" though surely with a hand in putting this evening together. And Michael Waldman and Melanne Verveer and, as always, the vice-president. Gore was saying hello and, as ever, assuring me that he knew exactly who I was (I knew he knew, and he knew I knew he knew, here again was that awkwardness). "Mr. Indispensable," he said lightly, but I hardly heard him. Such phrases no longer meant much in this house of flattery. "Do you know how much the president liked your memo?"

I didn't know. Michael Waldman, now chief speechwriter, had called several times before Christmas soliciting input for the president, who would be traveling to Renaissance Weekend and a Caribbean holiday afterward and who wanted material to read prior to that quasi-vacation. Whatever residue from the NEH business lingered in my mind, it clearly was business as usual in his White House. I had submitted a paper making my now rather tired arguments on behalf of unifying vision—just before the Monica story broke:

> The 1998 State of the Union offers an extraordinary opportunity—perhaps the last of your administration—to offer a unifying vision, one which can weave together and thus explain and justify the many incremental measures already taken (much of the criticism results not from distaste for the individual programs, which are popular, but from an absence of understanding about how they fit into a coherent and cumulative strategy). At the same time, a coherent vision can project an active agenda for the balance of the term, putting to rest the notion that you are marking time or playing out the term conservatively while cultivating a so-called "legacy."

I went on in this vein for six single-spaced pages, spelling out ideas that might provide "thematic coherence" from the Memphis, the Georgetown, and the Princeton speeches in 1997 (to all of which I'd contributed my two and a half cents). My call was for an arching rhetoric around the challenges of internationalism and the need (in light of the defeat of the president's bill for "fast track" authority on international trade treaties by a Congress in which too many members had never held passports)[1] for a clear portrait of what America's interdependence meant for ordinary Americans. That was the only way NAFTA could be sold to old-line Democrats. NAFTA was the president's bold and (for a Democrat) courageous North American trade treaty that acknowledged free trade as a necessary posture for a new economy America in a global market society. Clinton had secured its victory against the unions and much of the Democratic Party's congressional leadership, and had paid a high price, in part because the treaty had not taken the full measure of global worker safety and environmental concerns. An internationalism that was only economic would not ultimately be palatable to Americans who preferred the larger context of civic and political democracy. I was also, at painful length, combating what I had come to regard as the "lists as legacy" approach to presidential achievement championed by small-bore aides like Dick Morris and astute policy wonks like Bruce Reed, who believed that a sufficiently thick catalog of smallish policy innovations would put a noticeably impressive bulge in history's record of presidential accomplishment.

I ended my written peroration with a "model" of the kind of rhetoric I was urging. Here, I wrote to the president, is the sort of speech you might give in reporting on the State of the Union in 1998:

In a world where walls are everywhere coming down, we cannot and we will not build new ones. We will protect America not by building walls but by opening up new roads and constructing new bridges; ours will be an architecture of interdependence, in which we do not close ourselves off from the world but use our influence and, yes, our power too, to assure that the world does not close itself off from us. We lose our sovereignty in the anarchy of unregulated global markets; we rediscover it in the civic interdependence of nations working together.

In the past we have "protected" ourselves by hiding behind two

---

[1] A recent *New York Times* poll suggests this has changed. Nine out of ten congresspeople travel abroad nowadays, on an average of twice a year.

great oceans and the limitless space above them. But the oceans are now highways to the world, the new technologies skyways leaping over them, and America must now do with and for the world what it once did without or in spite of it. . . .

As we approach the millennium with a mixture of hope and anxiety, we approach an age of true internationalism—for better or worse. After all, global markets can reinforce our strengths, but they can also uncover our weaknesses. They will be a boon to many of us, but will seem perilous to others. Yet they will not go away, and we cannot go away from them. Our challenge is how to make them work, work for us rather than against us; how to civilize them and make them engines of democracy as well as prosperity. . . .

Free markets are a first step, sometimes painful but ultimately rewarding, which force us to acknowledge that interdependence. But to succeed, free markets must be associated with free institutions and a commitment to a free international civic culture and global justice.

As capitalism has flourished in America under the watchful eye of a democratic people, so in the global marketplace, we will need democratic eyes and prudent regulations to assure that development is fair and the distribution of benefits just. We cannot simultaneously globalize *and* privatize without putting democracy at risk. . . . Freedom is a word associated with government and culture and not just markets; [which is] why we must have international democratic and civic institutions alongside our international economic and fiscal institutions. We need an international system that serves citizens as well as it serves consumers, that speaks to our need for comity and justice as well as our need for raw materials and consumer goods.

We do not need to change our values to become part of an interdependent world: we need to make sure that our best values—political liberty, social equality, economic mobility, cultural diversity, civic pluralism, ecological prudence—become part of that world . . . .

In many ways, this has been the American century. But the years that will inaugurate the coming millennium cannot belong to any single nation, however powerful. They can mark an epoch in which not America but the values and ideals that shaped America, become global. In which planet earth becomes an open society. In which not America but the idea of America becomes the governing norm of peoples everywhere. In such a world, belonging to all of its peoples, America will flourish.

This is the sort of thing the president had to put up with to secure a little outside counsel. Yet, according to aides participating in this evening's work, he really liked this particular contribution. I later wondered why its themes and spirit appeared, if at all, as faint echoes in the speech he actually gave. Perhaps because it focused on an internationalist subtext taboo in political campaign texts and State of the Union messages. The only international accent to our dinner discussion that evening would be my banter with Clinton about our dogs. We shared a love of chocolate labs, their Buddy and my Billy. Clinton later whispered to me in mock conspiratorial tones that the Arabs and Israelis were nothing compared with the challenge of Buddy and Socks. It was a light moment, probably inappropriate to the tragic gravity of the Middle East, but not altogether malapropos either. Clinton's peacekeeping efforts on both fronts, trivial and tragic, remained unsuccessful, perhaps for the same reason: he was trying to move by dint of will realities on the ground that were impervious to will. In what was probably the best piece of advice I gave him in five years, I suggested to the president that he give up mediating the quarrel between his pets and leave it to Socks to train Buddy. That's what cats do. Good advice for the Middle East as well? Maybe. I don't think he listened to me on this one either, not even insofar as it touched on Buddy. He went on trying to bully Socks and Buddy into an unnatural amity, just as he went on trying to seduce Arafat and Barak into an unprepared peace. By the end of his term, bitter hostility still enveloped the futile Middle East peace negotiations, while he was being forced to negotiate a permanent partition for Socks and Buddy (different homes).

Because the president hadn't arrived until seven-thirty, nearly an hour after the appointed time, we didn't go in to dinner until eight. When they entered, the president and the first lady were glowing in the aftermath of their Caribbean vacation. They seemed in total possession of their lives, of the White House, of this era. They were in their prime. It was only a few days before the Monica scandal broke and brought it all tumbling down around them.

The president bestrode the table's midsection, and on his right was Sam Beer, on his left, the Columbia law professor and *Nation* columnist Patricia Williams, a sharp-witted but soft-spoken African-American academic who, like Rorty, seemed distinctly uncomfortable in these surroundings. I was seated next to her, and spent a good deal of the period before the official discussion began calming her anxieties about how to proceed, how to make the most of the moment. I didn't tell her that the hardest thing would be dealing with the common cashew bowl, but then she was not a nut person like Clinton and me.

In his sense of security, and perhaps because Sam was sitting next to him as a physical remembrance of things past, the president was waxing historical. He starting by commenting on the sculptures and paintings in the dining room like a fluent tour guide (different room but same spiel as at the arts dinner—he apparently did a lot of this), recalling that the primary entrance to the White House had once been from the garden into this room. He segued into a discussion of our comparative reading lists. I was reading Donald's biography of Lincoln; he was reading a biography of Grant (he aspired to be Lincoln, but perhaps worried in his heart he would end up like Grant). I asked him how he liked the biography of Daniel Webster he was also reading because someone had mentioned during the cocktail hour that Sid had given the president the new Webster biography. What biography? asked Clinton, puzzled. Not me, said Sid later, I never gave him a Webster biography. The White House is no different than any other big family house: gossip reigns. But where history is watching, rumor has a higher price. No wonder presidential biographers find it so hard to nail down larger truths, if a book title is so vulnerable to interpretive variation. No wonder they invent alter egos and pretend to be childhood witnesses to secure a tenuous hold on the truth. Who gave which book to whom? What constitutes plausible denial? What exactly did the president say, and when? All of these questions come back to me now as I try to reconstruct events and conversations for this memoir. Am I working in the name of the power of truth or merely pandering to the truth of power? Hard to say. Am I to be trusted? Not necessarily.

Sid gaveled us to order with his orderly voice. He was not going to follow Galston's presentational mode: he wanted a live debate, and instead would raise, seriatim, a number of significant questions and invite discussion. This made for a much livelier, if rather less productive interaction; perhaps Sid had figured out that liveliness rather than productivity was the point. It also meant shyness would pay an even greater price than normal and boldness would be rewarded out of proportion to whatever wisdom might be attached to it. His first query was about the nature and role of government, and he invited the president to respond first. The president gave what seemed to be a not quite canned reply that rehearsed his positions on government after the end of the era of big government, where public-private partnerships and coresponsibility by the civic and private sectors as well as individual citizens would leave government as a facilitator rather than the sole actor on stage.

Sid invited Sam Beer to comment, and he did so by putting the challenge of government in a historical context, arguing that the nation and its health was more important to the reputation of government than government itself. He spoke with the slow deliberation of a man who knows what he's saying and figures others can wait to hear him out if they are interested. "The nation," Beer said, giving a now trivialized idea more dignity in the mere saying of it than most Americans do in their interactions with it, "is more than the government: it encompasses the very citizens who feel excluded by the goings-on in the capital. We can get to them by appealing to it." It wasn't a suggestion or a plea. Simply how it was. The certainty wasn't in the claim but in the manner in which Beer asserted it. Matter-of-factly. Deliberately. As in "you want to get to New York? Take the Metroliner."

Rorty jumped in, more, it seemed to me, out of nervousness than a readiness to join or confront Beer's quiet argument. He might have done better to wait. His broad invocation of liberal practices as worthy even in the absence of liberal foundational principles came across as particularly arcane and remote following Beer's salient historical remarks. Having apparently decided to forgo philosophical sharp-wittedness in the name of political relevance, he was insufficiently political to seem anything but vague. He must have sensed the puzzlement, the impatience, with which his provocative philosophical position was received in this highly political audience, for he concluded in a hurry and fell silent for the remainder of the evening. He dashed off the moment dinner concluded. This was not the performance of Voltaire at the court of Frederick the Great, though this is probably a tribute to rather than a criticism of Rorty's demeanor. If the philosopher's true political vocation is resistance to cant and convention, a redefining of what's relevant, he was true to that vocation. He avoided the small compromises we made on the way to trying to "influence" power. We assumed a popular style, simplified ideological complexities, tacked strategically to the center to get those in the center to move slightly in our direction. Rorty simply rehearsed his philosophical position as if he were addressing a graduate seminar in political theory. Since in the end we probably had as little to show for our compromises as he had to show for his diffidence (or indifference), his was perhaps the more prudent strategy.

The issue raised by Beer and then joined by Sandel, who countered him (Harvard vs. Harvard), and Michael Lind, who buttressed him, was ultimately the quarrel between Hamilton and Jefferson—federalist vs. antifederalist. Did American democracy reside in the collective soul of a united nation, not so much a central government as a coherent and united people? Or did it reside in the decentralized empowerment of ordinary citizens in the governance of their communities and everyday lives? Was liberty defined by the moral whole that was America (Lincoln's formula) or by the actual involvement of responsible citizens in local affairs (Jefferson's and later Tocqueville's formula)? Sandel was playing Jefferson; Beer and Lind portrayed a national voice that bridged Hamilton and Lincoln. The "people" as People, as an abstract moral collectivity in which ordinary individuals could see themselves reflected? Or the "people" as people plain and simple, real bodies with actual lives for whom democracy meant a sharing in responsibility and power?

These two positions were not exactly polar and needed not exclude each other (the dialectical point I kept trying to make), but they did suggest rather distinctive directions with respect to government and its role. Beer's celebration of the American nation afforded national government a legitimacy that was expansive. Sandel's focus on decentralization and local community demanded a shrinkage of national government to leave space for localism. The president seemed torn—drawn to Beer's rich account of national power as any president must be (he is president of the United States of America, not its fractious parts), but seduced in his New Democrat incarnation by the importance of subsidiarity and local power.

Of course, historically, Jefferson the antifederalist had created a powerful national democratic party, and with his purchase of Louisiana and his sponsorship of the opening through the Northwest Passage to the Pacific (the Lewis and Clark expedition) had provided the thirteen colonies with the wherewithal to create a powerful nation that would stretch across the continent. Writing his own speeches and elaborating in letters on his own policies, Jefferson never gave a fully adequate account of the new ideology of national power. He practiced that ideology as president, but eschewed it as a theorist of antifederalism. Lincoln, on the other hand, practiced what he preached. He revered the moral content of union and invoked the mystic chords of memory to denote a moral wholeness, though in the end there is no moral union without individual autonomy and the liberty of individuals. (These early presidents were not quite the literary solitaries we make of them; they did have collaborators in their speechwriting—Secretary of State Seward provided a draft of the second inaugural, from which the "mystic chords of memory" phrase derives; but Lincoln not only embellished and perfected these texts but often wrote his own from scratch, as with the Gettysburg Address.[2]

Sid interrupted the arching historical debate and asked us to consider its implications for what he called the current cultural and moral crisis: the debate over values and the family. Bill Galston, finally freed from the responsibilities of neutral chairmanship, spoke with forceful eloquence. With what must for the president have been an ironic and painful emphasis, he described the collapse of traditional families and conventional marriage and its corrosive effect on society. As sociology, what he said was undeniable, though there was an elegiac tone in his portrait that evoked nostalgia—as if we might solve our current crises of teen pregnancy, the incarceration of too many minorities, and school dropouts with a return to a storied past when men worked and women raised children and did charity work. I reminded Bill that nostalgia for this world that never was had been a neocon excuse for refusing to confront the reality of social, religious, and political change in an ever more diversified society. The traditional family offered the consolation of solidarity and a sense of place but at the price of structural inequality and the disempowerment of women. Nor was there any way "back" to such a world, even were it desirable.

I turned to the president: "The family remains society's indispensable building block. But we need a new story of the family, a way of talking about it commensurate with new, more diversified familial experiences with multiple marriages and 'steps,' as well as single-parent house-

[2] William Safire, our nation's speechwriter emeritus and pundit laureate, notes that Seward suggested texts that Lincoln transformed from "oratory to poetry." See his "Parsing Gore's Speech," *New York Times*, August 21, 2000, p. A30.

holds. *Heather Has Two Mommies* [the New York City school board's controversial choice for a multicultural primary school reader] is probably *not* the story we're looking for here; at least it probably isn't the hook you're looking for in the State of the Union to hang your 'values' argument on. But any approach to American values must be marked by tolerance for diversity, by a willingness to accept pluralism. That is the new America." The president nodded, and well he might; for it would be precisely this new, multicultural America that would stick by Bill Clinton in the hard months to come, when cultural moralists as well as many legalistic critics thought sexual infidelity in the White House, and lying about it, were sufficient grounds for putting the popular president out of business.

Then, always the arbitrator, the president added, "This country has always been divided by those who think government has to espouse morality, and those who think its job is to protect the diverse expression of morality." Again, it seemed clear that he understood well enough which view would support and which undermine his claims in the coming months.

The vice-president jumped in enthusiastically but not quite at the right moment, diverting us to his own agenda in a way to which I had become accustomed. Savvy, articulate, but slightly off-point, as if following a menu of topics the same as ours, but always a course or two behind or ahead, he spoke with deep feeling and earnest good will. But he left us thinking, "Yes, I see, and very sensible too; but, er, how exactly does this speak to the debate at hand?" Someone else had to connect the dots.

The president seemed always to fidget and look uncomfortable when Gore spoke. Not because he was being upstaged by him or because he disagreed with what was said, but precisely because it seemed the vice-president was *always* a tad off-target, diversionary, moving us away from rather than toward our objective. Gore was going on about values but in a different context—technology, the future, the need for adaptation. Important points—in a different debate. Clinton grew impatient and broke in, as if to steer us straight again.

"The Court, let me say something about the Court," Clinton began in what initially seemed a serial non sequitur to match Gore's: "Have you noticed, every decision the Court passed this year was an assault on the presidency, and thus an attack on government?" He meant that this

Supreme Court had been systematically attacking presidential prerogative—as it did notably in 2000 when it declared all executive regulation of tobacco in the absence of legislative authority invalid, and undid two terms of work against big tobacco. But he was focused here on the absurdity of a decision that insisted in the case of Paula Jones there could be no harm in permitting a civilian to bring a civil suit against a sitting president. The Court had justified its position by declaring that for the president to respond to Jones's controversial charges would "take no more than a half hour" (sic) of the president's time. Clinton was nearly apoplectic: "Well, we're the only ones still fighting for a belief in a role for government. The courts, the Congress, they're on the other side. But 65 percent of the American people support us." Yes, they did. And would. All the way through that assault on government called the impeachment hearings.

Clinton was struggling to contain his undisguised rage by linking his grievances back to party history as we'd been debating it: "Today the Republicans want to tear down government to liberate private power and private interest. Democrats, though sensible to the need for change, still believe government can serve justice and remedy inequality. It's ironic, isn't it? Because the difference today between Democrats and Republicans inverts the nineteenth-century model Sam Beer was talking about. Then the Republicans stood for national government. What's happening today, it's the reflection of a two-hundred-year-old struggle, starting with the Federalists, and coursing down through Lincoln's battle for union. Yes, it's this legacy of Lincoln the modern Republicans have betrayed. And then, in the twentieth century, the Democrats, once champions of disunion and confederation, fighting for a national government capable of rectifying injustice."

He looked around. We were dead silent. Waiting. As if it were our fault. But he was the one who had given succor to government's enemies, proudly proclaiming the "end of the era of big government." As if reading our thoughts, he rebuked us:

"Yes, I pronounced big government finished, but that's been misconstrued by those who thought that to reform overbloated government, to *reinvent* government, meant a war on all government." (This is what I had urged him to clarify back then.) "We won't make war on government; we will make it a lean and efficient instrument of justice."

Prompted by rage and leavened by insight, his words hung in the air—residual embers of a fireworks display falling gently to earth well after the explosions are over. Stunned by his extemporaneous eloquence, I grabbed a three-by-five card from my briefcase and scrawled the words "What you just said, that's your State of the Union Address" and passed it to him. He read it, glanced at me, nodded slightly, and stuck it in his notes. If only he could be persuaded actually to write his own text—not to massage an overwritten compilation of a speech after it was done (as he tended often to do); not to depart from text and improvise a few passages to clarify his personal view; but actually compose the core of a speech ex nihilo, on a blank sheet of paper. Or let someone record his extemporaneous speechifying for more formal occasions.

When he spoke again a little later in the discussion, he acknowledged that prior to the '96 election he had felt compelled to avoid "philosophy" and stay concrete. Focus groups always faltered and lost interest when he waxed theoretical, and registered enthusiasm when he got into the small-bore stuff that affected their daily lives, and though it bored the media, it had become his signature of success. "But I don't care anymore," he said. "They don't like it when I talk foreign policy either, but foreign policy is crucial today." He was prepared to speak generically, speak historically. "Ben Barber wrote me this really good letter telling me I can't mollify fear with facts, and he's right. I'm ready to speak in a different way. About interdependence . . ."

He's listening, I kept thinking. The skeptics are wrong. Ideas can make a difference.

Sid wasn't quite through. By replacing the discipline of a speaker's list with the discipline of a set of related themes, he'd engaged us in as high-level a discussion as we had had. Now he wanted us to finish up by joining the issues of nationalism, cultural conflict, and interdependence to the challenges of multiculturalism and identity politics. Easy for him to say! We were tired. The late start meant it was already 10:30 P.M. and counting. A few random comments—too few to introduce a new debate—and a summary observation from Sam Beer, our éminence grise tying together the centuries as well as the topics—and we were done.

The president offered his thanks, solicited additional comments in writing—"but get them in soon, the State of the Union's on the twenty-seventh"—and said goodbye. When Clinton said goodbye, I knew by now, he meant goodbye to this part of the evening, hello to the next part. He lingered in the reception room to chat and extend the arguments he'd been making. And lingered. And lingered. I stood at his left as he spoke to the small group that lingered with him—Sandel, Lind, Sunstein, and, of course, Bill Galston and Sid. Clinton leaned into me as he formed his thoughts, an unspoken fraternity between us justifying the near-violation of my private space his proximity threatened. Me and Clinton, brothers, comrades in arms, ready to argue the world. Having been mainly a careful listener for two and a half hours, he exploded into garrulousness.

**THE WHITE HOUSE**
WASHINGTON

January 22, 1998

Dr. Benjamin Barber
1019 River Road
Piscataway, New Jersey 08854

Dear Ben:

Thank you so much for joining me for the Leaders and Thinkers Dinner.  I was glad to get your ideas.  These types of sessions are helpful not only for my State of the Union preparations, but also for thinking through how to carry out our plans over the long term.

I welcome your continued counsel.

Sincerely,

He'd suffered our historical and social science lectures and was ready to indulge his own views on politics. He fell from the imposing, even haughty grandeur of his public statements of philosophy at dinner, descending happily into the muddy, dirt-stained ground of the political.

He'd talked in the abstract about the Court, the Congress, their attack on government, and he'd managed to conceal to a degree his bitterness in the scholasticism of our discourse. Now he allowed himself to be just plain incensed, getting on the Republicans in a personal and vindictive manner. He must have seen the ghost of Christmas to come. "God, they hate me," he said, seeming to relish the viciousness of it. "I mean they really hate me." He recounted the story of how Senator Alan Simpson (a distinguished Republican) had dropped by a while ago for an informal conversaton. The president had asked, "Now tell me the truth, Alan, do you really believe there's anything to this Whitewater thing? I mean, do you believe we did anything that wasn't moral? I don't just mean not legal, but not moral?" Simpson smiled. "Of course not, but we got a federal prosecutor out of it, didn't we?" They laughed together, but to Clinton it conveyed a brutal truth. He grew still more harsh and partisan, as if fully digesting Simpson's jest for the first time. Then he let it go, smiled, relaxed. "You know what someone told me yesterday? I really like this line, they told me, 'Democrats, they're guilty about what they earn; Republicans, they think they're entitled to what they steal.' "

The president talked on, relishing the intimacy that allowed him to sink into the kinds of crass partisanship he never was permitted in public. Three-quarters of an hour had passed since we left the table, and the first lady and the staff had vanished. Only Sid had stayed behind: it was his evening. But now he was trying to get us out so that the president would leave. Buddy started barking from a nearby room, as if calling his master to more important responsibilities (like Buddy!). Sid tried the press conference tactic: "Thank you, Mr. President," indicating final closure to us. The president's inertial momentum kept him rolling through a few more agitated sentences, and then he stopped. Buddy and Sid were nipping like sheepdogs at his heels, and he turned reluctantly to go, waving to our little group of ardent listeners.

I turned to leave with the others, but felt a hand on my shoulder. He was pulling at me, and I turned back. His voice was a hoarse whisper: "We did good, didn't we?" he asked like some novice assemblyman seeking reassurance.

"Great, great," I said, unable to quite believe the president needed this final word.

"This speech is really important," he added, still importuning me for something, I wasn't sure what.

"You know what the conclusion is, don't you?" I asked, falling into my fatherly role. He looked at me silently, quizzically. "That you have to write the first draft yourself. I mean write it *yourself.*"

He smiled wanly, satisfied at last. "Yes, I guess that's what I have to do."

Not, of course, that he actually did it. The State of the Union once again bore only a remote resemblance to what we had talked about, and its core was the usual laundry list written in group-speak. And the media dismissed it, and television viewers liked it. And who can remember it now?

It was close to midnight when Bill Galston and I hit the fresh air outside the east gate. It was odd having him leave with us. He was *them.* But not anymore. He was a civilian again. Like me, he could put the White House out of his head and head home. I hopped a cab back to Mike Levy's town house east of the Capitol. I had started the evening before the White House dinner drinking with Mike, and now, well away from his job as deputy secretary of the treasury for political affairs, he was keen enough on gossip to let me keep him awake for another two hours. I was being mildly indiscreet, in order to let enough hot air out of my overinflated tires to go flat and feel sleepy enough to go to bed. When I finally sank into what I thought would be a deep sleep, I was troubled by presidential dreams in which—this was a dream I had over and over again during these years and still have today—I was courting his attention, sometimes getting it and feeling elated, sometimes being ignored and feeling mortified. The president did not choose on this night of dreams to pay me much heed. But the first lady stood by my side, and we talked animatedly through those brief seconds of REM sleep that always feel like hours. Then real slumber arrived, banishing the first family to the nightmares of Ken Starr and Christopher Hitchens, who seem more deserving of them.

# CHAPTER TEN

# Clinton vs. *Jihad* vs. *McWorld*

**HENRY KISSINGER**, starkly criticized by idealists (like me) for his cold-blooded realism, nonetheless was correct in his assessment of America's distaste for foreign affairs. One of his favorite stories, which he repeated to me in Philadelphia when we shared a World Policy Forum there in the summer of 1998, several years after our comical encounter at the White House correspondents dinner, concerned the sales of an early book of his on NATO called *The Troubled Partnership*. The trouble with *The Troubled Partnership* was that Americans had no interest in its esoteric, slow-moving discussion of the Atlantic Alliance—except in Chicago, where, inexplicably, it was "selling like hotcakes." When an agent finally visited the store that had made it a local best-seller, he discovered it had been shelved in the "Marital Problems" section. Clinton himself would later learn that extramarital affairs were of far greater interest to the media than foreign affairs. He might have done better by his intellectual agenda had he found a foreign mistress, so that media scandal mongering could also have served the purposes of a foreign policy tutorial.

Bill Clinton was in fact a president with a serious interest in foreign affairs, not for their own sake, but because he understood that they could no longer be conveniently hived off from the domestic agenda. I learned this in the most delicious way. An author has few public epiphanies. Such joys as are likely to lighten the overrated literary life tend to be solitary: a perfect title accidentally found, a fresh topic for an essay stumbled across, a nearly fresh metaphor (it's too late in the history of literature for completely fresh metaphors), a sense of achievement at the rounding off of a last paragraph of a last chapter of an endless book. Interactions in the public domain, on the other hand, usually take the form of disappointment: depressing reviews (even the good ones take back with a sneer what is first granted with a smile) or, worse yet, no reviews at all; inadequate sales (no sales at all). And the friendly questions from allegedly friendly readers of your work (often family members) who consistently misquote your perfect title or confuse your arcane portrait of Swiss law called *Alpine Constitutionalism* with some other, far more successful book on mountain walks called *Alpine Constitutionals.*

So to turn on C-SPAN and come across the president of the United States holding up a copy of *Jihad vs. McWorld*, my 1995 critique of globalization, and not only describing its argument with considerably more acumen than most reviewers ever display but appearing also to be shamelessly hawking it to a couple of hundred opinion leaders gathered as a captive audience at a White House religious breakfast—that is probably about as publicly epiphanic as it gets for an author. Although (to the dismay of the unions) Bill Clinton pushed hard for NAFTA and championed free trade, he was no mindless zealot of the global economy. He knew it had high costs and grasped that unless American policy could get "beyond McWorld and Jihad" (as he promised it would in the inscription he penned into the copy of his little volume of speeches called *Between Hope and History* he sent me), we would be in trouble.[1] For the globalization of markets that was a crucial feature of the spread of what I had called McWorld—America's fast food, fast computers, fast music, fast films—was leaving many ordinary wage earners fearful, and worrying (in Clinton's words) that no matter how hard they worked they still might "not make it." Unless the challenge of globalization's dark side was met, Clinton said publicly, it would become an ever more serious problem for Americans.

[1] His small collection of essays, subtitled *Meeting America's Challenges for the 21st Century*, is organized under those now familiar New Democrat rubrics "opportunity, responsibility, and community," and does little more than allude to the perils of globalization. However, his inscription to me confronts McWorld directly, reading (with what others will regard as fulsome overstatement but can only appear to the receiver as much deserved praise): "To Benjamin Barber, with appreciation for your wise counsel and your love for America—we will find a way beyond McWorld & Jihad."

*(Courtesy of C-Span.)*

It was more than a little remarkable to hear the president talk this way a few years after an election in which foreign policy debate was completely absent, and years before the media would put globalization on the international crisis map and demonstrators would hit the streets of Seattle, Philadelphia, and Los Angeles to protest what they understood as the high-handed and hierarchical policies of the World Trade Organization (WTO) and the International Monetary Fund (IMF), as well as the unwillingness of the two majority parties to even address the issues at their 2000 conventions. For, like most presidents who respond more to the American electorate's well-known parochialism than to any intellectual interests in the world they may possess, Bill Clinton came into office far less concerned with foreign policy than he later became—a striking example of the dominion of politics over ideas, since while almost all the interesting ideas were of necessity global (the very idea of the sovereign nation was eroding), all of the interesting politics were of necessity local. American parochialism probably also had something to do with the issue of empire: small nations are per force deeply concerned with the world around them. Empires are notoriously opaque to the domains they rule. Although they have every reason to be sensitive to the regions they conquer, especially when they have done so by culture and currency (in our case, the hot dog and the dollar) rather than by the battleship and the sword, empires frequently lose their grip, whether through insensitivity or inattention.

The irrationality of ordinary Americans on the subject of foreign policy is ridiculous to the point of being quite comical. In a now famous poll taken by the University of Maryland a year into Clinton's first term (1994), respondents were asked three questions: how much they thought the United States spent on foreign aid as a percentage of its budget, whether this was too much or too little, and what an appropriate figure might be.[2] The median answer to the first question was about 15 percent—a figure that, answering the second question, more than two-thirds of the respondents thought was far too high. They opted for a cut on the average to about 5 percent of the national budget. The trouble is, the actual figure for U.S. foreign aid is less than 1 percent! So that, in their obliviousness and antiforeign biases, most Americans were inadvertently requesting a fivefold increase in actual spending when they thought they were requesting a two-thirds reduction in spending on the basis of fantastic figures they conjured up in their nightmares.

For all the persistence of antiforeign biases in his constituents, for his own part Clinton did become as intellectually engaged in the neglected world abroad as in the favored world at home, if not in that first Camp David seminar, certainly by the time the Gingrich revolution swept through Congress (many of the new Republican victors were quasi-isolationists). Ideas led him there, and although they were not always evident in his politics, they surely contributed to his picture of the world, where he allowed ideas to lead. He did little, however, to apply politically and in practice the opinions about which he enthused in theory (a more general complaint about this president in nearly every sphere of action). His administration reacted to the world only as it impinged on the administration and the nation. Ireland, the Middle East, middle Europe, and the issues of war and peace they called up could hardly be avoided; and Russia (Chechnya, nuclear weapons, and economic ruin), Mexico (NAFTA and the economic crisis) and China (trade and more trade) obviously demanded attention, if only as an extension

[2] The poll was taken by the University of Maryland's Program on International Policy Attitudes.

of the American politics of economic policy. There was, these concerns notwithstanding, no systematic and proactive anticipatory framework for dealing with foreign affairs. There was Dayton for Yugoslavia and Wye and Camp David for the Middle East, but such marathon summits, though they displayed the charisma of the president and gave foreign leaders a glimpse of the seductiveness of which he was capable, proved unsuccessful in resolving in a week or two conflicts that had been bred by centuries of enmity and war. For the rest, American parochialism prevailed.

Historically, there have been those who welcome such parochialism, whether it is calculated or inadvertent. Isolationism was not just a matter of know-nothingism; it was born of the conviction that America had little to gain from meddling in the corrupting affairs of a world beyond its shores, and that its best foreign policy (the Monroe Doctrine) was to stay out of the other hemisphere and keep that world out of this hemisphere. The debate continues in America about whether, in a democracy, reactive pragmatism is not preferable to a five-year plan" style of holistic planning. This debate aside, for better or worse, Clinton was no Nixon, and he had no Kissinger to contemplate innovative global strategies on his behalf. Kissinger critics, including me, could only feel relieved about this initially, although we soon came to hanker for a more Kissinger-like and systematic approach.

The president allowed the small-bore parochialism that often served him quite well in domestic policy to prevail also in international affairs, where it had less fortunate consequences. There had to be a place between visionary imperialism and stutter-step reactivism—a place for a kind of far-horizon pragmatism that took into account the long term without trying to impose some rigid paradigm on the rapidly changing international scene. Clinton's staff reinforced only the reactive, short-term tendencies, however, with all the foolish intellectual pettiness and wise political acumen of men and women dedicated to politics as provincialism. Not that there was anything novel about self-important parochialism.

Back in 1977 I had commiserated with friends working on the foreign policy side of the Carter administration who had daily to confront Carter's Georgia mafia provincialism. Gary Sick, who was the point man on the National Security Council on Middle Eastern Affairs and actually became semifamous during the Iranian hostage crisis, and

William Maynes, who was deputy secretary for international security affairs at State and a clear voice of reason on foreign affairs in the administration, both had to swim against the tide of the Georgia parochials who ran Carter's White House. President Carter (a southerner like Clinton) was little engaged in foreign policy issues. In the American heartland, Midwest or South, away from the oceans and the borders and the immigrants, it is understandably easy to feel comfortable with parochialism. It's harder in the Southwest, where Mexico beckons from across the Rio Grande, or on the two coasts, where New Yorkers and Angelos per force are confronted with the world across the two oceans that lap up to their doorsteps, yielding a regular tide of immigrants year in and year out.

White House journalists are often more cosmopolitan than the people they cover. Bill Shirer (*The Rise and Fall of the Third Reich*), with whom I had shared a sailboat and weekly gin and bitter lemons during the last ten years of his life when we had become friends, was a shining example of cosmopolitanism in times when, ironically, both the United States and Nazi Germany shunned cosmopolitanism and made a virtue of their splendid isolation. Although one was a great democracy, and the other a fledgling tyranny, neither belonged to the League of Nations, and both played at moral righteousness disguised as diffidence—despite the power both exercised. Reporting from Berlin in the thirties, Shirer bridged the gulf, insisting that know-nothing democratic Americans should know more than they wanted to know about know-nothing fascistic Nazis in the new *Reich*.

In the 1970s Roderick MacLeish was doing much the same for American radio audiences, traipsing around the world after presidents who would have rather stayed home, and helping Americans figure out why it was important that presidents didn't stay home. I was a senior Fulbright scholar in Britain in 1977 when Carter's first summit was held in London. MacLeish took me along to the *New York Times* London Bureau chief Johnny Apple's flat, where Carter's senior staff had repaired for R&R after a first, exhausting day. Embodying the smalling parochialism of presidential staffers ever since, the future chief of staff Ham Jordan regaled us with the keen insights of a first-time traveler: "Damn, did ya know they drive on the wrong side of the road?" and "Have you tasted the beer? I mean it's warm. Warm! Would you believe?" or "Is that supposed to be English they talk? Damn if I can understand a word." Jody Powell, Carter's rather more worldly press secretary, was a little more reticent, nodding in a kind of circular head rotation that left it ambiguous whether he was embracing or disdaining the dribble coming from Jordan's fatigue-loosened mouth. The man responsible for organizing, advising, and supporting the free world's democratic leader at that leader's first summit at the height of the cold war then summed up his impression of America's closest ally: "Well, maybe they talk English, but I'm telling you this is a foreign country, about as foreign as it gets." The mood was light, the journalists were laughing at this powerful rube's pugnacious naïveté, but his words come back to me every time I hear some White House staffer or Capitol Hill congressman complaining like a fraternity boy on a mandatory junior-year-abroad bus tour about the "damn fureneers" who forchrissakes can hardly speak English, and when do we get to go home to good ol' Alpha Epsilon on the Potomac anyway?

Was this how presidents carried on with their staff in private? Was George Bush's vomiting at a state dinner in Japan a public clue to his private views of the world beyond America? Does his son's revanchist cold war unilateralism betray the same disdain? What were we to make of all those congressfolks who never had occasion to apply for a passport, all those White House aides sitting in our semicircle in Johnny Apple's modest flat, cursing our allies? If the Brits are bad, imagine what would be said about the friggin' frogs! about the whole despised world outside the U.S. of A., nothing but a bunch of goddamn foreigners with their anti-American envy festering just below the surface of their pro-American rhetoric and their hypocritical private greediness for the American goodies they loved to put down in their public rhetoric.

The idea of America seemed to exclude the ideas of the world, interdependence, and integration. Ham Jordan was the vulgarian version of Melville's Captain Delano—the commander of the American frigate portrayed by Melville in his *Benito Cereno* as disgusted to the point of incomprehension at the equally repugnant antics of a slave boat crew and its rebellious cargo of slaves.

Now, Bill Clinton surely was no vulgarian on the model of Ham Jordan on such issues. He'd been a Rhodes scholar at Oxford and as a student had gotten around Europe. His natural curiosity and his ubiquitous empathy for the strangeness of others made him a favorite of people elsewhere in the world. Yet, for all his earnest protestations on behalf of American workers and third-world peasants likely to react violently and jihadically to first-world market depredations, for all of his subtlety in his portrait of McWorld's dark side, his foreign policy was mostly shortsighted and simplistic. Policy payoffs on the theories he spun were rarely evident in a foreign policy game where free trade always seemed the trump card and neoliberal laissez-faire market fundamentalism was obviously the ruling ideology.

Clinton was no bumpkin, but his foreign policy practice seemed to be at some distance from his own vision, as if he put on the tourist's ugly-American suit every time he stuck his head out the door. It was never clear whether his elevation of trade to trump card status was the result of political opportunism (the president serves American business first and unions, jobs, and third-world children last), the path of least resistance (globalization is inevitable and ubiquitous, so go with the flow), or a consequence of carefully considered strategic planning (we have weighed all the alternatives and concluded that support for free trade is in America's and the world's long-term interest, even after its considerable costs are calculated). What was clear was that Clinton never got around to walking the talk he had so eloquently trotted out on behalf of my critique of McWorld at that September religious breakfast in 1995. He failed as a hard-nosed free trader: he got only forty, or one-fifth, of his own party in Congress to vote for his failed "fast track" legislation (which would have given him discretion in negotiating trade treaties—Bush will try again). He wasn't much more successful as a soft critic of hard-nosed free trade. His calls for transparency and democratization came to seem like meaningless rhetoric in light of the actual policy positions adopted by his trade and economic deputies and hence his administration. That is why Ralph Nader seemed so convincing—on this issue and this issue alone—in the 2000 presidential campaign where he insisted there was nothing to distinguish the two parties or their candidates in the arena of the global economy. It's also why street rebels picketed *both* party conventions with equal vitriol.

Yet what a rhetorical job Clinton did the morning he hawked my book! Had he only found a way to inject some part of his democratic reluctance to incorporate McWorld into his policies and allowed the caveats he entered with respect to the IMF and the WTO to influence his legislative agenda, Nader would have been deprived of his entrée into campaign politics and Al Gore would be president today.

The annual prayer breakfast appearance at the White House that year had a Cal Ripkin theme. Ripkin had just broken the baseball record for consecutive games played, and had become an exemplary text for Clinton's frequent paeans on behalf of persistence and reliability, which Clinton saw as underrated moral values in our fast-moving, promise-averse society. Yet the new global economy, with its emphasis on "flexible labor" (read no unions, no pensions, no security!) did not always recognize loyalty and good-faith effort. We need "to include all Americans in the bounty of America," he said—inclusion was a litany in his administration—but it's not always so easy to do. Then he said something about how he'd cited a study of religion by Stephen Carter (a participant in one of our seminars a couple of years earlier), and now wanted to cite another relevant book.

"I've been reading this . . . a fascinating book by Benjamin Barber, whom I have the privilege to know," he said—and then, like a spirited carnival broker, he actually held up the book, title out to the cameras, and looked at it approvingly as he scanned its title. The consummate performer, he sounded out the syllables Arkansas style—"Ji-haad versus Mac-World," he said, with a "funny title, huh?" lilt in his voice, and then waited for the little trickle of laughter that his emphatic pronunciation of so peculiar a phrase would surely (he knew) elicit and quickly did. He went on, anticipating Seattle's blustery outrage against globalization by four or five years, to limn the book's themes: "Now let me tell you what the essential argument is, let me tell you why I believe it's important," he began, still waving the book.

"Mr. Barber is arguing that democracy and the ability to hold people together and have reliable, predictable good lives for people who work hard and do the right thing [Cal Ripkin] is being threatened today first of all by the globalization of the economy, which has a lot of benefits for those of us who have good educations and can benefit from it . . . with the movement of money and technology all across the world." Clinton had it exactly right.

"But it's elevating consumerism to even higher and higher levels and promoting short-term gains. We watch this money, we watch it every day, billions and trillions of dollars moving across the globe in the split of an eye. . . . It's very hard in those conditions to preserve even in the wealthy powerful countries the conditions of stable ordinary lives." In his schoolmarm mode now, the president was a superb explainer.

"Therefore you see what happens in America, we have seven million new jobs, we have all these things, and what happens is that the good but mostly hourly wage earners are working harder for the same or less than ten years ago. And a lotta people feel insecure in their jobs because the economy is changing so much, and they have no confidence that if they lose the job they have, they can get another one that's just as good or better." Now he was ready to put it all together—Ripkin, McWorld, the winners, the losers, the costs to democracy:

"So we're moving in this global economy and where there are a whole lotta women . . . a lotta people who think even if they do just like Cal Ripkin and the Virginia bus driver [another paragon of reliability Clinton was referencing during this period] do, they think they may still lose. That's a big problem for America. People think: they're willing to show up every day, they're working hard, they're doing right by their kids, they wouldn't break the law, they wouldn't cheat the government out of a nickel on their taxes, they wouldn't begin doing anything wrong, and they still may not make it. This is a problem for Americans."

Yes, it is. It was then, it is even more now. It was this "problem" that fueled the protests in Seattle, that energized both Pat Buchanan's and Ralph Nader's 2000 presidential campaigns, and that today gives union protectionism the glow of democratic idealism. President Clinton saw early on, saw it and understood it brilliantly. But he didn't do much about it. The political winds were blowing buckets of money the other way, and there wasn't much political gain to be had from worrying about "Mollie's job," the kind William Adler recently described in his touching and disturbing book with this title about the migration of jobs to Mexico: jobs that once raised up and sustained aspiring working-class American families—black and white—but today merely exploit low-wage Mexican workers without sustaining them or their families at all.[3] Union members like Mollie were no longer sovereign in the Democratic Party (union membership was down from over 30 million to fewer than 12 million, and white non-union workers had become a critical swing vote), and many of those most vulnerable to globalization's

[3] See Adler, *Mollie's Job: A Story of Life and Work on the Global Assembly Line* (New York: Scribner, 2000). This and other recent works are discussed at length in my "Globalization and Its Discontents: Winners and Losers in the New Economy," *Los Angeles Times Book Review*, August 12, 2000.

costs were undereducated nonvoters or foreigners. By the end of Clinton's presidency, the "problem" had worsened and left the presidential candidate Al Gore wondering how to hold off a wave of protectionism from the populist Right as well as the populist Left without having to give up on free trade. Clinton himself had grown more vocal on the issue, upsetting his own trade team with a call for a more transparent, inclusive, and democratic WTO in Seattle in 1999. But other than for the inconvenience of a little moralizing rhetoric, the banner of free trade flew freely in both political parties, and an intellectual assessment of its potential costs had little impact on the practical assessment of its economic gains—particularly in an era where economics trumped politics, and Clinton's own politics of the market economy trumped the moralizing in which he tended to engage at high-minded events like our seminars and the annual religious breakfasts.

I had tried to bridge the gap between moral posturing and practical politics, spending a good deal of the precious currency I had in exchanging ideas with the president advancing what I hoped was a realist argument for the growing meaninglessness of the boundary that separated national and international. Traditionally, frontiers were territorial, physical. The new economy was virtual, however, and transnational interactions, whether around ecology or disease, financial speculation or crime, trade or drugs, investment or terrorism, had little respect for such antique barriers. I wanted the president to use his schoolmarm manner to educate Americans to these new realities. After all, he was Robin Williams in that anti-academic hit film *The Dead Poets Society* rather than Mr. Chips, Britain's heroic but hide-bound scholastic. He was carpe diem all the way, the subversive, seductive teacher grabbing destiny by its lapels and shaking it—a teacher to whom foreign-policy-averse Americans might actually listen. He could show them that their isolationist realism, once so well grounded, had been overtaken by time. The bridge to the twenty-first century crossed national frontiers and spanned a virtual world.

Yes, America's traditional parochialism, even in its most fabulist incarnation, had once had a kind of convincing realist base, rooted in eighteenth-century notions of a young and innocent nation of Puritans protected from the corruptions of a decadent, history-burdened Europe by two vast oceans and an Edenic ideology that cast America as a place where one might literally (Tom Paine) "start the world over again."

That was the source of Captain Delano's New England disdain for the slave ship shenanigans in *Benito Cereno*. The world had changed, however. ICBMs, computers, and then the Internet along with the economic interdependence that these innovations had spawned had destroyed such geographically grounded dreams forever. In 1995 there was no longer anything "realist" about fables of innocence and isolation. Though some still thought (and think) a missile shield might replace the oceans and wrap America in a kind of technological cocoon, a virtual ocean that rogue states and evil tyrants and corrupt societies will never cross, they now sound less and less like hard-headed Puritan warriors and more and more like fools. Not that fools do not, as ever before, abound.

Yet surely a modern man, a boomer like Clinton, knew better and could bring the message of the necessity of interdependence to a public schooled in radical individualism and the idea of absolute independence. His own vice-president was a champion of global environmentalism and a protagonist of the new telecommunications technologies. So it didn't seem a stretch for me to make the case over and over again, in memo after memo offering textbook speech examples of "local" problems that had global antecedents (such as pollution), and in drafts of speeches showing how national policies could be successful only when they were internationalized (as with trade sanctions). It was not the arrogance of unilateralism—whether isolationist or interventionist— that was the problem, it was that it didn't work. As the new administration is learning the hard way.

Still, Clinton ultimately seemed as trapped in the imagined cocoon of an island America as Reagan had been and George W. Bush would be. His intellect roamed freely and his capacity for seductive personal interaction clearly knew no cultural or parochial boundaries. He had few of the enemies abroad he had garnered at home and, despite the absence of major successes toward the end of his term, had a sterling reputation beyond American shores (except in the Islamic world). But his politics trapped him, not only because they were local rather than global but also because they failed to see that the local could no longer be distinguished from the global. The slogan "Think globally, act locally!" might work for neighbors and citizens, but for a president it was the other way around: what was required of Clinton was that he think locally but act globally: that he show how and why internationalism mattered in the neighborhoods, how the global impacted on the local, and then, projecting American power, act globally. A politics of poll-driven compromise that followed rather than led could never let him move very far from the public he should have been educating. Too often he ended up acting unilaterally, or exclusively in terms of American economic interests. Unilateralism in international affairs is simply a particularly nefarious version of parochialism. As Americans were parochial, Clinton was parochial. As they reviled foreigners, he simply ignored them except when being leaned on by the State Department or the National Security Council.

BETWEEN
HOPE AND HISTORY

To Benjamin Barber

with appreciation

for your wise counsel and
your love for America —
we will find a way beyond
McWorld + Jihad.

Bill Clinton
9-7-96

I'm not sure he shared Reagan's Hollywood innocence, but at the end of his second term he seemed to embrace the Reaganesque fantasy of an America rendered forever safe from the crafty and depraved tyrants of the outside world by the very technology that had made America so vulnerable. He did not make the missile shield a priority, as George W. Bush would do after him, but probably only because the tests were so disastrous—hitting a missile with a missile, especially when the incoming missile is accompanied by dummies and decoys, is very, very hard—and the opposition of scientists (which in most matters would be decisive for him) was so intense. Nonetheless, like Reagan, he conceived of New Star Wars as a combined product of American ingenuity and American beneficence—a shield not only for innocent America but for all nations of good will. He never could figure out why those whose interests our beneficence would supposedly benefit were so ungrateful, how it could it be that not just Russia and China but Germany and France—our allies!—saw the shield as provocative and destabilizing. But Americans never really see themselves as others see them: the powerful discount their own power and inflate the significance of the moral rationales they deploy to legitimize such power as they admit to having.

Bill Clinton also shared with Ronald Reagan the conviction that personality might drive foreign policy, that his regal sun might actually melt the hard and frozen facts on the ground that defined intransigent foreign policy conflicts like those in Yugoslavia, Ireland, and The Middle East. He thought he might literally *will* change, might budge immovable realities by dint of pure volition. In a final display of that illusion, he ended his term believing he might impose his vast personality on the stark enmities and interest oppositions of the Middle East. He cajoled Prime Minister Barak of Israel and dragged Chairman Arafat to Camp David to reach a final settlement for which the ground had not been prepared (as Arafat told him). Like a parapsychic working his will on a rigid spoon, he was sure that persistence could eventually get it to bend, and in the last weeks of his term he mounted a final, futile offensive aimed at Barak and Arafat. But he could not talk the world into peace anymore than he could talk his own country into forgiveness for scandal and prevarication. He was a great and efficacious seducer, but there are arenas of contention not subject to the seducer's wiles. Words can change realities on the ground, but they also can be undone by those same realities and in turn screw up the "realities." At Camp David the president tried to seduce men into arrangements that instead, ungrounded and undid the men. When narcissism wrapped in words works, it appears nearly miraculous. When it fails, it can be catastrophic.

Problematic affairs, whether international or personal, are produced by more than words, and words cannot undo the harms and grievances they precipitate. In Philadelphia, Kissinger had warned against pursuing a policy of mere words. I sent Clinton an account of Kissinger's performance in Philadelphia, a performance in which he endorsed the visit to China that Clinton had just concluded, but warned, "You can't give the impression that a two-hour conversation, that ten days of tourism plus homilies, can take the place of long, hard negotiation." Would that Clinton had recalled this Kissinger homily before insisting on a Camp David finale to his Middle East interventions. Indeed, had Clinton but pondered his own baseball metaphor, he might have eschewed so recklessly heroic an effort. His model, after all, was not to be the home run hitter with the .350 batting average who, a loner, sets team records for a club that never wins; it was instead Cal Ripkin showing up every day, year in and year out, with a decent batting average and a strong slugging percentage, someone who's there all the way through, and can perhaps help his club win a pennant over an entire season.

I don't blame Clinton for ignoring Kissinger; I've spent much of my life resisting power realism. But on method he had a point. You have to do the little things in global affairs to be relevant at the big moments. A president wedded to drama may not have patience for the little things, the "long, hard negotiations" that must pave the way to real agreements signed at summits. Nor did Clinton seem to have many staffers who understood this. Weaned on the photo op and well-placed morning newspaper coverage, they did little to combat Clinton's impatience and his faith in his own power to seduce and hence to settle intractable conflicts by sheer personality.

I had a couple of immediate experiences of the short-term provincialism of a protective staff. The context was trivial but perhaps for that all the more telling. Twice I had urged the president's staff to welcome at the White House eminent foreign intellectual journalists—once for an audience with Clinton, once with Mrs. Clinton. Both times I was rebuffed (not a surprise) with silly and shortsighted pro forma explanations (more disturbing). The bottom-line response in both cases was the same: why on earth should the president or the first lady waste his or her time on *foreigners*? (Unless, of course, they are in power and must be seen for reasons of protocol, alliance strategy, or policy.)

My first candidate was Jean Daniel, the founder and longtime editor of the distinguished French weekly *Le Nouvel Observateur*, a cross between *Time* magazine and the *New Republic* (in its more liberal days) that had become, if not France's most eminent weekly, certainly among its best. I had meet Daniel in Paris in the midnineties because, like Clinton, he had read and liked *Jihad vs. McWorld* and had organized and participated in a public debate on the French edition that included the former prime minister Michel Rocard and myself at the legendary Cirque d'Hiver in Paris. In France, where politicians are often intellectuals (no one goes through tortuous self-reflection about it), proposing an idea to a political figure is second nature (of course, that may explain why French policy so often goes off the rails). Not long after my public debate, Jean Daniel was preparing a special issue of *Le Nouvel Observateur* on the United States, and he had the notion that he would interview Clinton for the cover story and bring to his French readers an intimate sense of a leader about whom, during his first term, the French knew little. This seemed to me to be of potentially tremendous usefulness, because France remained the fly in America's European policy ointment. Whenever Germany and England said yes to the United States, France said no. Although France was America's "sister republic" and had in the early years of the Republic been an even more loyal ally than England, it also was frequently the bee in America's NATO bonnet and the thorn in its foreign policy side. It had refused overflight rights when the U.S. Air Force was bombing Libya, insisted long ago on developing its own independent nuclear force (*force de frappe*), resisted American culture with its left hand (subsidizing its film industry and trying to impose quotas on American films as if they were vegetables), even as it welcomed it with its right (bestowing honors on celebrities like Sharon Stone and Sylvester Stallone and other less gifted actors who really were vegetables), and generally getting in America's face every time America stuck that face into Europe. In this climate of endemic anti-Americanism, a sympathetic Clinton cover story in the leading French leftist newsweekly would surely be a blessing, especially in a period when the Republicans had just won the Congress.

There was a personal side as well to Jean Daniel's desire for an interview, one that I imagined would make overtures doubly welcome in

Washington. Daniel, who had come out of the French resistance during the war and been catapulted into a glittering career as a writer, intellectual, and journalist in the fifties, had founded the *Nouvel Obs* as part of a unifying progressive vision for Europe. As a young editor he had won an interview with a young president named Kennedy, who leaned toward and was adored in Europe. This interview had helped launch the large reputation of both Daniel and his magazine and had contributed at least a little to Kennedy's somewhat inflated reputation in Europe. Wouldn't it be an inspired closing of time's circle if (as he explained it to me) Jean Daniel, now approaching the end of his career, could interview the young Clinton, as once he had interviewed the young Kennedy, whom Clinton so admired and with whom Clinton had himself won a much publicized audience when he was but a boy? Surely the serendipity of this overlay of historical events would astonish and please both Daniel's French readers and the president's legacy-hungry handlers—and, above all, Clinton himself of course.

There were, however, no Bouviers or Salingers or Schlesingers with their French connections, no Jackie Kennedy with her French confections, no Francophile interlopers to make the case for Europe's importance to Bill Clinton. To the bighearted but small-minded staffers around the president, Europe wasn't important and Daniel was just some foreign reporter trying to weasel his way onto the busy president's schedule, using the not very subtle and certainly not very effective tool of me, a sometime outside "adviser" who apparently thought he had more influence than he did. The '96 elections were approaching, and my friends in the White House said things like "It's a good idea, Ben, but let's face it, how many votes does Daniel bring? I mean it's not like Hungary or Italy, where maybe there'd be some indirect political payoff." Or "Look, Barber, France is not exactly our closest ally in Europe, and if the prez does *that* magazine, how many other overseas guys are gonna be lining up for an interview?" Quite a few, I hoped; that was the point! Free international publicity, foreign policy on the cheap! Then I'd rush past the forming frowns of this or that staffer, insisting it was exactly because France wasn't our most reliable ally that the president's interview would count for something. And then, this was my closer, I'd recite the Kennedy story again and say how surely Clinton wouldn't want to do less than Kennedy, and how Daniel would inevitably flatter Clinton by writing about him in the glow of Kennedy's Camelot legacy—I mean, Clinton could surely use a little Camelot imagery abroad, could-n't he? "We'll get back to you," they'd conclude in a tone that made clear I'd tried their patience and they'd never actually get back to me at all on this request. And they never did. And the president never made the cover of the *Nouvel Obs*. And nobody noticed or cared.

With Mrs. Clinton, I thought I had a better shot. My candidate for an interview was not a suspect Frenchman from a country with few immi-grant American voters but a celebrated dissident who had helped bring democracy to a country that was extremely well represented in the Democratic Party's electoral demography—Adam Michnik, Solidarity's hero and today the editor of Poland's largest and most influential news-paper. In addition to his heroic Polish identity, Michnik was a leading European intellectual with considerable influence in scholarly and journalistic circles. We had spent several beer-lubricated European evenings arguing in variously inflected bad French about the responsi-bility "model" democracies like America had not simply to "export" their indigenous institutions to emerging post-communist societies but to support local civil society and encourage something more than free markets open to Western investors. When Michnik wrote to say he wanted an interview with Hillary during a visit she was making to Poland, I was thrilled on behalf of the White House. I naïvely assumed Michnik was the sort of democratic figure whom the first lady and, yes, the president too, would want to invite to the White House even if Mich-nik had shown no interest in coming, someone about whom the Com-munications Office could boast, a figure worthy of the president's own formidable intellect and of the first lady's penetrating intelligence. And all I was asking for was half an hour for Michnik with the first lady. I fig-ured they'd probably welcome the chance and ask, to boot, whether the president could take part.

No deal. Michnik was another foreigner. Nobody I spoke with seemed to know who he was, though they shook their heads appreciatively at the mention of Solidarity and nodded with the grave respect due to a long-dead uncle who had once done something admirable though nobody could remember exactly what it was. They didn't really take much of an interest when I tried to explain his hero's pedigree and cur-rent standing in Poland (where, like Clinton, he'd moved somewhat to the center, making him an even more useful interlocutor for the White House). It simply wasn't going to happen, I was told. Sorry.

Now, the president and first lady of the United States have schedules from hell and have to say no to a great many worthy proposals. I understand that. They also have to entertain all possible varieties of domestic citizens' groups and civil associations in the White House—champion sports teams, select Boy Scout troops, irate consumer representatives, touring Young Democrat fan clubs—especially where a photo op with one or another such group can highlight a significant issue or provide cover for a controversial policy initiative, and this can eat up a schedule pretty quickly. But to refuse interviews with heavyweights as considerable as Jean Daniel and Adam Michnik simply because they were not American in the face of the procession of domestic featherweights who passed regularly through the White House struck me as a pathetic emblem of all the contradictions from which America's reluctant imperialism suffered. If this was to be written off as one more consequence of an unavoidable provincialism, how costly it was!

Or perhaps it was because those like me who use words and ideas always overestimate their value to those who work the world successfully without them. The Congress was widely acknowledged to be a home both to intellectual indifference and to arrogant parochialism. Until recently, fewer than half of the members of the House of Representatives and scarcely a single member of the gang of eighty Gingrich had brought to the House in 1994 had ever even applied for a passport—unthinkable in any other Western parliament and no longer the case in ours, I am relieved to report. But the White House carried the responsibility for the conduct of foreign policy, and dealt primarily in the currency of words (what else did it have, unless it actually deployed the Marines?). Surely it had to compensate for the provincialism of the other two branches with a passion for what went on beyond America's shores. Surely it had to be eager to make its case when the wordsmiths from overseas came calling.

Or not. President Clinton, like many of his predecessors, seemed in the end to prefer a hardy unilateralism: a standoff foreign policy that mimicked the better-safe-than-effective standoff strategy of the U.S. Air Force in Serbia, where our planes maintained an altitude of at least fifteen thousand feet, beyond the reach of antiaircraft fire and missile defenses, if also effectively beyond the range of their own weaponry. We lost not a single pilot, though, as it turned out, Milošević lost precious little of his military arsenal either, and emerged remarkably unscathed from his confrontation with the great empire, falling only years later to the democratic aspirations of his own restive population, which continued to revile the United States even as it ousted him.

Reactive not proactive, standoff rather than engaged, prophylactic in the technical sense of wearing a condom but rarely preventive, America under Clinton simply didn't have a foreign policy commensurate with Clinton's own analysis of the global situation. As in so many other domains, he seemed to subordinate his innate intelligence to the demands of a dumber, but perhaps more efficacious politics. Neither Warren Christopher nor Madeleine Albright was a visionary (Richard Holbrooke had perhaps the clearest worldview but was stuck like Adlai Stevenson and Arthur Goldberg in the dead-end post up in New York that was the U.S. Mission to the United Nations). The dominant players were process mavens, and pretty efficient ones to boot. Both Christopher and Albright made the right noises about democracy, and toward the end of her term Albright helped engineer a "Community of Democracies" caucus that brought together over one hundred "democracies" (it's actually impossible to find a hundred democracies in today's world, so count in Peru and Pakistan and their ilk) in conjunction with a world forum on democracy being held by nongovernmental organizations in Warsaw at the same moment. But this was mostly talk.

So was the Berlin gathering that Clinton and Blair and Schröder hosted, also in June of 2000, to debate the Third Way with a handful of allies, a gathering that produced a document whose main achievement was to replace the language of "third way" politics into the language of "progressive governance."[4] The declaration that issued from the meeting—"The Berlin Communiqué: Progressive Governance for the 21st Century"—contains mostly pleasant-sounding, if harmless, rhetoric along the lines of "the key task of progressive governance in the new century is to help people make the most of change, by providing the tools for them to fulfill their talents in the new world that is being created." Economic globalization and free trade were embraced with the proviso that they not become "a destructive race to the bottom at the

---

[4] Participating states included Argentina, Brazil, Chile, Canada, New Zealand, and South Africa, as well as, in Europe, France, Holland, Greece, Italy, Portugal, Britain, and Germany—all states with "progressive" governments on the new center left to which most older Labor and Social Democratic parties had repaired to rewin power in countries that had moved to the neoliberal right.

expense of environmental and worker protections" even though that was exactly what they had become. International economic institutions were recognized along with a call for more transparency and accountability and a "more inclusive and sustainable division of wealth and opportunity." Noises on behalf of humanity, while actual policies and institutions continue to grow and prosper at humanity's expense. The columnist Bill Safire once wrote that Clinton thought of himself as a "lovable old rogue who can make a centrist waffle look like red meat."[5] In foreign policy this sometimes has the ring of truth.

Yet part of Clinton's foreign policy problem was that actual sovereignty was passing from the political to the economic arena, from democratic states with public constituencies to private firms with private concerns and private constituencies. This erosion of state sovereignty allows privatized policy to bypass the government altogether or, within government, to privilege the secretary of the treasury and the trade representative's office at the expense of foreign policy experts whether at the National Security Council or the State Department. As sovereignty has passed from the political to the economic domain, economic ministers have necessarily usurped some of the functions of political ministers. Robert Rubin was a more important player on NAFTA than Warren Christopher, Sandy Berger more key than Madeleine Albright on the initiative to allow China most-favored-nation status as a trade partner, and Alan Greenspan, the keeper of the Fed, may have outranked even Clinton in his ability to control the American economy and hence to set the tone for stability around the world. No wonder Clinton seemed at times to have little control over foreign policy, or that when he criticized the WTO and IMF in Seattle he sounded more like an irate citizen critic than a chief of state in a position to alter the policies he assailed.

Yet this development, too, was foreseen by Clinton in his religious breakfast address. He made clear that the economic fortunes of the world might impact crucially on political stability and cultural civility. His astute reading of *Jihad vs. McWorld* noted that the Jihadic and tribal fundamentalisms rooted in anti-Western, anticapitalist antiAmericanism that so destabilized the world were not just reactions to McWorld but depended on the success of the new economy for its virulent opposition

[5] Safire, "Bill's Third Acceptance," *New York Times*, August 14, 2000, A21.

to it. McWorld precipitated Jihad not only in the Islamic fundamentalist Arab world but in modern Europe as well: in France, for example, where the government had launched an attack on "franglais" and Hollywood's global incursions into local culture, and a farmer recently (in 2000) vandalized McDonald's to launch a national protest ("Attaq!") against American beef and bio-engineered food and in favor of the so-called Tobin tax on international currency transactions; and also in Italy, where partisans of cuisine as a part of culture launched their own "slow food" movement to counteract the ubiquitous McDonald's.

Clinton recognized that what passed as independent acts of rebellion, opposition, and even terrorism in the name of anti-Americanism might be linked to the imprudent expansion of global markets and transnational corporate power, and hence to the loss of democratic transparency and accountability. This recognition meant that Trea-sury Secretary Rubin and Trade Representatives Larry Summers and Sandy Berger were not only foreign policy troubleshooters patrolling the new porous frontiers of the international economy, but indirectly responsible for policies that had political and cultural consequences—often quite reactionary—they seemed unable to anticipate or deal with. Consequently, even as these Beltway optimists rhapsodized about the glories of global trade, cantankerous pessimists such as Samuel Huntington were penning tomes prophesying a "clash of global civi-lizations" in which Chinese hordes backed by militant Islamic elites would make global war on isolated America.[6]

When Clinton described to religious leaders how globalization can threaten democracy, whereas its purpose should be to serve it, he limned a foreign policy that might have aimed at retrieving democratic sovereignty from the limbo of economic anarchy. A consistent strategy along these lines would place democracy and regulation of the inter-national economy in the name of public goods over the private interests of those who benefited from global markets and restore a modicum of democratic sovereignty to the anarchic international realm.

Of course, this would have brought the president up against the old debate in American foreign policy about whether a prudential pragma-tism wedded to interests (usually, although not always, economic) is not

[6] See Huntington, *The Clash of Civilizations and the Remaking of World Order* (New York: Simon & Schuster, 1996).

only a more effective but also a safer course for American foreign policy than the kind of moralizing that President Wilson employed on the way to a failed foreign policy, or that John Kennedy and LBJ used to dig the nation deep into the Southeast Asian quagmire. Many critics of America prefer a pragmatic and restrained imperialism based on tangible interests to a moralizing democracy in whose name whole countries are colonized or, worse, like Vietnam, destroyed in the name of rescuing them.

More important, pursuing a democratic rather than an economic internationalism would have brought the president squarely up against the powerful business interests with which he had finally reconciled the Democratic Party, and whose support he believed he needed in order to continue to govern as a New Democrat shunning "class war" and economic divisiveness. For better or worse, he was clearly not prepared to pursue so confrontational a strategy (nor was Al Gore, despite the warmed-over populism of the 2000 campaign). Without a degree of confrontation, no warm words about the perils of globalization and no glib internationalist rhetoric of the kind found in the Berlin communiqué will make much difference. The same old lesson: words may create policy, but they can't enact or enforce policy, and since the global economy is already fully enacted—an extant reality—it is well beyond the rebuke of mere words.

Words being this president's primary currency, however, I sometimes daydream about what Clinton will do with the storehouse of them he has accumulated, and with his seducer's potency to deploy them effectively, in his next life, the one after his presidency ends. That's what an affair with Clinton does for you: you end up dreaming not about your own destiny but about his, not about the interdiction of your own aspirations but about the realization of his.

My daydream about him is that he will become the first "president of the world." Not literally, of course. There's no such office, and even the most innocent World Federalist will hesitate to predict the coming of world government anytime in our own or our children's lifetime. But Clinton's empathy, his penchant for seductive and persuasive talk, his belief that words can somehow trump realities, lends itself to a kind of moral leadership on behalf of global civil society and global governance, if not global government. His popularity outside the United States is grand indeed, even where elites may regard him as a little naïve. But who

other than a naïve American could dream about an innocent pax demo-
cratica that united women and men across the world under the banner
of neither the United States nor the global economy but of a transnational civil society—an "international civic league" with its own
annual Davos-style networking meetings. Under Clinton's banner, this
league could energize the old national democracies to use their power to
recapture the international economy on behalf of public goods and to
fashion new international institutions that pool civic and governance
resources, giving peoples a framework for global cooperation and oversight—a pale shadow of global sovereignty, but far better than what we
have at present. A new global social compact (and that *is* what the Berlin
communiqué called for) would, like the traditional one, subordinate private to public power, and allow citizens to trump producers and consumers in making decisions about how the world is to be organized.

The intuitively internationalist statesman I heard riff on *Jihad vs.
McWorld* on C-SPAN, who spoke so movingly at half a dozen seminars
and sessions on the priority of democracy, and who displayed so infectious an intelligence in moving people to care as much about the sovereign "we" as about all the attention-grabbing "me's" is a man whose
democratic career is long from over. Despite the fragility of his legacy,
the ambiguities of his reputation, and the petulant rage of his adversaries, this is a man whose huge talents will be squandered if he contents himself, as he will surely be tempted to, with collecting back pay
from the corporate world he has served a little too well as president
instead of pledging himself to serve the global public goods about which
he has spoken so eloquently but done so little.

# CHAPTER ELEVEN

# Hillary Takes Over

**WITH CLINTON THERE ARE** always dreams. It's not just the cliché about how Monica's affair lights fires in every erotic imagination (though there's truth enough there). It's how easily Clinton's fleshy reality can reproduce its narcissistic omnipresence in the sleeping mind's eye. The stripping away of his public persona and the publicization of his private parts must surely make him the most dreamed-about president in the nation's history. George Stephanopoulos opens his memoir with a dream, and Philip Roth peppers *The Human Stain* with more than a few. In mine, Hillary is usually a presence secondary to the president. But in the one that disturbed my sleep recently (perhaps tracking her Senate campaign) it was Hillary who was ascendant: a warm maternal presence the clarity of which made the president seem fuzzy. My arm was around her waist with a kind of filial ease—I'm older than she is, but mothers are ageless, sons wither and die— while I chatted casually with her husband. It was on the steps of the White House portico, or perhaps it was a New York Club or Independence Hall standing in as a presidential venue. My psyche had seized on the woman the media didn't want to see, the female person they preferred to caricature as a steely-eyed ice bitch who had sold her defeminized soul for a Yale J.D. and a chance to ride her husband's career to the very end of ambition's horizon. They were wrong, of course (they are more or less always wrong). I say this not because she inhabited my dream as a suffusing female presence (a matter more of my wishfulness than of her reality) but because she so clearly inhabited her own life fully and powerfully without yielding her identity as a woman. She did the same, it seemed clear, in the president's life as well.

Wife or rival to Bill, his lover (for all the cynical detractors, that is not so improbable) or his nemesis, an inspiration or a scold, she is sufficiently embedded in his being to be part of his essence. And he part of hers. Which is why it was so hard for me to imagine—whatever the pain they inflicted on one another—that they could ever separate. Like Siamese twins in a premodern age, they'd bleed to death at the point where their two beings were severed, even if the surgery were performed with the best of intentions and in both of their interests.

So much of Hillary's ambiguous reputation seems to come from the ambiguity of feminism at the end of the century. Women are so much freer than they once were, and so much less free than they hoped to be or than men assume—in grumpy acknowledgment of the rights women have won—they are. Hillary was caught in the middle: the radicals hated her for her loyalty, which they understood only as dependency, while the conservatives insisted she was a rank opportunist, construing that same loyalty as a particularly raw variety of opportunistic careerism. She was too attached for feminists to whom liberty was impossible without total independence from men, but far too independent for traditionalists seeking some archetype of tribal motherhood and fealty to the patriarch. Chelsea was, they granted, living proof of Hillary's womanly adequacy, but Bill's promiscuity was taken as living counterproof, a devastating sign of her marital inadequacy—either because she couldn't keep her man or because she wouldn't leave him.

Enough. Such reveries belong to the dream domain that prompted them. They serve here only as a speculative prelude to the fugue that describes the complicated real-world dance between the two who, in almost every meeting I attended, appeared in tandem—except for the one I want to describe here. No wonder David Gergen spoke (without enthusiasm) about their "co-presidency." During the '92 campaign, candidate Clinton had said gaily, "Buy one, get one free." What changed was their relative positions in the evolving pas de deux they were forever executing. Sometime between the moment when President Clinton denied he had ever been involved with "that woman" and the moment his impeachment hearing ended three votes short of conviction, Bill Clinton's effective presidency more or less came to an end. He continued to be rhetorically active, to legislate and to enact small-bore stuff that made a difference, and to range around the world in search of last-minute peace accords that might secure abroad a legacy unlikely to be won at home. And he certainly continued to bully-pulpit popular opinion while straight-out bullying the Republican majority into various acts and deeds for which neither the populace generally nor the Congress in particular necessarily had much taste (like the opening of China to trade, which passed against the odds by an overwhelming majority in the fall of 2000). But though his numbers remained spectacularly high, he no longer enjoyed that comfort zone of leadership where he could expect success as a right or take chances in the name of principle (though he rarely did the latter under the best of circumstances). The hungry, but easily sated, collective psyche of America moved on. Clinton was deposed, a savory that had become too familiar. Those who hated him, no less than those who loved him, sought a fresh taste. The awkwardly earnest vice-president and the awkwardly ambitious first lady and, in time, that other deposed president's son with much more winning ways than his dad, George W. Bush Jr., would do nicely.

In late 1998 Al Gore began to emerge as an autonomous politician—a process completed at the Los Angeles convention a couple of years later. Qualities hard to detect when he walked loyally and quietly in Clinton's shadow, where wonkish fealty punctuated by occasional feints at independence were the only forms of self-expression he permitted himself, gradually came into view. His gifts as a political warrior, sublimated by the vice-presidential role, were less subtle but in fact fiercer even than Clinton's; they were fatally underestimated by Bill Bradley. George W. Bush Jr. also underestimated him initially, but eventually took his measure, pushed him back into awkwardness, and forced a close enough vote to defeat him by other means. Gore's stumbling self-consciousness, in which he could not even embrace his own authentic identity without rendering it somehow phony, came back into play at the worst possible moment. The presidential election of 2000 was not between Gore and Bush but between Gore the political warrior and Gore the media stumblebum, and the stumblebum vanquished the warrior by a hair's breadth.

The transformation of Hillary Clinton was even more stunning, not just because she toyed with and eventually became a candidate for the New York Senate seat vacated by her champion Patrick Moynihan, and not just because, where Gore lost, she won, but because by default she became to a degree the more politically active and perhaps the more politically relevant of the two persons who made up the first couple. They reversed their standard dance positions; she led while he followed. Some would say it was that way all along, others that it was his guilt exploited by her ambition that put her up front, and still others that he was faking it and, from behind the scenes, was still pulling all the strings. She certainly had a more loyal, maybe even more competent, staff than Bill Clinton, largely ignored by the media (as were White House women more generally). Monica they noticed, but Melanne Verveer's role in the White House has been largely neglected by the media, as have those of Ellen Lovell, Maria Echaveste, Ann Lewis and Elaine Kamarck. Why do journalists have such a hard time catching up with the Clintons when it comes to recognizing women of achievement? Hillary also adhered more firmly to principle than her husband—call it ideological rigidity or call it conviction. Either way, it was easier both to fix her nature and hence to trivialize it. When, in the normal course of a rough Senate campaign, she was forced to compromise and tack in order to walk a middle path, she did it with far less facility and authenticity than her husband (I mean this as a compliment, but I don't know to which of them).

I never felt anywhere near as close to her as I did to her husband, but I suspect that whatever little connection I had with her was more real (same thing with the vice-president). Too many people felt close to the president for it to be true: ubiquitous intimacy is an oxymoron, and it's probably just how we experience charisma. There was certainly no reason to expect just because she was married to him that Hillary would share the president's rare capacity for deep seduction of all those who came into his orbit—a capacity that in fact is only weakly captured by the term "charisma." The infatuated rarely see their seducer with clarity, and much of the intimacy they feel is generated by narcissistic *self*-proximity. I never worked directly with Hillary as I'd worked with the president—I was indirectly involved with her through the President's Bicentennial Commission, which she chaired. I had wholly satisfactory dealings with her (indirectly)—in no small part thanks to her chief of staff, Melanne Verveer, and her commission director, Ellen Lovell, two of the most level-headed staffers in the White House—loyal without being professional sycophants, tough but unbureaucratically humane.

I had encountered Hillary numerous times at our dinners and work sessions, and had been in the admiring audience when she discharged official duties (overseeing a bicentennial evening in the White House, touring a New England architectural restoration site, speaking at a community service event). But my interactions were mostly trivial: I had overseen a translation of pointed comments she made at the Davos World Economic Forum on global civil society for a French audience, and she had graciously made a "host" video and written statements for me to use at conferences I ran in France and America, cosponsored by the French and American Bicentennial Commissions. Otherwise, I had seen her mostly at the president's side—cohost, White House mistress, cool counselor.

I had one pivotal experience in her company that was telling, because it mimicked my experiences with the president and at the same time signaled her evolution into an astute and efficient politician in her own right. It also demonstrated how intractable was the underlying and undying and still undead debate between New Democrats and old Democrats that had defined White House policy evolution. The occasion of our meeting was the last of the White House seminars I participated in and one of the last held. The distractions of the impeachment hearings and the diminished openness of the White House in the last two years of the second term made the seminars dispensable. Ours that summer day in 1998 was noteworthy not because it was one of the last but because it featured not Bill Clinton but Hillary Clinton playing Bill Clinton—and beginning for the first time to find her own firm political footing. The first lady pulled off her new role with a panache that her earlier, tentative participation in seminars would not have led one to predict.

Our subject was (again) New Democrat ideology and its battle with old Democratic principles. We'd been at this for five years, and, despite the apparent White House victory of the New Democrats, there was still an appetite to do battle with the old—not because the old demanded it (they were far too weak to demand anything) but because the chief New Democrat was in this arena, as in every other, clearly still obsessed with bringing his adversaries into his camp, even at the expense of alienating his allies. Sid Blumenthal was orchestrating this meeting, but evidently following a script prepared by the Democratic Leadership Council itself. It was the summer of '98 just before the congressional

elections, and not only were the DLC's president, Al From, and its Progressive Policy Institute director, Will Marshall, present, but so were Bill
Galston, back in the academy but working with Barbara Whitehead on
a political "mapping" project surveying the Democratic Party's demographics in preparation for both the 1998 and the 2000 elections (the
so-called Blueprint series, eventually published by the Progressive
Policy Institute), and such old DLC White House hands as Bruce Reed
and Elaine Kamarck (who had departed the administration for Harvard's Kennedy School but would soon return to Al Gore's campaign
staff as a high-level policy counselor).

Although this was a full-blown strategic meeting at which senior
staff, including New Democratic friendlies like Ann Lewis, Paul Begala,
Michael Waldman, Melanne Verveer, and Maria Echaveste, were in
attendance, the chief New Democrat, President Clinton, was absent.
Notably absent, oddly absent, downright invisible. As if he'd been banished, had slunk off on a long vacation, and hadn't been heard from for
months. As if his presidency were over and Hillary now the president.
There she was, poised and upright at the head of the table (well, in the
middle), squarely in his place, listening discreetly, provoking us with
pointed questions, leading the discussion by purposeful indirection, a
Clinton all the way, but a Hillary Clinton. The (Bill) Clinton presidency
was dead! Long live (Hillary) Clinton!

Ann Lewis quickly dispelled the illusion—after all, she was the
administration's communications director, adept equally at spells and
disspells. She apologized for the missing chief executive. Returning from
China, she observed, he was heavily scheduled domestically, he had to
remind the country that he continued to attend to *its* business even as
everyone else was attending to his. He was always a public workaholic
on the nation's behalf, but since the Monica scandal, he'd made a
mantra of the boast that he'd "been hired to work for the American people and that's just what he intended to do, no matter what his enemies
thought of next." He couldn't just be absent; his absence had to be spun.
(I hated his corporatist references to being "hired," a New Democrat
affectation that turned the people's deputy into its CEO.)

We must not have looked reassured (though we actually knew in
advance it was to be Hillary's show), because in her most soothing and
effective mommy manner, the one she used when the press probed her
about Monica, Lewis rushed on to say, "Americans like their presidents

to look presidential abroad, but insist they be quite parochial at home."
Our look of puzzlement persisted. She talked even faster: "So, you see,
he needs to prepare to reclaim the domestic agenda, to get out among
people and do the job for which they elected him." Which is why he
can't be here was the unspoken conclusion. She couldn't actually say it
without implying that Hillary was merely a sub, and she knew as well
as we did that we'd been invited by Hillary to join with Hillary and that
the whole Bill thing was just a distraction. For Hillary was no mere surrogate, filling in at a diplomatic function for a busy husband. She was,
in some oblique manner, well, taking over. Sid had talked about a typical "seminar" six days earlier when he had called, and had said entic-
ingly, "Your civil society themes will be on the table." But by now both
he and I knew that "my themes" were White House pap—"public private partnerships" and "civil society" and "third way" serving as gen-
eral-purpose clichés rather than as engines of specific policy.

The real aim of the meeting—if the attendance list was any indica-
tion—was to clean up the blood spilled over welfare reform and health
care, and accommodate the party to the New Democrat ideology by
incorporating into it a wan and de-rhetoricized populism from which
strong democratic citizenship language was useful only insofar as it
provided bromides. In retrospect it is apparent that the meeting was in
effect (if not intent) preparation for the 2000 campaigns, in which Al
Gore and Hillary Clinton would have to embrace the base (still New
Deal/Great Society Democrat) without relinquishing their hard-won
hold on the New Democrat center (where all those independent, soc-
cer mom, urban blue-collar swing voters sat, telling pollsters over and
over again how very "undecided" they were). Gore would re-rhetori-
cize populism.

Hillary and later Al had taken up where Bill had left off in approaching the rift between old and New Democrats: in responding to the two
constituencies they would "do both" and in doing so perpetuate the
Clinton legacy of ambivalence that had been the key to his political success and the Democratic Party's rebirth.

The table was crowded. Along with those I've already mentioned
were old Democratic foot soldiers like Richard Leone, the president of
the Twentieth Century Fund, Paul Starr, a sociologist and editor of
the *American Prospect*, Barry Bluestone (a Gephardt associate), and
Nick Littlefield (long a Ted Kennedy policy aide) who, with their old-

fashioned liberal views, could be seen as standing in for the departed (defeated?) Robert Reich and those like Alan Brinkley and Theda Skocpol from that first seminar I had attended at Camp David back in 1995 who stood strong for welfare interventionism and aggressive, big-state interventionism. Ruy Teixeira of the Economic Policy Institute, Jack Donahue of the JFK Institute at Harvard, Ralph Whitehead, David Osborne, and the Brooklyn-bred politico Fred Siegel were also present, constituting a more disparate and less academic assemblage of talent than these seminars usually represented. Politics and policy would trump ideas and ideology on this afternoon, assuring an outcome the DLC could live with, maybe even run with.

Hillary entered only after we were all seated, apparently happy to forgo the preseminar schmooze that the president always found irresistible. She circled the table, greeting us like an efficient restaurant proprietor. Her skills in the flattery department had grown considerably (she must have been studying her husband). I told her I was pleased she was hosting the meeting.

"Any excuse to get you here, Ben; if we have to call a meeting, we'll call a meeting." And similarly to others around the table she knew, finding the appropriate flatteries (or not) as required by her profile of the guest in question. She even flattered Sid, seated opposite her (she was flanked by Galston and From; Sid had me to his left and Whitehead to his right across from the first lady), noting how she'd first met Tony Blair at his house. She regretted that the president wasn't able to be with us, but as the "Michael Jordan of politics" his presence was required at more populous venues (this was a variation on Ann Lewis's line about attending to the people's business). But that was the last we heard about the president. She recalled that at Sid's house the discussion with Blair had quickly moved to the need for a new progressive language reflecting the changed circumstances for liberal parties in the West. Blair's Third Way talk had dominated that informal meeting, she said, and been the formal topic of the meeting at Checkers (Blair's Camp David) that followed.

"You have to admire the Right for its ability to debate and disseminate new ideas," she said, urging us to do more than just engage in an in-house debate with one another. "We need to enlarge the audience—present our ideas, not just argue among ourselves."

The first lady was again propounding the virtues of the kind of civil society talk I championed, but the victory of this rhetoric had begun to worry me. Third Way language offered a vision of politics in which class was no longer so salient—who were the "workers" and who the "capitalists" in the new, global information society? In which the harsh and polarizing politics of the industrial age no longer captured what concerned an average American (most Americans, whatever their income, read themselves as middle class, but most, however "middle class," also lived with a sense of economic uncertainty, even foreboding). In which, between the caricatured abstractions of big government (public, coercive, bureaucratic) and big business (private, exploitative, bureaucratic), lay a viable third zone called civil society in which ordinary citizens went about their neighborhood business of playing, praying, volunteering, learning, creating, entertaining, and associating that defined the best parts of their lives.

I had argued that the virtue and attraction of civil society was that it was voluntary (freely associative, like the market sector), without being solipsistic and atomistic, and at the same time was public and communitarian (it engaged our social being, like government), without being coercive or remote from our actual lives. The Clinton administration had made civil society a buckle holding the public and the private sectors together. It had asked for "public/private" partnerships whose real locus was the neighborhood, where citizens worked together. This had been the magic of Americorps, facilitated by government, run by state governments and local nonprofits, and participated in by young citizens operating in the civic domain as volunteers. But it had also used civil society and personal responsibility as surrogates for public power and government responsibility. I worried that what started as a campaign to root government more firmly in citizenship and community might end as a campaign to replace government with them—which is what usually happened when Republicans got hold of Third Way language. Shared responsibility should mean strengthened government responsibility, not its wholesale privatization. The mood here today seemed oblivious to such complications.

Sid jumped in right after the first lady, reinforcing her message, as she had reinforced his. The point was not to rehash but to firm up the Third Way argument, to achieve sufficient consensus so that liberals could take on conservatives. As Hillary had punted the ball to Sid, he shovel-passed it to Al From. This all had a more scripted feel than earlier sem-

inars, as if the DLC veterans who believed they had gotten Clinton elected in the first place had caucused and diagrammed a rhetorical play
that would thrust us all into the end zone of their centrist principles.
Was this meeting really about finishing off the old Democrats in the
name of incorporating them into a consensus? Triangulation as (in the
words of a critic) strangulation?

Al From executed a straight-ahead move that carried us well into
DLC territory, riffing seamlessly about the many Clinton successes that
DLC ideas had made possible. Look at Eli Siegal (the first Americorps
chair), said Al. He was now working on welfare-to-work plans that
made it clear that New Democrat welfare reform was opening up rather
than closing down options for the poor. All that screaming about the
destruction of the welfare program when its abolition was finally actually empowering the poor! Then he shifted into a reaffirmation of those
now familiar pillars of New Democracy—community, opportunity, and
responsibility. "We've got to expand the winners' circle!" he exclaimed,
savoring the words that had become the New Democrat mantra for the
New Democrat economy. See, it's not about winners compensating
losers (the old redistributive Democratic politics of envy, as the Republicans would label it); it's about *everyone* becoming a winner (what can
the Republicans not like about that? and hadn't I called a book of mine
*An Aristocracy of Everyone?*).

Later in the day, when we moved from the White House to DLC
headquarters southeast of the Capitol to continue the debate and,
supposedly, solidify the consensus, Barry Bluestone did the opposite,
muttering angrily that this line of argument couldn't be impeached by
the Republicans because it *was* Republican. Much of the day's consensus was rooted in ideas indistinguishable from Republican principles.
How was a Democrat supposed to run on Republican principles? In my
mind I imagined Al From muttering, "Successfully!" But in fact what
From did was to defend the vestigal distinctions, saying that Bluestone
was exaggerating, that expanding the winners' circle wasn't just trickle-down economics by another name.

Yet the focus on the production of more wealth as the premise for its
equitable distribution did seem, well, Republican. Maybe that's why Al
Gore found himself running away from New Democrat ideas in his presidential campaign in favor of a more simplistic, but sellable, populism.
It is certainly why Ralph Nader abandoned the Democrats and ran a

self-absorbed third-party campaign more obsessed with destroying the Democrats than with defeating the Republicans.

My own caveats continued to rumble around in my belly like distant thunder, caveats I was reluctant to share (there is a coercive element in the drive for consensus). The very idea of "winners" entailed the idea of losers, even if the losers were being invited to become winners. Trickle-down had also said we could "all" win as a result of the big winners' winning even bigger. The central idea of egalitarianism, on the other hand, had always been *sharing,* and while it might be clever to turn the idea of "winner take all" into the idea of "we all can be winners," the shift to market metaphors deeply rooted in competition could only leave old Democrats—even well-intentioned ones like those at the White House that day who were seeking a tactical alliance with the New Democrats—feeling like ideological strays. Democrats were historically the prophets of public collaboration and social comity, but here we were championing the private, high-stakes horse race in which (this seemed an afterthought) everyone could (maybe) be a winner. An odd foundation for a theory of social justice, above all in a global market environment where the idea of joining the "winners' circle" was for most people around the world wholly risible.

Sid and Al knew, of course, that there was no consensus on these issues around the big table in the Map Room, and continued to orchestrate their appeal by turning to Nick Littlefield, a Ted Kennedy liberal now practicing law in Boston. His endorsement of New Democrat ideology would surely be seen as a resounding legitimation of its supposed liberal credentials to old Democrats (just as in 2000 the support of Jesse Jackson and NOW for Al Gore was intended to legitimize his supposed liberal credentials to Nader runaways). Nick avoided a substantive discussion—his goals were tactical, and maybe he wasn't anxious to sell out substantively if he didn't have to. He directed his comments to Mrs. Clinton, seeming to seek not her approval per se but *her* legitimation, just as Sid was seeking his. He urged us to organize and sharpen the message and then to "market" the hell out of it.

I reacted more viscerally against the idea of "marketing" a message about social justice than against the New Democrat take on social justice. But that was not an argument I was likely to win in a country where long ago the distinction between politics and marketing had disappeared, and so I remained silent, trying to control the grimace into which, I knew, my mouth was tightening. As early as the 1960s the "selling of the presidency" had become a cliché in a book title and an emblem of the vanishing of what was supposed to distinguish citizen politics and consumer marketing. Why spit into a gale?

Still, as the marketing metaphors continued, I was torn between compliance and an outburst. I wanted to serve the first lady's wishes and play the consensus game according to the rules, but I also wanted to register some level of protest against this convenient yielding to slick New Democrat ideology. Like the president, from whom I had learned so much, when I finally spoke I managed to do both—concur a little and rant a little. Yes, I said, civil society affords us a new rhetoric that moves us off old class paradigms and substitutes for exploited and exploiter the language of the citizen, and for class conflict the ideal of civic cooperation, and for aggressively defended individual rights the related and empowering notion of civic responsibility. That was precisely the message the first lady had offered in a striking address to the participants at the Davos World Economic Forum the preceding winter.[1] So much for consensus. But, I added quickly, we have to take care not to embrace a conservative antigovernment construction of civil society, the sort of thing Republicans purvey when they attack government and call for the outsourcing and privatization of its functions. Neoconservatives had, after all, made civil society an argument about substituting voluntary action for government action. They construed voluntarism not as a complement to but as a surrogate for common civic action and so integrated it into their attack on democratic government; if we played that game, we would find ourselves bereft of the very democratic tools we needed to combat private power and market injustice.

Unlike earlier seminars, this heavily scripted meeting was dominated by short presentations from the visitors, who acted as if they were reading testimony into the *Congressional Record* rather than engaging in a deliberative debate. There were too many people around the table, too much posturing (me too!) in an effort to get in a key point or two. No one replied directly to my (too gentle) warning. Instead, the modest little for-the-record speeches continued.

[1] I had worked with my French publishers Desclee de Brouwer to have the address translated into French in a volume I put together on civil society that includes passages from Tocqueville.

Richard Leone worried about the way in which economic divisions were creating not class distinctions but two walled-off societies nearly invisible to each other across the divide, let alone capable of talking to each other. Paul Starr of the *American Prospect,* perhaps envying Bill Kristol of the *Weekly Standard* his cause, observed that the Republican Party had made itself a "cause" and that Democrats had to do the same. Bill Galston, his muscle memory reviving the weariness he must have felt in his last years at the White House, spoke lethargically, his low-key energy making him sound almost despondent as he implored us to focus on common "core ends" and so elude the radical disagreements that emerged when we spoke about means. Recrimination creeping into his darkening voice, he added, "You all must know what I mean, I was damned and denounced by folks here today for *my* views on Social Security privatization." (He had violated the liberal taboo prohibiting any change in the public character of Social Security early on.)

New Democracy was apparently still troubled by old demons. The trouble with Galston's "core ends," however, was that they quickly became high-minded clichés on which everyone, Republicans and Democrats alike, might agree ("We need a Social Security safety net"), without in any way mediating the divisive debate over means that incensed the media and polarized citizens ("Should it be publicly financed or privatized?"). To bracket the debate over means was to pretend to a meaningless consensus—not to mediate but to evade the real conflicts. When Gore and Bush actually debated the "means" two years later, it animated an otherwise dull campaign.

Richard Rothstein must have been tracking the same anxiety I was feeling. "We always begin by admitting 'failure,' whether on welfare, Social Security, or education, and that loses us our audience if not the battle." It was education he wanted to focus on: "We haven't failed with public schools," he scolded, sounding like a teachers' union rep. "The test scores between whites and blacks are narrowing, black SATs are going up, the polls all show an education 'halo' effect (public schools stink, except *my* public school, which is great). When Ford improves the Taurus, it doesn't say what a dreadful car the Taurus is; it says how it's *improving* an already great car."

Again, the allusions to the market. Why is everyone so hell-bent on imitating private corporations? On privatizing everything left that's public—schools, prisons, culture, the military? The president as the nation's hireling? Is there really just one ideology left in America, hovering around a right-of-center "middle ground" defined by markets? Robert Kuttner observed bitterly at the end of the second term that the Third Way means meeting conservatives halfway, over and over again, until there are two conservative parties. Is this the centrist meridian Hillary Clinton thinks she must stand on to escape her "liberal" reputation and wage a "balanced" campaign?

Elaine Kamarck jumps in, Rothstein having pushed a button about effective communication: "We all condemned Newt's TV class thing [while Speaker, Gingrich had taught a much criticized cable television course offering his own highly politicized, some would say skewed, version of American history], but, you know, what I said was 'Why didn't Bill [Galston] and I have that idea?' Why not do it Newt's way, put your view of history on TV!" We seemed to be moving well beyond shame.

Barry Bluestone, the only certifiable full-blooded liberal in the room, tried to slow down the "let's do it the market way" talk. Expanding the winners' circle is fine, but what do you do when there are no jobs in the inner city? he queried. The African-American sociologist Bill Wilson has been saying forever that it's about jobs, not race. Sure, growth solves all problems, but in those places where there's not enough growth . . . ? What happened to "investment in people," the slogan of the first two years of the first term? Capitalism was brilliant at producing wealth, but much less efficient at producing lifelong jobs and piss poor at distributing wealth equitably.

David Osborne, as conservative as Bluestone was liberal (the old ideological terms that don't apply anymore still apply), cut in and pulled the conversation back on the DLC fast track. He wasn't about to let us move off of the privatization talk that put market forces front and center. "The global economy's great; we have to embrace it!" "And those who can't keep up?" he added, as if to query himself (he was reading my mind). "The ones who can't keep up, they need a hand up, not a handout!" Yes, community, opportunity, and responsibility are fine, he said, civil society's great, but we need new forms of government, forms that embrace free trade and use the market more aggressively. He looked at Galston: "We do need to privatize Social Security!" Heads began to shake—even the New Democrats were getting nervous. This just drove Osborne deeper into his neoliberal corner: "Schools too; they need to be forced into being competitive!" The old Democrats were beginning to froth, the head wagging growing vigorous, and much as I admired the political viability of New Democrat ideology, I was beginning to feel like an old Democrat as well. No wonder Barbara Ehrenreich would write two years later in an election week op-ed—defending her defection to Ralph Nader—"We didn't choose to abandon the Democratic Party in its hour of need; the party chose to abandon us."[2] And paid dearly.

"Charter schools are great," exclaimed Osborne, charging on, "but the teachers unions all oppose them." Down with the unions! Down with government! You want to go back to losing by embracing hopelessly outdated principles or go on winning by tacking to the great and glorious American center? That was the question Clinton's victories absent Clinton had posed and whose subtexts were being ripped open in our debate.

Before opponents of the emerging Republican line could give voice to their escalating resistance, Will Marshall, the DLC's Progressive Policy Institute president and a thoughtful and effective occupant of the middle ground leapt in: "I couldn't disagree more with Rothstein; the schools *have* failed. We don't need ideology [liberals talk ideology was the implicit message]; we need problem solving and public remedies [New Democrats talk pragmatic realism]." Trouble is, I thought silently, your opponent's pragmatic solutions always look like ideology and your own ideology always seems pragmatic and realist. And besides, pragmatism is not a new paradigm. Dismissing the old paradigm is not a new paradigm. We truly did need a new paradigm, as the failures of 2000 would show, but New Democracy, although it had delivered us decisively from the old, was not it.

As the heat rose, Hillary intervened, but not to cool us down. While I was thinking someone needed to call a truce, she was apparently feeling that we were verging on too much consensus and was urging us not to be afraid to clarify and debate concrete differences. But Ralph Whitehead had already accepted Hillary's challenge and was racing on about how the quarterly-reports approach to evaluating change, which we condemn when corporations use it, is the same approach government uses. We've got to push out the time lines. The Right has all those think tanks—what about us? With us it's too much tank and not enough think. "We don't need big bucks; we have a think tank right here in this

[2] Ehrenreich, "Third Party, Mainstream Hopes," *New York Times*, October 26, 2000.

room," he concluded. "Let's convene a virtual think tank with the resources right here." He was right: no paradigms without pondering, if we wanted to get beyond spin.

Whitehead brought a wry, informal, Lake Wobegon style into the Map Room, except that it ended up more style than substance. He seemed to be saying because we're the good guys, we can do for free— and with equal clout—what the Right spends millions to do. Whereas conservative foundations have no scruple about funding expressly rightist agendas, liberal foundations get all weak-kneed when faced with what they imagine is "partisanship" in grant making. They abjure not only explicitly party-oriented research (an appropriate concern) but every hint of anything practical or programmatic on the left. The asymmetry between what is available to the two sides is huge, and has impacted significantly on the capacity of progressives to engage in long-term reflection and planning.

Fred Siegel finally got in a word or two for the frustrated liberals in the room, but seemed to edge toward a more conservative tone as he talked. He started strong: "We're the first 'mass upper-class society' in history," he declared. "Travel Florida, what do you see? Miles of McMansions. Forty-five percent of all new jobs are in the top one-third tier of salaries. Only 20 percent are in the bottom one-third. But free trade *hurts* the bottom third, even though it isn't a majority." Siegel was onto the oldest democratic dilemma there is: majority tyranny. When the masses represent the underclasses, majoritarianism is always on the side of progress, and democracy is a force for social justice. But what happens when the underclass falls into a minority— Siegel's "mass upper-class society"? Then democracy begins to work against social justice, content to add to the benefits of the already privileged majority, even at the expense of the ever more exploited and underrepresented minority.

Siegel drew the picture with disturbing accuracy. He didn't stay for an answer, however. He didn't want to be a troublemaker, either, and despite Hillary's invitation to air differences, consensus beckoned. He segued to multiculturalism (the new majority will be multicultural), complaining with New Democrat irritation about those diversity curricula that in serving multicultural special interests are destroying the "common" in common schooling. This was Arthur Schlesinger Jr. material, the dividing of America along our differences at the expense of a celebration of our common civic culture. There was an important issue here worth arguing, but I couldn't see how it helped resolve the majoritarian paradox Siegel had rightly introduced earlier—a paradox underscored by his closing line about how there was still 10 percent unemployment in his native Brooklyn at this otherwise extraordinarily prosperous moment of "full employment."

Barbara Whitehead again tried to strike a balance, appealing to New Democrat conscience (and maybe to Mrs. Clinton's "village") by talking about kids. You want a foundational theme? she asked, looking at Mrs. Clinton: it's kids. She didn't have to enumerate the statistics, which were well known to this group of policy experts: one out of five children live in poverty; schools are in chaos. There's more construction of jails than of schools anyway. Teens of color are far more likely to go to prison (or die) than to go to college. The statistics were all implicit, and Barbara pushed on: "But all we talk about nowadays is what's *wrong* with kids. Why are we so 'tone deaf' on the subject? Don't we know that we've avoided Europe's demographic stagnation because of immigration and the rate at which immigrants are having kids? Yes, government may get in some people's way, but it protects the unprotected, the vulnerable, the weak. It's *good for kids!*"

It was great stuff, and Mrs. Clinton had to like it. Republicans always figured her "village" that it took to raise kids was government, and they were right. Because government was the best and most faithful ally children had in a market world that targets them as customers but otherwise neglects their needs and interests, leaving so many in poverty even in our land of cornucopia. To call government the ally of children speaks to its virtues, not its vices.

Still, the appeal didn't seem to make much headway among the tough New Democrats at the table. Kids, I tell Barbara later over lunch, the reason kids never really work as a political issue is that they are a minority (part of Siegel's minority underclass) and, poor and invisible, and without a vote, where's the payoff in electoral terms? As compared, say, with Medicare beneficiaries. Moms with school-age kids are often young, single, and politically inexperienced. QED: kids tug at all the right heart strings and are guided by the appropriate moral guy wires. But, unfortunately, are politically irrelevant. It may take a village to raise kids safely and well in a global market society, but it takes a bank— dollars and votes (not the currency of kids)—to elect a politician or motivate an investor. Maybe this is why Gore cloaked the interests of kids in the oblique language of "working families" in his campaign.

Mrs. Clinton was ready to bring us to a close. Maybe she wanted to leave us thinking about the underrepresented children. Maybe she just needed to head out to the next stop on the day's busy schedule. We were going to continue over lunch at the DLC headquarters anyway. She urged us to face the "hard issues." Public education? How do we unpack and deal with the differences between Dick Leone and Will Marshall? she asked. Free trade? She pushed us to have a look at the president's World Trade Organization speech, which had been ignored by the media but was fairly tough (relatively speaking) on the WTO and full of new ideas. Bring more people to the table to talk about and get behind more-stringent labor and environmental standards in the global marketplace, she urged.

Then she too was inadvertently deploying the neoliberal metaphors that had dominated the conversation all morning. We had to "market" our resources as effectively as the Right had done. Get the message out. Her friend Tony Blair, she reminded us, was set to "rebrand" English politics and market it to a British nation. I recalled that he'd said something fairly repellent about how it was no longer going to be "Rule Britannia" and instead would be "Cool Britannia," and shuddered. "We've got to rebrand our politics too," she added. Another shudder. Branding was how corporate markets merchandized unnecessary goods to people who had no need for them, how the postmodern economy manufactured not the goods we needed but manufactured the needs themselves so we would want all the goods. Productivist economies focus on manufacturing; consumerist economies, on merchandizing. Now Tony Blair was mimicking an advertising executive, merchandizing his nation to indifferent consumers, and we were being urged to follow suit. We should be condemning this commercial trivialization of the political, I thought; instead we were being urged to cultivate it. But why not? Millionaires like Jon Corzine (the ex–Goldman Sachs chair who bought Lautenberg's New Jersey Senate seat with a $70 million investment) were no longer anomalies in a postmodern politics that was fast becoming the least reputable branch of the otherwise all too reputable consumer economy.

Hillary was nearly done. We need more of this, she concluded, her hand sweeping across the large Map Room table. She seemed to be indicating us. "Where can we continue the conversation? How can we extend the debate? With whom?" She was all questions, so many open-ended invitations to us to keep it up. It was a deft performance, not quite as probing or recreationally interactive as the president's would have been, but perhaps even more successful. Clinton's seminars were riveting and mostly irrelevant. This one had been more fractious, less cohesive, certainly not so inspiring. But like the first lady herself, it had also been more real and palpably pertinent. Despite its verging on the rancorous, or because of it, our debate was capturing the Democratic Party's unfinished business, exposing the threadbare and incomplete character of the new consensus, revealing the degree to which the truce between left and center depended on the president's personal charisma and his conviction that we, like him, could surely "do both."

Under the more realistic circumstances of a merely smart politician finding her way to a political strategy, and confronted with angry adversaries still vying for the soul of the party, things had fallen apart. They would stay apart throughout the next couple of years, and condemn the Democrats to a campaign in 2000 that would veer like a car out of control between an imitative Republican politics of compromise and an old Democratic politics of rant and rage. The party divided could stand but could not win. Without Clinton it lost. Why became visible to me for the first time that hot August day when Hillary Clinton took over from her husband and brought the party back down to a merely ordinary level of being, where it no longer could spread Clinton pixie dust in the eyes of the voters. The demographics still favored the Democrats, as did the issues on which demographics impinged—abortion (lots of unmarried heads of households and single women who were ferocious about choice), immigration (a closed society implicitly marginalized recent immigrants already inside)—but the illusion of a third way in which the battles of the past would vanish was over. Now Democratic contenders would have to decided either to be Democrats and abandon the burgeoning apolitical center where so many Americans felt comfortable, or abandon the base for that center and risk losing the real Democrats to apathy, cynicism, or, worse, Ralph Nader–style third parties. The center-left was in command, the "new majority" won the election in 2000 (between them, Gore and Nader won a decisive 52 percent of the electorate), but it was divided along the lines of our debate with the first lady. This in turn left the party vulnerable to a well-organized, center-campaigning Republican minority, which secured its minority victory with the blessing of the Supreme Court. Under Bush's Clinton-lite leadership, the Republicans set about rendering our Democratic debate moot by building a bridge to the 1970s—one that overlept all of the eighties and nineties debates with a single backward-looking orgy of cabinet-building senioritis.

Al From nodded at each of Hillary's questions, seeming to take her literally. Where can we continue the debate? Why, we can continue it at our DLC headquarters! When? Right now, over lunch! You're all invited. It seemed a pretty partisan venue for a "heal the rifts" session, but no one wanted to decline further interaction, let alone a free lunch, and an afternoon at the DLC headquarters had in any case clearly been scripted along with everything else. Maybe the headquarters was now a wing of the new White House S.W. I dumped a copy of my newly published essay on civil society, called *A Place for Us*, into the First Lady's outstretched hand (she was graciously trying to say goodbye and now it was me, marketing *my* brand). "Yes, thank you, Ben. I'll look forward to reading it." Then she was gone, and I was joining Al From and Bill Galston for the quick drive in Al's luxury import over to the DLC's place across town.

On the way over, we passed the courthouse where Ken Starr was holding court. Al was tweaking Sid: "Sorry, but we got to drive *right by!*" Not amused, Sid launched into an attack on Republican witch-hunts. He was nearly as exercised as Clinton on the subject, and his anger carried over and made him a little too defensive and partisan in the afternoon meeting. Avenging the persecution of Clinton was always getting mixed up with establishing a new center-left agenda in the second-term White House, probably to the detriment of both. We spent three hours that afternoon in the conference room at the DLC trying to meet Hillary's requirement—airing the disagreements—while Sid went on looking for a united front so we could effectively attack the Republicans. This brand of attack politics was the kind of stuff the American people really didn't like, above all the majority that continued to support the president because it already knew he'd been the victim of partisan attacks when he didn't deserve it (which had delegitimized the attacks he'd suffered when he did deserve it). Had they been able to observe us, ordinary citizens would probably have welcomed our rehearsal of that morning's disagreements even where, in the first lady's absence, we aired them with rather too much vitriol. But they would have been impatient with our politics in the attack mode and wondered how it squared with the new centrism being touted. If we were tacking to the center to pursue a tactical politics of accommodation, how could we justify vilifying the Republicans? Clinton's personal politics were tainting the DLC's tactical politics, which in the long run would help Ralph Nader and George Bush more than Al Gore or Hillary Clinton.

Happily, the American public I worried about was not actually listening in on our conversations. But we were listening in on the American public in an indirect sort of way. The highlight of the afternoon was a presentation by Bill Galston and Barbara Whitehead of research from their "Blueprint" project suggesting that generational change was transforming the Democratic Party's base. Only about 8 percent of the electorate was left in the old liberal camp shaped by the progovernment views of the New Deal and war experiences. This comprised the remnants of Tom Brokaw's "heroic generation" and Robert Putnam's "joiners" who had actively contributed to the building of the nation's record store of social capital in the first half of the twentieth century.

Bill and Hillary Clinton were born on the fault line between that generation and the one that squandered the precious capital and lost its zeal for democratic politics. Clinton was elected in 1992 by the last of the old electorate, Hillary would be elected in 2000 by the new electorate. That electorate was made up of boomers and Xers with no entrenched loyalties to the Democratic Party. Suburbanization dominated the new demography, and while as a people we were ever more diverse, we were also less politically engaged, less partisan, and less civic minded. All this spelled danger for Democrats—problems for the base constituencies of both parties, but especially for liberals. The electorate was more up for grabs than ever before. Kamarck parsed the new demographics for us: Democratic primary voters are progrowth and protrade, but they also worry about economic security long-term. The poor are Democrats but don't vote. "We won't have another Clinton," Kamarck concluded, "so we have to identify policies that will secure the new populations."

As things turned out a few years later, we had "another Clinton" in the race, as well as a Gore weaving his way rather indelicately through Clinton country, trying to stay free of any taint yet still to absorb the fragrance. Yet while Hillary won her election, Clinton's successor lost his.

But only because Al Gore failed to hold together the new coalition Clin-
tonism had forged and for which, with Hillary's help, we had tried to
find a formula that would work in the absence of Clinton's personal
magic back on that summer day in 1998. Gore's loss—yes, without
Nader, without a conservative Supreme Court, without those old and
fallible voting machines in Florida's poorer counties, he would have
won, but history will record he lost—reaffirmed the new American
demographic but suggested we failed in our search for common ground
among New and old Democrats. As Ruy Teixeira (with us in the meeting with Hillary) and John Judis and even conservative observers like
David Brooks and Ramesh Ponnuru would note, the country was now
dominated by a center, center-left coalition of new Americans in which
blue-collar non-union voters, middle-class Latinos, and working
women held the decisive swing votes. Hold that coalition together
against the old male, Protestant, southern/midwestern/western suburban America, and you could win every national election. As David
Brooks concluded after the Bush victory, "the Republicans have a geography problem, stronger in the center of the country but weaker on the
coasts, where there is the most population growth." Even the young
conservative Ramesh Ponnuru wrote in the *National Review* that
"whatever they may say, conservatives know in their bones that their
position is weak. . . . [A]t a level of politics deeper than the fortunes of
political parties, the ground is shifting away from them."[3] That's why
Republicans needed the electoral college to stay in the race, even where
Nader was stealing Gore votes; that's why Bush had to tack hard to the
center in the general election, even where his primary campaign and
his actual presidency were animated by more conservative principles.
Nonetheless, Gore was unable to exploit the demographic advantage
and allowed those non-union blue-collar whites who had once voted for
Reagan and had been won over by Clinton to migrate back to Bush and
give him his razor-thin edge in states like Florida.

As Clinton had said with such eloquence at our seminar at Camp
David, American progressivism cannot succeed without including poor
whites in its agenda. How to include them had been at the heart of all

[3] See Brooks, "An Emerging Democratic Majority?" *Weekly Standard*, December 18,
2000, pp. 26–29; and Ponnuru, cited in E. J. Dionne Jr., "Did Clinton Succeed or Fail?"
*American Prospect*, August 28, 2000, p. 44.

of our subsequent debates—not least of all, the battle between old and New Democrats at Hillary's table in the Map Room two years before Al Gore and George Bush battled to be Clinton's successor. Clinton's insight at Camp David had in fact also been a prophecy: he had called the election of 2000. He who wins the constituency of his good ol' working boys—too poor to be loyal Republicans, too resentful to be loyal Democrats—wins the presidency. Not even Gore's own blue-collar constituents in Tennessee had given him a mandate. He went down in West Virginia. The demographics did not fail Gore; Gore failed the demographics.

Hillary, however, laid the foundation for her successful bid that summer day in 1998. She prepared herself for negotiating the tough New York State byways that connect Manhattan and the suburbs, Westchester and the rural counties of the west, and Albany and Buffalo by seeking some common ground on which old and New Democrats could walk, if not with confidence, without too much resentment. In doing so, she not only secured the foundations for her victory; she underscored her husband's legacy as the savior of the Democratic Party. By making the journey from the liberal left to the pragmatic center-left that included those the old coalition omitted, a journey she had earlier disdained, she signaled the victory of New Democrat thinking, and proved that under the new demographics the Democratic Party can not only survive but even flourish.

Whether democratic principles can survive New Democrat success is, of course, quite a different question, whose answer lies well in the future and beyond the scope of this memoir or of the dreams conjured by it. An answer to the question will, however, surely turn as much on what Mrs. Clinton does in the next dozen years as on what Mr. Clinton did in the last dozen. And if Hillary ends up as the greater part of Clinton's legacy, if one day "the Clinton co-presidency" turns out to be more than a metaphor for an intimate partnership as dazzling and profound as it was troubled, Bill Clinton will surely have few complaints.

# CHAPTER TWELVE

# The End of the Affair and the Legacy Question

**AS I WRITE** the Clinton presidency is not yet quite over, but my affair with the president is. Playing an indifferent Hamlet to my preoccupied Rosencrantz, he will not notice that, as he haunts all of those who experienced him even casually, he will continue to vex my memory. But he will himself be vexed by what we—in the abstract and as a nation—think about him too: the ongoing question of legacy, a question that will linger well into another man's new term of office. Will his two wildly vicissitudinous terms in office inspire only retroactive fatigue (as it did a year before it was over) or something more—grudging respect (he survived!) or even a certain admiration for what could turn out, after all, to be historic accomplishments? A lot depends on how history treats his affair with Monica. Whether, as Clinton's many enemies surely hope, it petrifies into a symbol of all of his vices and inadequacies; or, as his supporters will insist, endures only as a symbol of what his enemies tried to do to him and hence a monument to what he accomplished in spite of those enemies and his own frailties. Either way, sex, lies, and the impeachment trial will loom large.

Like so many who have known him, I may have had my own intellectual version of an affair with Clinton, but that doesn't qualify me to comment on Monica's, which (I trust it is clear) was of a rather different nature, though perhaps not as different as I'd like to think. I gave far less, asked far less, and meant far less, although, as with so many people who knew him, including Monica, he necessarily occupied my imagination to a degree no one could occupy his. Such is the skewed nature of power, charisma, and narcissism in the age of mass media.

In any case, as a memoirist and political philosopher ruminating on ideas and power, I don't have a lot to say and don't wish to say a lot about the sorry episodes in Clinton's presidency that turned on his sexual needs. Where fools rush in (take Richard Posner, for example), I am pleased to tread ever so lightly. However momentous the politics of the impeachment trial—it was unrelated to the president's ideas and ideology (other than to obscure them, quite another matter). The media were, of course, right in the middle of things, creating the scandal as they pursued it, shaping the outcome as they decried it. Like Bill Bennett and other conservative cultural critics, they blamed the majority of Americans who remained agnostic for not blaming the president, but (playing both sides) also derided the partisan rancor of the agitated minority of "Puritan" Americans who assailed Clinton even more vehemently than the media did. Having helped create the story they breathlessly condemned, the media simply did not seem to understand what the American majority was doing, since the American majority was obstinately refusing to do what the media expected or wanted it to do. Bertolt Brecht had once declared with memorable irony at the time of the 1953 workers' uprising that it was time for the East German Communist government "to elect a new people." In 1998, quite without irony, the American media seemed anxious to do the same thing.

Not that the American majority so keen on supporting the president was getting much help from the White House. Like its predecessors under siege (Carter during the Iran crisis, Nixon during the long twilight of the Watergate tragedy leading to his resignation), the Clinton administration had drawn up its wagons and few outsiders were being talked to about anything. Staffers, themselves betrayed by presidential lying, were not ideally situated to mount a defense (though they tried). Ideas, new or old, were hardly the issue, and intellectual friendlies not only were not being consulted but were being pretty well shut out (given the special prosecutor's penchant for issuing subpoenas, perhaps for our own sake). I had only a couple of interactions during the period, but they did convey something of the controlled hysteria that afflicted the White House staff and the president, mirroring the uncontrolled hysteria that reigned on television and in the media—what Philip Roth has called "the ecstasy of sanctimony."[1]

The meeting that seemed, in retrospect, most telling was with Sidney Blumenthal. I had been acquainted with Sidney since well before he joined the president's staff in the Office of Communications and liked and admired him. His sharp coverage of presidential campaigns for the *New Republic* had been a highlight of that magazine's otherwise deteriorating (or do I just mean right inclining?) political commentary in the late 1980s. At the *New Yorker* he had continued to write sharp if increasingly partisan commentary on the Clinton White House. No doubt his apparently unbounded affection for both of the Clintons contributed to the invitation he received to join the White House staff. Once there, Sid played the part of ardent partisan and worked hard to gain favorable coverage for White House positions and, as things unraveled, to put as favorable a spin as possible on the unraveling. He was a little too slickly handsome and unshakably confident for the purposes of his job—awkwardness and middle American ordinariness might have made his spinning more palatable. Nor was the job itself enviable, but he did it loyally (the only way it could be done at all) and hence well, as indicated by the venom with which he was excoriated by the president's howling legions of enemies.

I met with him after the Lewinsky accusations had been made but before the president had admitted to wrongdoing. We sat together, as we had a number of times, in his West Wing basement cubbyhole. It pleased Sid that the tiny room he occupied just off of the warren of low-ceiling media offices housing White House communications (that is, public relations) had once been the White House barbershop. "Barber" jests aside, it didn't please me quite as much, because the old barbershop had a mirrored wall, and the mirror reflected my image back to me and, though Sid was in the middle of the picture, gave me the impression that I was talking to myself. Here was (literally) a mirror of the architecture of an office devoted to spin where, as someone instructed you on how you might react to this or that, you seemed to be conversing solely with yourself.

[1] Roth, *The Human Stain*, (Boston: Houghton Mifflin, 2000), p. 2.

The cozy office was well positioned in the West Wing basement. Many other important communication functions, including speechwriting, were housed in the Old Executive Office Building across the west driveway from the White House, where their remoteness from power was compensated for by an architectural grandeur, which, however, had no value whatsoever in the currency of White House influence. In the high Middle Ages, courtiers and philosophers (Machiavelli was one) wrote "mirror of princes" tomes to reflect and inform the behavior of kings: Sid's little den was a perfect setting for his preoccupation with providing the media with a new mirror of princes image suitable to the Clinton presidency.

Sid seemed remarkably relaxed under the circumstances of siege in which he worked both professionally and (since he had been falsely accused of scandal in his own life and subpoenaed by the Starr office to boot) personally as well. He seemed almost as perplexed as the rest of the country about what was happening to his boss, and when I asked him point-blank whether he thought the president was lying, he had no easy answer. Rather, he seemed to be mulling it over with me. Finally, he said no. No, he didn't think the president was lying. How could he think such a thing? he asked back earnestly. "Clinton is president of the United States, and he is my president and my boss. He told me the charges are not true. Of course, I believe what he tells me. I couldn't work here if I believed anything else." That seemed sound judgment to me. Clinton *was* president of the United States, and he *had* looked Sid in the eye just the way he had looked the American people in the eye, and he *had* said to both of them, "Didn't do it and that's the truth." And he had lied. But it was neither naïveté nor blind patriotism to believe him. It was a necessary condition of working in the White House. Moreover, Sidney had himself experienced vilification by groundless lies that nevertheless were enthusiastically spread by the media, and he knew they could seem both credible and damning, and yet be quite untrue.

Still, to believe his boss he needed an account that made sense of the contradictions and inconsistencies of what was already on the public record. This, I think, was the origin of that story about Monica that got him (and the president) into such trouble with hardboiled Clinton critics like Christopher Hitchens and Rush Limbaugh, those demon dogs of the Left and the Right who, on this occasion, discovered they ran in the same pack. Sidney offered me more or less the same story he offered Hitchins, which Hitchins will probably conclude damns Blumenthal (and me to boot) but which I believe undermines Hitchins's cynicism. Might it not be possible, Sid ruminated, might it not explain the crush of contradictions emerging about Monica Lewinsky, that she was an overwrought young person with a crush on the president, someone whom the staff and the president liked and with whom he had—perhaps foolishly—gotten overinvolved in trying to help her out? Not that she was a stalker (there, the word was on the table), but she could be fixating on wishes, contriving fantasies from unrequited desires, exaggerating feelings until they felt like truths and had all the insidious effect of half-truths. Might not the refusal of the White House to explain or clarify what had transpired, Sid concluded, might that not actually be its way of trying to protect Monica from herself?

Where did this story, soon to be revealed as preposterous as well as insulting, come from? It seemed a crucial question since it embodied the underlying controversy about who, besides the president, knew about and colluded in his sexual indiscretion and (more important) the lying about it that would lead to impeachment. Did this imaginative narrative originate with the president, who could then be seen, knowing the truth, as willfully misleading his staff? Were the staffers making stuff up to cover for what they knew to be his guilt? Or were they trying to reconcile appearances with their own conviction that the president would not, could not, lie to them—he was president of the United States, for God's sake!—and so there had to be some such complicated narrative that accounted for the appearances? No way for me to know, of course. Nor for Christopher Hitchins to know. Run with your own interpretation, based on your own long-standing view of the man. Clinton supporter, Clinton seducee, I was inclined to believe it was an account conceived by goodwilled staffers trying to make sense of the contradictory evidence, an account hardly invented by, but conveniently indulged in, by the president. Clinton hater, Clinton basher, Christopher Hitchins seized on the same account and believed he had found another bumper car for his Clinton demolition derby. Everybody spins. Everybody's spun.

Don Baer, long gone from the White House when this particular hell broke loose (and was he ever glad!), suggested to me not long after my meeting with Blumenthal that the account Sidney had proposed was actually Don's own effort to make sense of what seemed to be happening, and that it had been taken up by the White House staff only after Don had introduced it to them. Neither Sid nor Don ever even hinted that the story was the official Clinton version perpetrated on gullible staffers by a manipulative president. I didn't feel used and didn't have Hitchens's passionate conviction that the president was using Sid to use Christopher (and me and others) to mislead the American people. Rather, Sid gave the impression of a loyalist searching for an explanation that would allow him to make some sense for himself out of an emerging embarrassment of major proportions, gave the impression that he was trying out this account (perhaps borrowed from Don) not just on me but on himself. It worked for me because the metaphor of seduction seemed to operate everywhere in the Clinton modus operandi; and because it worked so well as metaphor—I too felt "seduced," I too was having an "affair" with the president—the obvious fact that with Monica it was more than metaphor eluded me, as long as I had a plausible way to read it as metaphor.

In retrospect, the only aspect of the story I found offensive (in the same way the media found *everything* said and done by the president offensive) was the way in which it not only exonerated the president and shifted the onus to Monica (he was the victim, she was the fantasy monger if not the stalker) but also made him out as a kind of martyr to the effort to save Monica from herself. Knowing what he knew, the president might have plausibly wished to let his staff make him a minor figure in or a reluctant party to or even the modest victim of the story: but to allow the staff to cast him as a kind of gentleman hero trying to rescue a fantasy-lumbered damsel from the distress of her overheated imagination? That was more than unsavory; it was the kind of hubris that had brought down as mighty a king as Oedipus, and Clinton (if not his staff) surely should have known that this story—the hubris of shifting of the guilt to Monica—would be far more lethal to his presidency than the foolishness of the original dalliance. If it wasn't his story to start with (and I've suggested it didn't seem to be), he still should have nipped it in the bud. His lie didn't require that he blame Monica for the story.

This was Clinton's burden of guilt to bear, however. I left the West Wing believing in my heart, if not quite in my head, the story I'd been told, and (yes, this is Hitchens's complaint) I repeated it to others who saw me, affecting the insider's knowledgeability, misleading them in good faith as I had allowed myself to be misled in good faith by others. Whether I was a well-spun sucker or merely a prudent sympathizer, the American people were way ahead of me—and of Sid and the president as well. They were ahead of all the other insiders and wannabe insiders, and they were ahead of the intellectuals and professors who had been involved with Clinton, because they were not really much interested in whether there had been an affair or not, whether the president had dissembled, stonewalled, or lied outright. When I called my fellow seminarians who at one time or another had been in the White House, they tended to be incensed, outraged, indignant—just like me. Incensed at Clinton for his stumbling betrayal of our cause, outraged at the other side for turning the scandal into a constitutional crisis (the constitutional standard for impeachment of high crimes and misdemeanors just couldn't be met by private sex and its accompanying cover-up), indignant at the media for the obvious pleasure they took in watching the country (with their fulsome support) tear itself to pieces. The American majority, on the other hand, seemed measured and calm in its response.

This was not because, as some of his defenders had it and Clinton clearly believed, the whole Lewinsky scandal was merely a pretext for the president's enemies to attack him (though there was some truth in this). And not, as his detractors insisted, because the American people had lost their moral bearings and, rolling in prosperity, were immune to presidential salaciousness. Rather, a majority of the American people had placed the scandal in a larger context that drained it of its poison. That larger context was the American Constitution and the liberal principles of separation of private and public associated with it. I don't mean to say the American people are natural constitutional authorities or adept lawyers; only that they had and have an intuitive grasp of the entailments of their civic faith. What I think they knew, and what allowed them to be uninterested in explanations and stories of the kind Sid and I needed, was that this stuff was not really relevant to why they went to the polls or whom they voted for. The impeachment trial—the failure of the Republican managers from the House of Representatives to secure even a simple majority on either the count of perjury or that of obstruction of justice (let alone the two-thirds required by the Constitution)—in fact represented a triumph (if a costly one) for the American people and the constitutional system. While the president was contriving half-cocked rationalizations and permitting his staff to engage in earnestly half-baked explanations, roughly 60 percent of America was calmly insisting that the president's outrageous conduct wasn't really an issue. Nor the lying.

This new majority, what its critics dubbed a new "immoral majority," sensed that the "crime" failed to meet the standard inherent in the impeachment provisions of the Constitution. It had elected him because of who he was and what he stood for and was not about to support his removal on the basis of his private sex life, whatever scandalous sexual indiscretions he'd committed and whatever he'd said or not said about them. He had done what he had done, and it was probably a terrible thing he had done, especially for his family and for the poor kid whose fantasies he had indulged and turned into fateful realities, but those out to destroy him didn't care a fig for what he had done, only that they finally had—after they had come up empty with Whitewater, Travelgate, the Vince Foster suicide, and other selected pretexts—what they thought would finally be the instrument of his undoing. However much grist he had provided the Republican campaign mill against him, the real beef of his partisan critics was precisely with that growing majority in the country that supported him. Clinton's critics and the Clinton majority both knew this. Wisdom lay with the people. Not with their representatives in whom the founders had laid their trust, but with the "howling mob" the founders had thought representative government would silence.

In fact, the trial's outcome turned on its head the ancient formula James Madison had concocted for representative government. With his typical founder's distrust of democracy, Madison had decried pure government of the people as a reversion to those ancient direct democracies that Madison disdained as nurseries of faction and discord, in which an ignorant rabble might trample reasonable and prudent governance. As the 1787 Constitutional Convention's youngest and most prudent critic of democracy, Madison had introduced the quasi-aristocratic innovation of representation, which, he believed, would act as a noble "filter" for the base passions and noisome prejudices of the inexperienced multitude newly empowered by "popular sovereignty." In this fashion a nominally democratic constitution would be saved by the representative system from its tendentious democratic tendencies.

Yet, in the case of Bill Clinton, the American people had apparently

grown up and out of Madison's formula for disabling their alleged pro-
clivity for prejudice. For it turned out that those who actually saved the
Republic were not prudent representatives filtering and correcting the
passions of a crass and unseeing people but a prudent people filtering
and correcting the passions of crass and unseeing deputies and their
frenzied media spinners. What the president had going for him was not
zealous party fidelity or a fervent commitment by Democrats to his policies or the economic good times they had produced—the sorts of loyalties that drove Don and Sid and other loyal White House staffers, and
that drove me as well. Nor was it a matter of "tout comprendre, c'est
tout pardonner," for he was not forgiven because he was being too well
understood and sympathized with. It wasn't about Clinton per se at all;
it was about the people.

What Clinton had going for him was exactly what the once grand old
Republican Party had going against it: demographics. The demographics, I have suggested, that Hillary Clinton rode to victory in New York.
The demographics that deserted Gore when he couldn't work Clinton's
magic and hold together old and New Democrats, allowing Ralph
Nader to insert his deadly wedge. The demographics that Bush courted
in moving to the center and going after Clinton's favorite down-home
blue-collar constituents. The demographics that the liberals John Judis
and Ruy Teixeira along with the conservatives David Brooks and
Ramesh Ponnuru refer to when they read the depressing writing on the
wall left behind for conservatives by the new America.[2] Immigrants,
working women, people of color, single family household heads, gays,
ethnic blue-collars, and Latinos were disproportionately on Clinton's
side. Those his policies benefited and those his views reflected—that
long list of so-called special-interest groups—all the minorities that had
emerged as the new American majority.

Since his first campaign crisis in 1992, when then Governor Clinton
was compelled to admit to (if only obliquely) and apologize for (if only
diffidently) his affair with Gennifer Flowers on national television fol-

[2] Along with the pieces by Brooks and Ponnuru cited in chapter 11, see Judis, "The
Spirit of '76: Why W. Won't Stop an Emerging Democratic Majority," *New Republic*,
November 6, 2000, pp. 27–30, and the new book by Teixeira and Joel Rogers,
*America's Forgotten Majority: Why the White Working Class Still Matters* (New York:
Basic Books, 2000).

lowing a Sunday night football game, this majority had chosen to support a man whose personal life was known to them to be less than spotless (literally)—as a matter of fact (more or less like their own?) something of a shambles. When further "bimbo eruptions" (one thanks the media for the studied detachment with which they label these things) became likely as a consequence of the Paula Jones lawsuit and the Supreme Court's astonishing conclusion that it would not "divert" the president from his business for more than half an hour or so, this stolid American majority retained its composure. And when the affair with Monica first appeared as gossip, and then as an accusation, and finally as factual truth, the majority refused to change its position. Right through the impeachment trial, a clear and consistent three-fifths of the nation opposed first impeachment and then conviction—a view the Senate ultimately upheld. Indeed, this majority remained supportive right through the end of Clinton's second term, and probably would have put him back in the White House for a third term had not the Twenty-second Amendment prohibited it.

Critics of this majority from the right, such as the cultural conservative and values champion William Bennett (once Reagan's education secretary and drug czar), condemned the people for their absence of moral spine. Bennett rued (in the title of his book) the "death of outrage" in this "immoral" majority, suggesting it was "complicit in Clinton's corruption" and writing off support as a sign of ethical complacency—complacency reinforced by the stupor-inducing fumes being given off by the turbo-driven stock market. (Rising tolerance for immorality tracks rising share prices!) I believe, however, that Americans supporting the president were moved not primarily by boom-time self-interest or the complacency of moral indifference but by their intuitive grasp of three simple liberal truths. These truths were rooted in their own sense of who they were and how the American system embodied their identity. That is to say, the small-t truths they embraced tracked the small-d demographics they reflected.

The first truth was that the president, for all his faults (perhaps because of those faults), was a lot more like them than the men who assailed him in the name of their own supposed virtues, an imperfect brother who did well by them rather than a putatively perfect father whose every virtue was shadowed by hypocrisy. The second thing they grasped in their plainspoken common sense was that impeachment, rooted in the separation of powers, could surely not have been intended by its creators to permit a partisan bunch of ideologues to bring down a popular president who had violated no public rules of governance or constitutional principles (and good try, but no, lying about sex does not violate such rules or principles either). And finally, they seemed persuaded that the Republic was unlikely long to endure (anymore than their own reputations could long endure) a blurring of the public and the private realms, in which sexual misconduct in the latter domain became the basis for political condemnation in the former domain. It was not just that democratic government would be unlikely to survive so stern a test of human frailty but that the whole American experiment in republican governance and the separation of church and state was organized around the conviction that moralistic crusading across the boundaries separating private from public was the very thing that had nearly destroyed Europe in its era of religious wars and from which many of the founders of the United States and those who followed them across the seas in subsequent centuries had fled.

Americans wanted no part of a system of politics on the model, say, of England in the seventeenth century or ex-Yugoslavia last week, in which cultural war replaced pluralistic openness. America was no longer (it had never really been) a land of white Anglo-Saxon Protestants manning the sea-lanes in their cultural frigates to defend national unity and American purity against Catholics, Jews, Irishmen, and Italians and the even more "foreign" waves of Asian and African and Latino diaspora who were forever taking the invitational inscribed on the base of the Statue of Liberty at face value and teeming ashore from rickety steamers, third-world 707s, and barely seaworthy rowboats. The new America had its lion's share of traditional WASP families, but was also constituted by single mothers, multicultural immigrants, gay couples, working women, green-card workers, nontraditional families, middle-class African-Americans, newly settled Latinos, and blue-collar ethnics, and although their political ideologies were anything but pre-cooked or uniform, these Americans saw in Clinton an emblem of tolerance, openness, and good will that allowed them to claim America as their own. Toni Morrison could thus call him the "first black president," and—for all his shameful shenanigans—working women and single mothers could see him as their spokesman for choice, whether choosing to work, to remain unmarried, or to terminate a pregnancy.

The real wonder of the Clinton impeachment trial is that these three old-fashioned American liberal truths have actually prevailed. Yes, their victory may have served a too cynical and combative president who, after all, was guilty as charged but, after all, had been charged with nothing impeachable. But the triumph of the majority over an overheated system bent on self-destruction was a significant victory for the viability of American democracy. A majority of Americans had understood Clinton perhaps better than Clinton understood himself. A jest about the president that had been around way before the Monica story broke caught just the right balance of cynicism and hope with which many ordinary Americans read (and forgave) Clinton. This is a man, the joke that circulated in Washington during the second term goes, who wakes up every morning thinking about three things—golf, pussy, and what's wrong with America.

As I read it, this is a backhanded compliment. Most of us think a good deal more than our Puritan forebears would have liked us to about the first two (de-gender them as fun and sex, and they probably apply across the board). Few of us, and this includes too many politicians, think very much about the third. Those obsessed by the moral lassitude that can be occasioned by the first two—those who, in H. L. Mencken's phrase, are forever worried that somewhere, somehow, someone might be having a good time—often manage to remain oblivious to the third. Cheating on your country is so much easier to get away with than cheating on your spouse. Clinton's unruly appetites are easy to moralize about. The American majority preferred to admire his disciplined commitments—the devotion he showed in trying to right what was wrong with America. (There is nothing that is wrong with America that can't be fixed by what's right with America, he had said in his first inaugural.) That most Americans understood the difference between chasing a president from office because he had sex on the brain, and rewarding him with two full terms because he had his country close to his heart suggests to me not the corruption but the maturation of the American citizenry as well as the viability of their democratic Constitution. The system had worked. And works.

Not necessarily thanks to the president, however. In my own direct personal interaction with him around these issues at a brief meeting at New York University in October 1998 where the president was participating in a law school roundtable with Prime Minister Blair and other dignitaries well after he had acknowledged the Monica affair, his focus was turned entirely outward. Organized by the law school's dynamic dean, John Sexton, the roundtable was scheduled, as it happened, on the very day the special prosecutor released the transcripts on the Internet. During the formal proceedings both Clinton and the first lady had acted as if nothing were amiss beyond the red brick walls of the law school, and it must have been a solace to be talking about global civil society with a handful of foreign dignitaries, including Tony Blair and a bunch of lawyers more obsessed with the law of nations than with sexual misconduct. But at the law school reception after the conference, where we spoke for a few minutes, the president exploded. As if the net had been scrolling its endless pornographic texts down the front of his eyeballs throughout the day, even as he tried to focus on our academic discourse about civility. His cheeks were even more ruddy than usual, flushed with barely concealed rage. A guest had asked him about the release of the records, and he was stammering out a reply. He saw me, and pulled me toward him, still stammering. I broke in, anxious to signal a sense of intimate solidarity: "Don't let those fuckers bring you down!"

Clinton nodded furiously, his arm thrown around my shoulders drawing me even closer so he could deliver a kind of raspy and whispered shout into my ear, "I won't! They won't! They won't bring us down." He went on, heaping scorn on the Supreme Court for its blithe naïveté, its unworldly opaqueness in ever allowing the Paula Jones case on the docket, reasoning, as it had, that such a suit would scarcely divert the president from public business for "more than a half hour."

He was right, of course, though there was something inappropriate about his being the bearer of this indisputable truth. The old saw about the parricide complaining about his status as an orphan. For while it was true that the Court's stubborn indifference to how politics actually worked in Washington had set the table for the debacle that followed, the consequences played out only because the president had been wildly foolish—not just in his dalliances but in refusing to settle the Paula Jones suit when he knew (as presumably his lawyers and others did not) that her suit was only the likely hors d'oeuvre in what, if the matter was pursued, could become a true banquet of scandal.

Perhaps it was just, as Camus had written of his protagonist in *The Fall*, that Clinton "had a modern heart, which meant he couldn't stand being judged," a less kind way of describing his (and his constituents') aversion to moralism and cultural condemnation. When he rued the death of outrage, Bill Bennett was only rehearsing the critique of post-modern relativism advanced by Allan Bloom in his *The Closing of the American Mind* fifteen years earlier. Yet moral judgment invokes pious complacency and makes war on diversity, and, for better or worse, it has been the modern and the postmodern view that—if and when toler-ance and judgment come into conflict—an open society is more pre-cious than a morally pure society. That's how the American people voted when they opted to support their president. Clinton was of his times, exquisitely modern in just the sense Camus adumbrated. His detractors (the honest moral critics, not the rancorous partisans look-ing for an excuse) were of an earlier time. That earlier time might have been better for our morals, but these times are more conducive to democracy and an open society.

Clinton's legacy has also been hard to measure because the standard against which he needs to be measured is one of absence, not presence. By the measure of liberal expectations—the hope for a more egalitari-an economic policy, for a universal health policy, for a more equitable energy policy, for a reformed welfare system whose costs would not be borne by poor women and their children alone, for an arms budget con-sonant with the end of the cold war, for progress on race and gender and sexual orientation as bold as the talk about it—Clinton had come up short. That's why Ralph Nader ran for president in the 2000 election, and gave the election to George W. Bush.

Liberals were everywhere excoriating the visible legacy, all the things Clinton didn't do and should have. James MacGregor Burns and Geor-gia J. Sorenson complain, "In the end, Clinton was content to tinker, when he had a genuine opportunity to transform."[3] They seem blind to where America was in '94, when the opportunity to transform belonged to Gingrich, not to Clinton, and the transformation in ques-tion was in the direction of the radical Right. The president's legacy was not in what happened but in what he kept from coming into being on his watch. The invisible legacy. In the atmosphere of today's economic well-being, even in a moderate recession, and the return of the Democ-rats to electoral respectability, even with the loss of the White House, it

---

[3] In *Dead Center: Clinton-Gore Leadership and the Perils of Moderation* (New York: Scrib-ner, 2000).

is hard to recall how desperate the situation seemed in 1994 to Democrats, when after only two years of unsuccessful Democratic governance, the Gingrich revolution seemed poised to reinvent America on the model of the nineteenth century, returning the nation to its white, southern, economically libertarian, culturally reactionary, antebellum roots.

Brother Clinton from Arkansas, who knew and understood the sources of this revolution better than anyone, was the living White House fire wall between the troubled liberal nation and the conservative conflagration. In a way, he had to betray the southern breeding that allowed him to comprehend and even sympathize with Gingrich's rebels (no wonder they hated him so!) in order to defeat them. And so he ended up mortgaging his loyalty to the region that produced him to secure the fortunes of the country that had elected him. What he did was to breathe air into Langston Hughes's poem—"Let America Be America Again!"—letting the new, open America of a hundred cultures (and a thousand interests) prosper while easing the old, more homogenous America into retirement. He did this more by prevention than by invention. He took on Gingrich and all he represented in a deadly fratricide, and he prevailed. He made nothing new, but he allowed the new to continue to grow and evolve. He let the nation birth a new America by holding off the nostalgic reactionaries and fearful conservatives. No, he didn't help us across the bridge to the twenty-first century, but he prevented the past from crippling the present, and so kept us on course for a future that now is ineluctable. To every liberal who would skewer Clinton for doing too little for liberalism, I would say remember how much he did by outmaneuvering and outwitting liberalism's adversaries at a critical moment in its history. You may think he did little *for* progressives, but you may also guess from their passionate enmity how much he did *against* conservatives. You may excoriate him for not delivering us to the future, but the Right will forever condemn him for delivering us from the past. George W. Bush not withstanding.

In assessing the likelihood of a Clinton legacy, we cannot avoid the question of this president's remarkable and ongoing demonization at the hands of his adversaries, who seem as compulsively obsessed with him out of office as they were with him when he was in the White House. Reviewing the events of the winter of 2001, one has the feeling that it may have been the first ex-presidential "hundred days" in American history, the first time an ex-president got more media attention than the man who succeeded him. A month into the Bush administration, Clinton was still a national obsession—hero and nemesis, heartthrob and scoundrel, everyone's daydream, many people's nightmare. It looked as much like Clinton's third term as the not-quite completely legitimate George W. Bush's first.

What is it about this ex-president that occasions a never-ending media frenzy, that drives his friends to distraction and his enemies to folly? To be sure, Clinton branded his departure from the White House with actions—mimicking the worst rather than the best of his presidential behavior—seemingly calculated to incense his tireless adversaries. He cut a deal with the special prosecutor in which he admitted to something but no one is quite sure what; he pardoned unpardonables based on what seemed to be their cash reserves; he grabbed basketfuls of gifts that may or may not have been intended for him personally; he negotiated ostentatiously for the most expensive office space in the most expensive city an ex-president has ever sought, and then, when challenged, instead of humbling himself, thumbed his nose at the white rich power brokers by choosing an office in Harlem, which had to seem to his good ol' boy detractors like the exchange of one kind of hubris for another.

Yet while all of these instances of personal assertiveness are irritating, even offensive, they are ultimately minor peccadillos in the larger scheme of things. Lifting a few White House mementos for personal use pales next to perverting the Constitution for personal gain as Richard Nixon did, or purloining an election as the Supreme Court conspired in doing for George W. Bush. Pardoning potential or past donors smells but only in the way that all American politics now smells, and it looks pretty innocuous compared to pardoning people involved in the higher illegitimacies of the Iran-Contra scandal as George Bush the elder did.

This is not to excuse the bad judgment and possible venality of Clinton's transition to private life. It is to ask, when did we last look carefully at a president's exit pardons? Or check the financials of a post-presidency office lease? Or harass corporations who had the temerity to pay an ex-president to speak at a conference? Have we ever subjected another president to such scrutiny *after* he has left office?

The fuming critics who failed to humiliate him while he was in office appeared to be intent on doing so once he was out of office, and the media seemed pleased enough to encourage them since it kept what was presumably the best story they had ever had—the Clinton story— in the news for another hundred days. Except for President Bush, who urged folks to move on, the Republicans—in their haste to take their adversary to the mat one last time—seemed scarcely to care that their own man now sat in the White House or that the ongoing assault on Clinton was a diversion from Bush's agenda. So they scrambled to try to confiscate Clinton's perks, defund his office space, boycott his corporate sponsors, subpoena his pardon files, take away his secret service protection, and even consider reimpeaching him. Why? How can the president who presided over the longest boom in American economic history be cast as a demon?

There are at least some Americans who use the term "demon" literally and not just rhetorically. A caller caught up in the heat of Bush's inauguration hissed breathlessly to Steve Malzberg on one of the Disney Company's parade of right-wing talk radio shows on ABC, "During the prayer, when they were swearing Bush in, Clinton disappeared! I mean he vanished." Taken aback, Malzberg suggested maybe Clinton had gone to the bathroom or something. "No, no," the caller broke in, "I mean he really disappeared. You know you can't see devils when prayers are being said. There was a big empty space where Clinton had been." She was serious. But so was the conservative journal the *Weekly Standard* that greeted George W. Bush's inauguration with a cover story focused not on Bush the hero but on Bill Clinton the heel. The headline read "Our Long National Nightmare is Over." After eight years of peace and unprecedented prosperity, a "nightmare" comes to an end.

Clinton's sin may not be what he has done but how he's done it: his boldness, his bravado, his hubris. The *Weekly Standard* complained that "Bill Clinton left office unchanged." Refused to be shamed. He is one of those exasperating Americans in the public spotlight who insists on being whatever he is without apology or shame—like Isadora Duncan, nearly naked on the stage and proud to call her nakedness art; like Henry Miller or Erica Jong, each zealous in the belief that sexuality and pleasure are sources of joy rather than shame; like Elvis and Madonna, not merely exhibiting but flaunting their sensuality. Like Clinton, each of these American figures has been a hero to some but a moral viper to many others, above all because each refuses the refuge of that all-American moral tactic we call hypocrisy.

In an ironic tribute to our Puritanism, we Americans are expert hypocrites—hypocrisy being the tribute our frequent vices pay to our rarely practiced virtues. We have learned how to do as we please and then hang our heads in shame. Two would-be speakers of the House of Representatives left their posts for doing the sort of thing for which Clinton refused to abdicate his presidency. He whimpered no mea culpas and instead gave a sermon on the meaning of "is." His is a sincere shamelessness, far more irritating than hypocrisy. His adversaries shout "hypocrite" but their real beef is that Clinton has refused to take sanctuary in hypocrisy. Even in his apologies he seems downright pleased with himself. And so the humiliators feel humiliated. There is nothing more humiliating than a failed attempt to humiliate someone else.

So, the legacy question will turn on whether the president is judged by the morally ambivalent standards of our own democratic times or by the nostalgic and high-minded criteria of his more hypocrisy-minded and pious critics. And on whether he is measured by the goods he achieved or by the ills he obviated. But it will also turn on his personality—so unpaternal, so fraternal and democratic. Can so socially interactive and open a man secure the statesman's legacy he craves? Will those to whom he was a likable brother and a sometimes venal servant elevate him to father and leader? Greatness historically has often been linked to remoteness and a kind of populist dissemblance—to a studied hypocrisy. Lincoln and Franklin Roosevelt were leaders in whom citizens read their own visions of greatness, but they were hardly chatty friends to those they represented. Brothers are rarely more than buddies, even when they inspire their siblings. They are easily forgiven, but, as a consequence, unlikely candidates for historical sainthood. Those who worked with the president certainly wanted a legacy for him. Yet their praise is oddly compromised, like the man they intend to lift up. Their writing is weighed down by dejection, heavy with a sense of betrayal that is more than just the pique of the jilted lover (though it is that too). Even the ardent among his staffers speak with odd ambivalence. "The hopes [Clinton] set on that first election night in Little Rock were high, too high," remarks the president's speechwriter Michael Waldman, in the closing lines of what is probably the most judicious account of his presidency yet composed by an insider, ". . . but I am convinced history will show he met more of them than we realize today."[4] "Meeting more of his hopes than we realize today" is stunted praise from a true admirer. I found similar enthusiasm but little that could help in establishing a legacy for Clinton in a late-term meeting with Sidney Blumenthal.

I was in D.C. in the spring of 2000 for a NEA-sponsored meeting on suburban malls and civic space, and was to have dinner with Bill Ivey, Bill Ferris's twin, who was chairing the National Endowment for the Arts with the same gentlemanly southern civility (invisibility) born of the same folklorist's genteel and gentle scholarship that Ferris has brought to the National Endowment for the Humanities. Like Ferris, Ivey was a genius at preserving what had been won, but at the price of forgoing the securing of any new ground. Before dinner, I stopped off at the White House to chat again with Sid Blumenthal. Sid's greeting was cocky, edgy, showing not a trace of the nervousness that had afflicted him through the impeachment hearings. He left his desk to sit in a chair opposite mine as if settling in for a good long chat, but immediately started tapping his foot and looking vaguely pressed as if he were merely seated next to me in the waiting room for some root canal work with his dentist. I asked him how things were going in the White House, remembering that a few months earlier he'd disclaimed all interest in the Gore campaign—"I work for the president"—he'd said then, as if Gore were an adversary, George Bush Jr.'s vice-presidential pick. But today Sid was again a road warrior, and he responded in a boisterous voice, James Carville ranting on *Crossfire,* to a question I hadn't even asked about the campaigns: "We'll wipe the floor with Bush or, if not Bush, whoever." I stared at him. "And Hillary?" he added (I didn't ask about her either). "She's gonna whip Giuliani's butt. I mean, he hasn't seen the likes of her before; he doesn't know what tough is." If he was wrong about Gore—Clinton and Gore did finally become adversaries at a fatal cost to the Democratic Party—he was right about Hillary, but then Lazio was no Giuliani.

The wave of words pushed me back in my chair. With Sid you never get a chance to say anything good about the president or the administration, because he is always one step in front, saying it all first, making you feel that if you say anything half as nice he's just spinning you, so after trying to compete with the compliments I'm always lured into

[4] Waldman, *Potus Speaks: Finding the Words That Defined the Clinton Presidency* (New York: Simon & Schuster, 2000), p. 273.

being a little mischievous, asking hard questions I was perfectly willing to forgo before Sid weighed in on the president's behalf. I always want to say to Sid, "Save it, I'm a friend. Yeah, he's a great guy, I know, I know." But then maybe Sid's just practicing, trying out on friends stuff a little too fawning to drop untested on Ted Koppel or David Broder. Sort of as he did when he tried out the interpretation of Clinton and Monica that had her a stalker and the president a good friend going a bridge too far in an effort to save her from herself.

I asked Blumenthal how things stood with his former friend Christopher Hitchens. He waved his hand again (for a rather tightly wrapped package he waves his hands a lot, not a lot for an Italian grocer, but a lot for a tightly wrapped package). "Hitch? He's crazy, a flake, a liar to boot. The day he swore we had our conversation? I was out of the country for Christ's sake! Only I couldn't defend myself, because the point was to serve the president, not myself, which meant get the Starr thing over as soon as possible. I couldn't even respond."

Sid has an implacable sense of rectitude. What he knows, he knows. Hitch is a liar. Hillary will clean Rudi's clock. Won't make any difference if it's Bush or McCain, Gore's the next president. With a Democratic Congress. Full stop. He's right enough of the time to feel justified in his opinions, but less would be more. Spinning that hard isn't spinning at all. And if you're really winning, no need for all the spinning.

What about me, he wanted to know. What was I up to? "Writing something," I said vaguely, "something about intellectuals in the White House." Sid was a lousy intelligence agent, however. He was too PR and ever intent on persuading others and so never listened quite long enough to learn anything new. Before I could even finish revealing half my secret, he was plying me with figures and facts on the "achievements" of the administration. "Do you know how much we've accomplished?" As I allowed as how I actually did have an inkling, he was calling out for Sean, his new assistant: "Get Ben a package of that stuff on what we've done." Now it was me waving him off—he might just spin me *out* of writing kindly about the president!—but it was too late. Sean had vanished back into the Communications Office warren to assemble a heavy package of achievements.

It was impressive in bulk and heft, and it did suggest that all the small-bore stuff could actually be melted down and used to manufacture a pretty impressive heavy cannon. In 2000 alone, the president had proposed seventy-three new "small" programs in the State of the Union, eighty-three in his final budget recommendations to Congress, what Fred Barnes of the *Weekly Standard* had called "little big government." But all these aggregated proposals and constituencies were also troublingly indicative of the Clinton approach to special-interest politics (and in fairness to Sid, his spin was little more than the Clinton program accurately represented, the Clinton persona secondhand). The accomplishments were organized not around public goods but around the special constituencies and the "little big government" policies that served them. Just the way the State of the Union proposals never turned on a single intellectual axis but spun out as a list of discrete policy initiatives, cabinet department by cabinet department. Sid's ream of achievements were victories for women and victories for African-Americans. Victories for gays and lesbians. For senior citizens and Asian-Americans and Native Americans. For Latinos and labor. For the disabled. And (with its own special list of achievements) those suffering mental illness. This elementary approach to classification felt like the last thing it wanted to be—not a unitary national achievement but a kind of *Saturday Night Live* "skirts, minorities and nuts" caricature. Like cable TV, a channel for every niche market. All the groups that make up Clinton's new majority (I just enumerated them myself) were here, but splintered into special-interest factions and as a consequence diminished. There was nothing tying them together, nothing that tried to say what Clinton did for them all, in the aggregate, to honor the public good, to acknowledge a new and open America, to achieve a new country. Nothing that spoke to an enhanced common interest, though I would argue all the constituencies added up to one America with one American national interest, but somehow the administration never got around to finding the language to say it.

Putting the pages into my hand, Sid enthused about how the White House was starting to talk about the legacy question, adding, "You should be part of that conversation." I thought I *had* been part of the conversation. And my conclusion was you can't make a legacy ex post facto; it comes from how you explain what you're doing as you go along. That may be why Clinton had (and has) a legacy problem. Same thing as the speeches: perfect conversation pieces for selected audiences, brilliant rhetoric on the day of the event, but without gravity or historical weight for the long haul. Same thing as the policy achievements: lots of very good innovations and emendations, taken one by one, but hard to see the connections. Same thing as the "brother president": siblings don't get the respect dads do.

Legacy isn't only about what you do but about how you say it. "Achieving our country" means defining it.[5] Lincoln started out with partial vision, one eye on the Union, one on strategy, a sword lifted against the secessionists, a hand of welcome held out to slave states like Kentucky and Maryland that agreed to stay with the Union if they could retain slavery. No arching vision there. Early on, he insisted his intentions were only to save the Union, whether he freed the slaves or left every one of them in servitude. But later, at Gettysburg, he came to understand that the blood shed by both sides in the war was about more than a sectional economic conflict, about more than federalism and secession. And by the second inaugural he was reaching for the wrenching image of a wrathful God exacting punishment from an unrepentent nation for the sins of slavery. He was helping to shape the forming American national soul around loss and redemption. His legacy was not the war he fought and won to restore national unity. His legacy rested on the way he explained America to itself, showing it that from its fratricide could come a new birth of liberty in which the wounds inflicted by slavery might be healed and the blood losses of war redeemed. Salvation lay not in deeds but in the new self-understanding that, encoded in narrative, deeds afforded.

Lists aren't legacy. That's what Clinton didn't get. His legacy problem derived not from the small-bore eclecticism of his policy successes but from his perduring failure to show how they together constitute something more than a hundred-page catalog of incremental changes realized for particular constituencies served. There was nothing wrong with the multitasking policy wonk approach to programs that Clinton's staff admirers kept referencing, or with the necessarily small-bore centrist ideology on which this approach rested and which became the target of radical critics. What was missing was an envelope of meaning capable of giving the approach and the ideology historical weight. Grandeur on the historical stage derives not from what you do but from how what you do is understood.

[5] This is the title of a book by Richard Rorty, the pragmatist philosopher who had been at one of our seminars, called *Achieving Our Country: Leftist Thought in Twentieth-Century America* (Cambridge: Harvard University Press, 1998).

Much of the Roosevelt package never made it into legislation, and much of the legislation was overturned by an unfriendly Court, and much of what was not overturned fell short of its objectives. The Great Depression finally yielded only to the economic stimulation of a second great war. But with Roosevelt's help, America understood Roosevelt as having committed himself, before the real war began, to a metaphoric war against fear, a battle for the Four Freedoms, a campaign to relieve that one-third of a nation that went to bed hungry every night from its burden of poverty. The New Deal he offered the nation was a new way to understand the war against injustice, which served not to destroy but to heal capitalism. His "accomplishments" on a legislative agenda pale in comparison with his achievement in bringing the country to believe in itself again: to believe again it was a society capable of defending itself against injustice at home and against tyranny abroad.

It is true in every country, but true with a vengeance in this land of self-made myths, that to shape a nation is to shape its idea of itself. To be sure, that idea must find its realization in policies and legislation, but in the absence of the idea a legislative record will neither affect a nation decisively nor long endure. The greatest leaders find a way to frame a visionary idea and then realize it in action. Churchill when Britain stood alone but steadfast against the Nazi onslaught. But history affords the opportunity for such greatness only rarely, and in more ordinary times it is often impossible to do both. Then, history demonstrates, those who deploy a powerful idea in the absence of a record of concrete accomplishments will do better in the holy book of legacy than those whose myriad concrete accomplishments are without a governing idea to give them significance. That is why, perhaps unfairly—and for a Democrat like me, infuriatingly—Ronald Reagan may leave behind a more enduring legacy than Bill Clinton. If that happens, it will not be the small-bore incrementalism, or the cafeteria menu State of the Union speeches, or the conversational approach to rhetoric that does Clinton in; it will not even be the Monica Lewinsky scandal or the scandal of impeachment into which his enemies' political alchemy transmuted it; it will be the absence of a sufficiently large idea. Service was a start, Third Way talk was an engaging notion, public-private partnership was an innovative praxis, end of big government was a detour, and new covenant was a provocative promise. But a legacy is an intellectual mirror into which a nation peers, a mirror in which it can see its own shining face, not as it is but, on the days it is listening to its better angels, as it wishes it were. Small-bore and Third Way and civil society and community service are not enough. They must be hooped together by dreams and driven by anxieties that respond to larger aspirations. In this, and in this alone, I regret my precious time with this remarkable president. I wish the small band of intellectuals whose special provenance ideas were supposed to be, the handful to whom I was privileged to belong, who from time to time had a hearing in the White House—I wish we had made more of our chance.

I do not mean I wish I had spoken truth to power. That phrase, I hope I have shown, is almost always illusory, even dangerous. When we intellectuals make policy or—efficient mandarins—draw the ears of the people's representatives away from the loud voices of those to whom they are accountable so that they will attend to our whispered schemes rooted in some version of higher truth, democracy is almost always corrupted. Our task is to persuade the people at large, to do battle in the intellectual marketplace of ideas and move public opinion. It is the task of citizens and citizens alone, moved by us or not, to then elect delegates who share their persuasion, and to insist that those they elect remain faithful to them. The Medicis might have done well to listen to Machiavelli (they didn't), but only because the alternative was for them to heed their own selfish interests. In a democracy leaders must abide by the views of the electorate, even where wisdom may seem to belong to the mandarins. And while I would have preferred a more subtle democratic method than polling and a more representative spokesman of the people's interests than Dick Morris, better for Clinton to have erred in that direction than to have allowed self-appointed guardians of the truth like me to lure him into grand notions for which there was no popular mandate. If there must be seducers, better they are elected seducers accountable to the seducees than self-appointed ones accountable only to themselves and what they regard as truth. In all of the sessions in which I took part, or heard about, there was but one accountable democratic representative: the president. I do not, then, regret that we failed to speak truth to power; only that we failed to get beyond the truth of power—the truth that is power. Nor do I regret that we did not manage to persuade the president to do something other than what he actually did; only that we never found a way—as Adam through naming gave meaning to the world—to give through renaming a meaning to all that this astonishing and disappointing president achieved.

# INDEX

Page numbers in *italics* refer to illustrations.